Verse by Verse Commentary of

DEUTERONOMY

*Enduring Word Commentary Series
By David Guzik*

*The grass withers, the flower fades,
but the word of our God stands forever.*
Isaiah 40:8

Commentary on the Book of Deuteronomy

Copyright ©1996-2024 by David Guzik

Printed in the United States of America or in the United Kingdom

Print Edition ISBN: 978-1-939466-83-9

Enduring Word

5662 Calle Real #184

Goleta, CA 93117

Electronic Mail: ewm@enduringword.com

Internet Home Page: www.enduringword.com

All rights reserved. No portion of this book may be reproduced in any form (except for quotations in reviews) without the written permission of the publisher.

Scripture references, unless noted, are from the New King James Version of the Bible, copyright ©1979, 1980, 1982, Thomas Nelson, Inc., Publisher.

Contents

Deuteronomy 1 – Moses Remembers the Journey of Israel 7
Deuteronomy 2 – Moses Remembers the Wilderness Years 21
Deuteronomy 3 – Moses Remembers the March to Canaan 28
Deuteronomy 4 – A Call to Obedience 35
Deuteronomy 5 – Moses Reminds Israel of the Covenant with God 47
Deuteronomy 6 – Moses Reminds Israel of the Commandment 63
Deuteronomy 7 – Commands to Conquer and Obey 74
Deuteronomy 8 – A Warning Against Pride 82
Deuteronomy 9 – The Battles Ahead and the Failures Behind 89
Deuteronomy 10 – Israel's Restoration After the Golden Calf 98
Deuteronomy 11 – Blessing and Curses for Israel 105
Deuteronomy 12 – The Worship God Commands 113
Deuteronomy 13 – Keeping the Worship of God Pure 121
Deuteronomy 14 – Living All of Life for the Lord 129
Deuteronomy 15 – Laws Regarding the Poor 136
Deuteronomy 16 – The Three Major Feasts 143
Deuteronomy 17 – Laws Pertaining to the Rulers of Israel 151
Deuteronomy 18 – Priests and Prophets 160
Deuteronomy 19 – Concerning Criminal Law 172
Deuteronomy 20 – Instructions Concerning Warfare 181
Deuteronomy 21 – Various Laws 188
Deuteronomy 22 – Various Laws 196
Deuteronomy 23 – Instructions to the Assembly, Various Laws 208
Deuteronomy 24 – The Law of Divorce and Other Various Laws 217
Deuteronomy 25 – More Laws on Various Subjects 226
Deuteronomy 26 – Presenting Firstfruits and Tithes 232
Deuteronomy 27 – Stones of Witness 238
Deuteronomy 28 – Blessing and Cursing 245
Deuteronomy 29 – Renewal of the Covenant 257
Deuteronomy 30 – The Choice 266
Deuteronomy 31 – Some Final Instructions from Moses 274
Deuteronomy 32 – The Song of Moses 285
Deuteronomy 33 – Moses Blesses the Tribes of Israel 297
Deuteronomy 34 – The Death of Moses 309
Deuteronomy Bibliography 319
Author's Remarks 321

Deuteronomy 1 – Moses Remembers the Journey of Israel from Mount Sinai to Kadesh Barnea

A. Introduction: Moses remembers the departure from Mount Sinai (Horeb).

1. (1) These are the words.

These *are* the words which Moses spoke to all Israel on this side of the Jordan in the wilderness, in the plain opposite Suph, between Paran, Tophel, Laban, Hazeroth, and Dizahab.

> a. **On this side of the Jordan**: At this point Israel was camped on the great plains of Moab, able to see across the Jordan River into the Promised Land. This was the land of Canaan that God promised them but which they had not occupied for 400 years.
>
> b. **In the wilderness**: Israel had come through a long, and difficult journey from Egypt – made even more long and difficult because of their unbelief and the death of the adult generation which first came out of Egypt.
>
> c. **These are the words which Moses spoke to all Israel**: At this pivotal point in Israel's history – on the threshold of the Promised Land, and ready to adopt a true national identity, Moses spoke to Israel in this book of Deuteronomy. Trapp suggests that the entire book of Deuteronomy was delivered by Moses to Israel in ten days or less.
>
>> i. The name *Deuteronomy* means "second law." It was the second giving of the Mosaic Law, the first being at Mount Sinai (Exodus 20-23). Moses was compelled to bring this reminder of God's law to Israel because those ready to enter the Promised Land were only children – if they were born at all – when the law was originally declared at Mount Sinai.

d. **Which Moses spoke to all Israel**: Essentially, the book of Deuteronomy was a sermon or a series of three sermons, preached by Moses to Israel, and preached with a heavy and zealous heart.

i. Moses' heart was heavy because he knew that he would not enter the Promised Land of Canaan with Israel. His disobedience to God at Meribah (Numbers 20:1-13) meant that he would not see Israel's exodus from Egypt through to completion.

ii. Moses' heart was zealous because he knew that if this new generation (which was a generation of faith, unlike the generation which perished in the wilderness) did not obey the Law of God then God's covenant would work against them and curse them. So, the LORD passionately pled through a passionate Moses in Deuteronomy, pleading for Israel to *choose life!* (Deuteronomy 30:19)

iii. Deuteronomy is therefore a book of repetition and a book of preparation. God's people never outgrow their need to be reminded, as Peter said, *I will not be negligent to remind you always of these things, though you know and are established in the present truth* (2 Peter 1:12).

iv. In addition to being a series of sermons Moses presented to Israel, Deuteronomy was also a treaty between Yahweh and Israel. Many commentators point out the similarities in the structure of Deuteronomy and ancient treaties between rulers and subjects. "The terms used in these initial verses indicate the nature of the book. 'These are the words' (v.1) suggest a suzerain-vassal treaty preamble." (Kalland)

v. The three sermons recorded in Deuteronomy (1:1 to 4:43, 4:44 to 26:19, and 27:1 to 34:12) were given to Israel in a fairly short period of time, probably all in the same month. The amount of time covered in each of the four books relevant to Israel's exodus is interesting.

- Exodus covers about 80 years, from the birth of Moses to Israel's arrival at Mount Sinai.

- Leviticus takes place in the 1 year Israel spent at Mount Sinai.

- Numbers covers about 38 years, starting with Israel at Mount Sinai and continuing until they came to the plains of Moab, on the threshold of Canaan.

- Deuteronomy covers about 1 month, documenting three sermons Moses gave to Israel on the plains of Moab.

e. **Moses spoke to all Israel...in the wilderness**: Deuteronomy is also a notable book because it was useful to Jesus for instruction and preparation.

During His temptation in the wilderness, it seems obvious that Jesus meditated on Deuteronomy because in answering Satan, the Savior quoted from it three times. Deuteronomy was a precious book to Jesus, and truth from Deuteronomy was of practical help to Him.

i. When tempted by Satan to use His divine powers to turn stone into bread, Jesus answered Satan from Deuteronomy 8:3: *Man shall not live by bread alone, but by every word that proceeds from the mouth of God* (Matthew 4:3-4).

ii. When tempted by Satan to tempt God the Father into demonstrating Jesus as Messiah before it was time, Jesus answered Satan from Deuteronomy 6:16: *You shall not tempt the Lord your God* (Matthew 4:5-7).

iii. When tempted by Satan to short-cut the cross by bowing down to worship the devil, Jesus answered Satan from Deuteronomy 6:13: *You shall worship the Lord your God, and Him only shall You serve* (Matthew 4:8-10).

iv. Deuteronomy "was that silver brook, that preciously-purling current, out of which the Lord Christ, our Champion, chose all those three smooth stones, wherewith he prostrated the Goliath of hell in that sharp encounter." (Trapp)

v. "Deuteronomy is one of the greatest books of the Old Testament. Its influence on the domestic and personal religion of all ages has not been surpassed by any other book in the Bible. It is quoted over eighty times in the New Testament and thus it belongs to a small group of four Old Testament books [the others being Genesis, Psalms, and Isaiah] to which the early Christians made frequent reference." (Thompson)

2. (2-4) The journey from Mount Horeb to Kadesh Barnea.

It is eleven days' *journey* from Horeb by way of Mount Seir to Kadesh Barnea. Now it came to pass in the fortieth year, in the eleventh month, on the first *day* of the month, *that* Moses spoke to the children of Israel according to all that the Lord had given him as commandments to them, after he had killed Sihon king of the Amorites, who dwelt in Heshbon, and Og king of Bashan, who dwelt at Ashtaroth in Edrei.

a. **Kadesh Barnea**: This was the place where, in Numbers 13 and 14, Israel believed the report of the unfaithful spies and rebelled against God, refusing to trust God and enter the Promised Land.

b. **It is eleven days' journey from Horeb by way of Mount Seir to Kadesh Barnea**: The journey from Mount Horeb to Kadesh Barnea only took eleven days. But from Kadesh Barnea (the threshold of the Promised Land) back to Kadesh Barnea (back to the threshold of the Promised Land) took thirty-eight years.

> i. This was because it took thirty-eight years for the generation of unbelief (those who were adults when Israel left Egypt) to die in the wilderness, and for a generation of faith and trust in God to arise in place after them.
>
> ii. **In the fortieth year**: "This was a melancholy year to the Hebrews in different respects; in the first month of this year Miriam died, Numbers 20; on the first day of the fifth month Aaron died, Numbers 33:38; and about the conclusion of it, Moses himself died." (Clarke)

c. **After he had killed Sihon king of the Amorites...and Og king of Bashan**: Israel's great fear when they first came to Kadesh Barnea and had the opportunity to enter the Promised Land was that they would be crushed by the military prowess of the Canaanites. But when the new generation trusted God and went forward, God immediately gave them victory over two pagan kings (**Sihon** and **Og**). As soon as Israel was ready to receive it in faith, God gave them victory over their enemies.

3. (5) Moses the expositor.

On this side of the Jordan in the land of Moab, Moses began to explain this law, saying,

a. **On this side of the Jordan**: Delivering the message recorded in Deuteronomy was one of the last things Moses did to prepare the people of Israel to finally enter the Promised Land. Moses understood that God's people needed to know the word.

b. **Moses began to explain this law**: In Deuteronomy, Moses was an expository teacher to Israel. The Hebrew word translated **explain** comes from the ideas "to dig deeply" or "to mine." The word itself means to make bare, to make clear, to fully explain. Moses will mine out the riches of God's truth to the people, using it to prepare them to enter Canaan.

4. (6-8) The command to move on from Mount Horeb.

"The LORD our God spoke to us in Horeb, saying: 'You have dwelt long enough at this mountain. Turn and take your journey, and go to the mountains of the Amorites, to all the neighboring *places* in the plain, in the mountains and in the lowland, in the South and on the seacoast, to the land of the Canaanites and to Lebanon, as far as the great river, the River Euphrates. See, I have set the land before you; go in and possess the land which the LORD swore to your fathers—to Abraham, Isaac, and Jacob—to give to them and their descendants after them.'

a. **The LORD our God spoke to us in Horeb**: This departure from Mount Sinai (**Horeb** and *Sinai* are different names for the same place) was recorded in Numbers 10. However, the Numbers 10 account does not present the details recorded here.

i. The recounting of this journey from Mount Sinai to where Israel presently camped on the plains of Moab was an important testimony of God's faithfulness. In the coming months, they would cross the Jordan River and trust God to enable them to conquer the Canaanites. That took a lot of trust in God, but it was trust founded on recognition of God's past faithfulness.

ii. "If every *Christian* were thus to call his past life into review, he would see equal proofs of God's gracious regards to his body and soul; equal proofs of eternal mercy in providing for his deliverance." (Clarke)

b. **You have dwelt long enough at this mountain**: Simply, God told Israel to move on. A year at Mount Sinai was **enough**; He did not bring them out of Egypt for them to live forever at Sinai. It was time to move on in faith and take the land of promise.

i. Galatians 4 and Hebrews 12 symbolically identify Mount Sinai with the old covenant of works and law. For the Christian today, it is important to spend *some* time under the law as it teaches the believer (Galatians 3:24-25), teaching the holy character of God and the need for a Savior. But God never intended the Christian to live their spiritual life at Mount Sinai. In faith, the believer must move on to the Promised Land.

ii. Many Christians today should trust God to live under His grace, having **dwelt long enough** under a legalistic mentality. "The law is not for men to continue under, but for a time till they be fitted for Christ (Galatians 3:16-25). Humbled they must be, and hammered for a season; sense of misery goes before sense of mercy." (Trapp)

iii. Charles Spurgeon considered many ways that believers might have **dwelt long enough** and needed to move on.

- Some live long enough at Sinai, under the law – when they should move on to Calvary.
- Some live long enough at the mount of little faith – when they should move on to greater faith.
- Some live long enough at the mount of endless questioning – when they should find rest in the simplicity of Christ.

- Some live long enough at the mount of planning and scheming – when they should move beyond to action.

c. **Turn and take your journey.... See, I have set the land before you**: Though it would be a challenge, God had set the Promised Land **before** Israel – and Moses here remembered when the LORD spoke to them at Sinai and told them to move on and take the land.

i. "Their SOUTH border might extend to the mount of the Amorites; their WEST to the borders of the Mediterranean Sea; their NORTH to Lebanon; and their EAST border to the river Euphrates: and to this extent Solomon reigned; see 1 Kings 4:21." (Clarke)

ii. "Indeed, the ideal limits of the land stretched out as far as the Euphrates. Probably only in David's time was the ideal even approximately realized (2 Samuel 8:3; cf. Genesis 15:18)." (Thompson)

5. (9-18) When Moses appointed tribal leaders among Israel.

"And I spoke to you at that time, saying: 'I alone am not able to bear you. The LORD your God has multiplied you, and here you *are* today, as the stars of heaven in multitude. May the LORD God of your fathers make you a thousand times more numerous than you are, and bless you as He has promised you! How can I alone bear your problems and your burdens and your complaints? Choose wise, understanding, and knowledgeable men from among your tribes, and I will make them heads over you.' And you answered me and said, 'The thing which you have told *us* to do *is* good.' So I took the heads of your tribes, wise and knowledgeable men, and made them heads over you, leaders of thousands, leaders of hundreds, leaders of fifties, leaders of tens, and officers for your tribes.

"Then I commanded your judges at that time, saying, 'Hear *the cases* between your brethren, and judge righteously between a man and his brother or the stranger who is with him. You shall not show partiality in judgment; you shall hear the small as well as the great; you shall not be afraid in any man's presence, for the judgment *is* God's. The case that is too hard for you, bring to me, and I will hear it.' And I commanded you at that time all the things which you should do.

a. **I alone am not able to bear you**: Numbers 11 tells how Moses experienced this crisis when the people complained again about the food God provided. To help Moses bear the burden, God directed him to appoint seventy elders to assist him in holding up under the pressure of leading the nation.

i. As described in Numbers 11, these elders served a valuable role. They were to *stand there with* Moses (Numbers 11:16), to have the same *Spirit* as Moses, and to *bear the burden of the people with* Moses (Numbers 11:17).

b. **Choose wise, understanding, and knowledgeable men from among your tribes, and I will make them heads over you**: This describes the appointment of elders recorded in Numbers 11. Before that, there was a selection of judges to help Moses (Exodus 18), but that was a separate event.

c. **So I took the heads of your tribes, wise and knowledgeable men, and made them heads over you**: Moses chose the elders of Israel by using a combination of approval by the congregation, and approval by Moses himself. Moses then instructed the elders in principles of righteous leadership, and by this he relieved himself of many burdens.

i. **You shall not show partiality in judgment**: "Let not the bold, daring countenance of the rich or mighty induce you to give an unrighteous decision; and let not the abject look of the poor man induce you either to favour him in an unrighteous cause, or to give judgment against him at the demand of the oppressor. Be uncorrupt and incorruptible, for *the judgment is God's;* ye minister in the place of God, act like Him." (Clarke)

B. Moses remembers when in unbelief, Israel refused to enter the Promised Land.

1. (19-21) Moses remembers his exhortation to Israel at Kadesh Barnea.

"So we departed from Horeb, and went through all that great and terrible wilderness which you saw on the way to the mountains of the Amorites, as the Lord our God had commanded us. Then we came to Kadesh Barnea. And I said to you, 'You have come to the mountains of the Amorites, which the Lord our God is giving us. Look, the Lord your God has set the land before you; go up *and* possess *it,* as the Lord God of your fathers has spoken to you; do not fear or be discouraged.'

a. **So we departed from Horeb**: Israel's dramatic departure from Mount Sinai was described in Numbers 10:11-36. Organized into tribes, marching in the order commanded by God, guided by the pillar of cloud by day and pillar of fire by night, with the ark of the covenant leading the procession, Israel left Sinai.

i. They made the difficult journey through the wilderness to **Kadesh Barnea**. "There must have been great relief then in reaching Kadesh Barnea, a large oasis with abundant springs and pastures." (Merrill)

b. **Look, the L**ORD **your God has set the land before you; go up and possess it**: By the time Israel made it to Kadesh Barnea, they had seen God's faithfulness in enabling them to cross the land of the **Amorites**. Moses was ready to lead the nation into Canaan.

c. **Do not fear or be discouraged**: This encouragement was important because this was the critical moment for Israel. They were a little more than a year out of Egypt and ready to enter the Promised Land. It was there before them, ready for them to take by faith if they would not **fear** or be **discouraged**.

2. (22-23) Moses remembers Israel's suggestion to send forth spies.

"And every one of you came near to me and said, 'Let us send men before us, and let them search out the land for us, and bring back word to us of the way by which we should go up, and of the cities into which we shall come.'

"The plan pleased me well; so I took twelve of your men, one man from *each* **tribe.**

a. **And every one of you came near to me and said, "Let us send men before us"**: As Moses remembered what Israel had suggested to him, he looked back with regret. There was no compelling reason to send spies to the Promised Land.

i. God had told them that the land was good (Exodus 3:8, 13:5, Leviticus 20:24). Unless they did not believe the LORD, there was no reason to confirm this through their investigation. God had also told them they would occupy the land of the nations living there (Exodus 3:17, 23:23). Unless they did not believe the LORD, there was no reason to take a look at the enemies and see if God could defeat them.

b. **The plan pleased me well**: Moses must have remembered this with some measure of regret. The people suggested the plan to send the spies to Canaan and Moses agreed to it. The plan **pleased** him. Yet when ten of the twelve spies came back with a report filled with fear and unbelief, the nation believed the unfaithful spies, refusing to trust God's promise and take Canaan.

i. From reading only Numbers 13:2 it might seem that this plan to send spies into Canaan originated with God, not the people. But a careful look shows that Numbers 13:2 dealt mainly with the *number* of spies to send (12) and *how they should be chosen* (one from each tribe). Deuteronomy tells us the plan was first suggested by the people, then approved by Moses, then allowed and regulated by God. In a sense, the LORD responded to Israel with the thought, "If you are going to send spies, send twelve, and have them represent the whole nation by sending one from each tribe."

ii. "Noting the narrative in Numbers 13:1-3, in addition to what is written here, it appears that the people first suggested that this reconnoiter be made, then Moses approved the idea, referred the request to the Lord who agreed to it, and ordered that each tribe send out one representative." (Kalland)

3. (24-25) Moses remembers the journey and report of the spies.

And they departed and went up into the mountains, and came to the Valley of Eshcol, and spied it out. They also took *some* of the fruit of the land in their hands and brought *it* down to us; and they brought back word to us, saying, 'It is a good land which the LORD our God is giving us.'

a. **They brought back word to us**: Significantly, Moses didn't mention the evil report of the unbelieving spies (Numbers 13:28-29). It was almost as if the memory was so painful that Moses didn't want to think about it.

b. **They also took some of the fruit of the land**: The returning spies didn't only tell Israel how good the land was. They also brought back proof, including some of the remarkable **fruit** in Canaan. This included a huge cluster of grapes, pomegranates, and figs (Numbers 13:23). The name **Eshcol** can mean "cluster" or "bunch."

c. **It is a good land which the LORD our God is giving us**: It was enough that the nation of Israel had the report from the two godly spies, Joshua and Caleb. In addition to that, *all* the twelve spies were united in saying the land was good and was God's gift to Israel (Numbers 13:27).

4. (26-33) Moses remembers Israel's unbelieving rejection of the Promised Land, though he pleaded with them to take the land in faith.

"Nevertheless you would not go up, but rebelled against the command of the LORD your God; and you complained in your tents, and said, 'Because the LORD hates us, He has brought us out of the land of Egypt to deliver us into the hand of the Amorites, to destroy us. Where can we go up? Our brethren have discouraged our hearts, saying, "The people *are* greater and taller than we; the cities *are* great and fortified up to heaven; moreover we have seen the sons of the Anakim there."'

Then I said to you, 'Do not be terrified, or afraid of them. The LORD your God, who goes before you, He will fight for you, according to all He did for you in Egypt before your eyes, and in the wilderness where you saw how the LORD your God carried you, as a man carries his son, in all the way that you went until you came to this place.' Yet, for all that, you did not believe the LORD your God, who went in the way before you to search out a place for you to pitch your tents, to show you the way you should go, in the fire by night and in the cloud by day.

> a. **Nevertheless**: In this context, this was a haunting word. It was the exact word in the mouth of the ten fearful spies when they began to give an evil testimony to Israel (Numbers 13:28-33).
>
>> i. Essentially, the ten spies and all Israel said, "We went into the land of Canaan and found it to be a wonderful land, just as the LORD said it would be. God's word was true on that point. **Nevertheless** (despite all that), we don't believe God when He said He will enable us to overcome the enemies of the land and to possess it."
>>
>> ii. It is a great tragedy when the people of God have seen that His word is true, nevertheless they fail to trust Him for great things in the future. "Remembering the mercies of God in the past, we may rest assured concerning the present and the future." (Spurgeon)
>
> b. **You would not go up, but rebelled...you complained in your tents.... you did not believe the LORD your God**: God had repeatedly proven Himself faithful to Israel. They could not point to one instance where He had forsaken them, though the journey had not been easy. Yet they answered God's faithfulness with rebellion, complaining, and unbelief.
>
>> i. They were not persuaded of the love of God, and they found it hard to trust a God whose love they doubted. Christians today should also be persuaded of the love of God. Many believers are hindered in their walk with God because they are not genuinely convinced of God's love for them. They should ask, "What would it take to finally convince me that God really loves me?" We don't wait for God to give us everything we want before we love Him. That would be the selfish demand of a short-sighted child, like the child who thinks their parent doesn't love them because they can't have all the candy they want.
>>
>> ii. God has already given the ultimate demonstration of His love: *But God demonstrates His own love toward us, in that while we were still sinners, Christ died for us* (Romans 5:8). The death of Jesus for guilty sinners was and is the ultimate demonstration of God's love; He can do nothing greater than what He has already done in Jesus. Now, it is up to us to simply receive His love.

c. **The LORD your God, who goes before you, He will fight for you, according to all He did for you in Egypt before your eyes**: With these words, Moses did his best to encourage the people to trust God. He called on them to specifically remember God's past faithfulness and consider that He was able to give them victory in the conquest of the land of Canaan.

i. The spiritual adversary of the believer (Satan) loves to make the believer *forget* what they should *remember* (the past victories and miracles of God on our behalf). He also loves to make the believer *remember* what they should *forget* (the past of sin and self-life).

ii. **You saw how the LORD your God carried you, as a man carries his son**: "Never a day without its cross, its lesson, its peril; but never a day that God does not bear us up in His hands, as some mighty river bears up the boat of the missionary explorer." (Meyer)

d. **Yet, for all that, you did not believe the LORD your God**: In a sense, it was not *sin* that kept Israel out of the Promised Land. Instead, it was *unbelief* (though certainly, unbelief is sin). Israel's sin could be covered through atoning sacrifice, but their unbelief and doubt of God's love for them made them unable to put their trust in God.

i. Believers often think that it is some particular sin that hinders them going on with the LORD. It is true that the LORD wants to deal with such sin and get it out of the way, but the way that happens is by deepening the relationship of love and trust in the LORD. Unbelief and lack of trust are the real enemies.

C. Moses remembers the aftermath of Israel's rebellion at Kadesh Barnea.

1. (34-40) Moses remembers God's oath of judgment against unbelieving Israel.

"And the LORD heard the sound of your words, and was angry, and took an oath, saying, 'Surely not one of these men of this evil generation shall see that good land of which I swore to give to your fathers, except Caleb the son of Jephunneh; he shall see it, and to him and his children I am giving the land on which he walked, because he wholly followed the LORD.' The LORD was also angry with me for your sakes, saying, 'Even you shall not go in there; Joshua the son of Nun, who stands before you, he shall go in there. Encourage him, for he shall cause Israel to inherit it.

Moreover your little ones and your children, who you say will be victims, who today have no knowledge of good and evil, they shall go in there; to them I will give it, and they shall possess it. But *as for* you, turn and take your journey into the wilderness by the Way of the Red Sea.'

a. **Was angry, and took an oath**: In response to Israel's unbelief and lack of trust in God's love, God swore an oath (Psalm 95:11) that the adult generation which came out of Egypt would not inherit the Promised Land, but would instead die in the wilderness.

b. **Except Caleb the son of Jephunneh**: The only exceptions were Caleb and Joshua. These were the faithful two among the twelve spies who came back with the report from the Promised Land (Numbers 14:6-10).

c. **Even you shall not go in there**: Even Moses himself would not enter the Promised Land. Though this was not specifically announced in Numbers 14 (coming later in Numbers 20), it could be inferred then, because Moses was not among the only exceptions named (Joshua and Caleb).

d. **Joshua.... he shall cause Israel to inherit it**: Moses was one of the great men of the Bible and all history. Yet, as great as Moses was, he could not and would not lead Israel into the Promised Land. That was left up to one who came after Moses, Joshua.

> i. **Encourage him**: God commanded Moses to **encourage** Joshua, even understanding that Joshua would succeed him. It was good for Moses to give the encouragement, and it was good for Joshua to receive it. The work of Moses in leading Israel to Canaan would be completed through Joshua.

> ii. Moses was the great lawgiver and represented a relationship with God through the law. This could give a person a "wilderness" kind of relationship with God but could never bring them into a "Promised Land" kind of relationship with God. Only Joshua could do that. It is significant that the Hebrew name Joshua exactly corresponds to the name *Jesus*. Only Jesus can bring us into a Promised Land relationship with God.

e. **Moreover your little ones and your children, who you say will be victims...they shall possess it**: Israel's great excuse for their unbelief at Kadesh Barnea was, "If we attempt to take the land, our children will be killed" (Numbers 14:3). God answered their unbelieving excuse by saying, "You will be killed, and your children will possess the land."

> i. "Anything, in fact, will serve as an excuse, when the heart is bent on compromise." (Spurgeon)

> ii. It is sobering to consider how easily, how quickly, and how completely, God sees through the excuses people offer. We often feel confident in our excuses because other people find it difficult to challenge them. But God sees through excuses and understands everyone's true motivations.

2. (41-46) Moses remembers their half-hearted repentance and futile invasion attempt.

> "Then you answered and said to me, 'We have sinned against the LORD; we will go up and fight, just as the LORD our God commanded us.' And when everyone of you had girded on his weapons of war, you were ready to go up into the mountain.

> "And the LORD said to me, 'Tell them, "Do not go up nor fight, for I *am* not among you; lest you be defeated before your enemies."' So I spoke to you; yet you would not listen, but rebelled against the command of the LORD, and presumptuously went up into the mountain. And the Amorites who dwelt in that mountain came out against you and chased you as bees do, and drove you back from Seir to Hormah. Then you returned and wept before the LORD, but the LORD would not listen to your voice nor give ear to you.

> "So you remained in Kadesh many days, according to the days that you spent *there*.

    a. **We have sinned against the LORD; we will go up and fight**: After hearing the consequences of their rejection of God, Israel had a change of heart. Yet they went out in their own strength and not in faith, because God did not lead them.

        i. "True to human nature, as soon as access to Canaan was denied that early rebellious generation (vv. 35, 40), they decided that that precisely was what they would do." (Merrill)

    b. **Rebelled against the command of the LORD**: They did this *amid their supposed repentance*. Their sorrow was not over grieving the heart of God but over thirty-eight more years in the wilderness. God therefore saw that even in their shallow repentance, they **rebelled against** His command.

    c. **The Amorites who dwelt in that mountain came out against you and chased you as bees do**: The invasion attempted in their own wisdom and strength ended in disaster. After their total defeat, *then* they wept. But again, this was over the consequences of getting caught, not over grieving the heart of God, and not over their sin of not trusting the great love of God.

        i. "The Amorites' pursuit 'like a swarm of bees' describes numerical greatness, persistence, and ferocity." (Kalland)

    d. **So you remained in Kadesh many days**: The rest of Deuteronomy will say nothing about these many years when Israel started at **Kadesh** and then returned there, yet mostly traveling as nomads in the broader wilderness. Even the book of Numbers gives very little record of what happened in these more than thirty-five years. Numbers makes mention only of the rebellion of Korah (Numbers 16:1-40), the complaining of Israel (Numbers 16:41-17:13), the death of Miriam (Numbers 20:1), and Israel's rebellion at Meribah (Numbers 20:2-13).

i. "Even though the way of the wilderness had been a terrible one, they had not been left to grope their way through it alone. God had constantly moved before them, choosing them the place of encampment at every pause, indicating where they should pitch their tents." (Morgan)

Deuteronomy 2 – Moses Remembers the Wilderness Years and the March to Canaan

A. Moses remembers the wilderness years.

1. (1-7) Moses remembers the journey through the land of Edom.

"Then we turned and journeyed into the wilderness of the Way of the Red Sea, as the LORD spoke to me, and we skirted Mount Seir for many days.

"And the LORD spoke to me, saying: 'You have skirted this mountain long enough; turn northward. And command the people, saying, "You *are about to* pass through the territory of your brethren, the descendants of Esau, who live in Seir; and they will be afraid of you. Therefore watch yourselves carefully. Do not meddle with them, for I will not give you *any* of their land, no, not so much as one footstep, because I have given Mount Seir to Esau *as* a possession. You shall buy food from them with money, that you may eat; and you shall also buy water from them with money, that you may drink.

"For the LORD your God has blessed you in all the work of your hand. He knows your trudging through this great wilderness. These forty years the LORD your God *has been* with you; you have lacked nothing.'"

> a. **You have skirted this mountain long enough; turn northward**: Deuteronomy 1 ended with Israel refusing to take Canaan by faith and penalized with circling in the wilderness until the generation of unbelief had died. In his telling of the story, Moses quickly advanced to the end of the 38-year period of wandering, as God now directed Israel to advance **northward** towards the Promised Land. Even as they suffered under their unbelief and disobedience, God did not forsake Israel and still directed their journey.

i. "He leads us by no unnecessary pathways. There are a meaning and a value in every stretch of the road, however rough and tortuous it may be. We learn lessons in the region of Mount Seir which can be learned nowhere else; we discover God in the country of Moab as we could do in no other region. Let us, then, ever rejoice in His commands, however much they disturb us." (Morgan)

b. **You are about to pass through the territory of your brethren, the descendants of Esau**: The **descendants of Esau** were distant relatives to the people of Israel (400 years earlier, the brother of Jacob was Esau). God didn't want Israel to take the land that He gave to Esau and his descendants, the Edomites. **Edom** was a nickname for Esau and became associated with his descendants.

i. Perhaps the most famous descendant of Esau in the New Testament was Herod the Great. According to the ancient Jewish historian Josephus, Herod the Great was an Idumean (*The Antiquities of the Jews*, book 14, chap 15, section 2), a people descended from the Edomites.

c. **Do not meddle with them, for I will not give you any of their land**: As they marched towards Canaan, Israel wasn't just another conquering army, out to get whatever land it could take. Israel was probably strong enough to simply take the land of Edom, but Israel only received what God had promised to them. God had provided for Israel (**you have lacked nothing**), they didn't need to plunder Edom, their cousin nation.

i. "The divine commands were not uniformly instructions to go forward or to fight. Israel was to conquer some areas and by-pass others. In this way the precise extent of the land to be occupied was defined by God and selfish human ambitions were restrained." (Thompson)

ii. **You have lacked nothing**: "God, as a liberal Lord, gives not some small cottage or annuity, for life, to his elder servants, as great men use to do, but bountifully provides for them and theirs to many generations. Who would not serve thee then, O king of nations!" (Trapp)

d. **You shall buy food from them with money…you shall also buy water**: God commanded Israel to treat the Edomites with respect, even though they could have dominated them as a stronger nation (Numbers 20:14-21).

i. How someone treats those weaker than themselves is always a good measure of character. When someone can dominate or abuse others and does not, it is one evidence of good character. For some of these reasons, God commanded Israel to treat the weaker nation of Edom well.

ii. **Buy food from them with money**: "Jarchi tells us that this exhortation meant that they were not to pretend to be poor. You know how many do so when it is likely to save their pockets. When the tribes came to the Edomites they were not to say to them, 'We are poor people, and have no money; you must not charge too much for the water, for we cannot afford to pay you at full rates.' No, no, no; it must not be. Supplied by the infinite God, the children of heaven dare not pretend to be poor." (Spurgeon)

2. (8-15) Moses remembers the journey through Moab.

"And when we passed beyond our brethren, the descendants of Esau who dwell in Seir, away from the road of the plain, away from Elath and Ezion Geber, we turned and passed by way of the Wilderness of Moab. Then the Lord said to me, 'Do not harass Moab, nor contend with them in battle, for I will not give you *any* **of their land** *as* **a possession, because I have given Ar to the descendants of Lot** *as* **a possession.'"**

(The Emim had dwelt there in times past, a people as great and numerous and tall as the Anakim. They were also regarded as giants, like the Anakim, but the Moabites call them Emim. The Horites formerly dwelt in Seir, but the descendants of Esau dispossessed them and destroyed them from before them, and dwelt in their place, just as Israel did to the land of their possession which the Lord gave them.)

"'Now rise and cross over the Valley of the Zered.' So we crossed over the Valley of the Zered. And the time we took to come from Kadesh Barnea until we crossed over the Valley of the Zered *was* **thirty-eight years, until all the generation of the men of war was consumed from the midst of the camp, just as the Lord had sworn to them. For indeed the hand of the Lord was against them, to destroy them from the midst of the camp until they were consumed.**

a. **Passed by way of the Wilderness of Moab**: The Moabites were also distant relatives to Israel. They descended from Lot, the nephew of Abraham. As it was with Edom, God did not want Israel to **harass Moab, nor contend with them in battle** – their land was not the land God intended to give Israel.

i. One of the more famous Moabites in the Bible was Ruth (Ruth 1:4). She was a Moabite woman who married an Israelite man named Boaz. Ruth became the great-grandmother to King David and one of the ancestors of the Messiah.

b. **The Emim had dwelt there in times past**: The Moabites were of note because they defeated a Canaanite people known as the **Emim**, who were a large, fearsome race, as mighty as the **Anakim**. The Moabites were not the first to inhabit those lands; they had displaced people who came before them.

i. The term translated **giants** here is the Hebrew word *rephaim*. The term *rephaim* is often translated "giants," but simply means "fearsome ones."

ii. The **Rephaim** were a group of large, warlike people who populated Canaan before the Israelites. In the area east of the Jordan River, they were known by many names: The Moabites called them **Emim**, the Ammonites called them *Zamzummin* (Deuteronomy 2:20).

iii. "Probably they were a hardy, fierce, and terrible people, who lived, like the wandering Arabs, on the plunder of others. This was sufficient to gain them the appellation of giants, or men of prodigious stature." (Clarke)

iv. "The noun *repaim* occurs in Psalm 88:10 (11, Heb.); Proverbs 2:18; 9:18; 21:16; Job 26:5; Isaiah 14:9; 26:14, 19 in the sense of the shades of the dead in Sheol. It is possible that the Israelites might have applied the term to the early inhabitants of the land as persons long since dead." (Thompson)

v. The **Anakim**: "The name Anak was an ancient one. It is known on the Egyptian execration texts of the twentieth and nineteenth centuries BC (cf. 1:28; Num. 13:22, 33; Josh. 11:21, 22; 15:14)." (Thompson)

vi. "And if God cast out those Emims, or terrible ones, before the Moabites, will he not much more cast out these Anakims before the Israelites?" (Trapp)

c. **Thirty-eight years**: In these brief verses, Moses covered thirty-eight years of Israel's time in the wilderness. This was a period when they didn't accomplish much more than survival, making little progress, and waiting for the generation of unbelief to die so that the generation of faith could enter the Promised Land.

i. **Just as Israel did to the land of their possession which the LORD gave them**: "It is possible that the narrator here was employing the so-called 'perfective of confidence,' used to speak of a future event that is as good as done inasmuch as it is promised by the Lord. Second, the statement could be a later addition to the text by an authorized individual understood to be directed by the Lord." (Merrill)

B. Moses remembers the nations Israel encountered on their way to Canaan.

1. (16-23) Going through the land of the Ammonites.

"So it was, when all the men of war had finally perished from among the people, that the LORD spoke to me, saying: 'This day you are to cross over at Ar, the boundary of Moab. And *when* you come near the people of Ammon, do not harass them or meddle with them, for I will not give you *any* of the land of the people of Ammon *as* a possession, because I have given it to the descendants of Lot *as* a possession.'"

(That was also regarded as a land of giants; giants formerly dwelt there. But the Ammonites call them Zamzummim, a people as great and numerous and tall as the Anakim. But the LORD destroyed them before them, and they dispossessed them and dwelt in their place, just as He had done for the descendants of Esau, who dwelt in Seir, when He destroyed the Horites from before them. They dispossessed them and dwelt in their place, even to this day. And the Avim, who dwelt in villages as far as Gaza—the Caphtorim, who came from Caphtor, destroyed them and dwelt in their place.)

    a. **When all the men of war had finally perished**: This marked the end (or the near end) of the generation of unbelief, that at Kadesh Barnea had refused to trust God's promise and take the land of Canaan by faith (Deuteronomy 1:19-33). Now, God would lead the generation of faith to conquer Canaan.

    b. **I will not give you any of the land of the people of Ammon**: As with the Edomites and the Moabites, the land of the Ammonites was also not for the people of Israel. Under the leadership of Moses, Israel was directed by God. They did not attack and conquer as they pleased, but as God directed.

    c. **A land of giants**: This again uses the Hebrew word *rephaim*, referring to a tribe of large, warlike people who populated Canaan before the Israelites. The Moabites called them **Emim** (Deuteronomy 2:11).

        i. **The Caphtorim, who came from Caphtor**: "The exact location of *Caphtor* is not known but it was possibly Crete. Elsewhere in the Old Testament (Jer. 47:4; Amos 9:7) it seems to refer to the sea coasts and islands of the Aegean Sea. The Philistines were part of the Sea Peoples who invaded the eastern Mediterranean coastlands in the thirteenth century BC." (Thompson)

2. (24-37) Moses remembers the conquest of Sihon, king of the Amorites.

"'Rise, take your journey, and cross over the River Arnon. Look, I have given into your hand Sihon the Amorite, king of Heshbon, and his land. Begin to possess *it*, and engage him in battle. This day I will begin to put the dread and fear of you upon the nations under the whole heaven, who shall hear the report of you, and shall tremble and be in anguish because of you.'

"And I sent messengers from the Wilderness of Kedemoth to Sihon king of Heshbon, with words of peace, saying, Let me pass through your land; I will keep strictly to the road, and I will turn neither to the right nor to the left. You shall sell me food for money, that I may eat, and give me water for money, that I may drink; only let me pass through on foot, just as the descendants of Esau who dwell in Seir and the Moabites who dwell in Ar did for me, until I cross the Jordan to the land which the LORD our God is giving us.'

"But Sihon king of Heshbon would not let us pass through, for the LORD your God hardened his spirit and made his heart obstinate, that He might deliver him into your hand, as *it is* this day.

"And the LORD said to me, 'See, I have begun to give Sihon and his land over to you. Begin to possess *it,* that you may inherit his land.' Then Sihon and all his people came out against us to fight at Jahaz. And the LORD our God delivered him over to us; so we defeated him, his sons, and all his people. We took all his cities at that time, and we utterly destroyed the men, women, and little ones of every city; we left none remaining. We took only the livestock as plunder for ourselves, with the spoil of the cities which we took. From Aroer, which *is* on the bank of the River Arnon, and *from* the city that *is* in the ravine, as far as Gilead, there was not one city too strong for us; the LORD our God delivered all to us. Only you did not go near the land of the people of Ammon—anywhere along the River Jabbok, or to the cities of the mountains, or wherever the LORD our God had forbidden us.

> a. **Sihon king of Heshbon would not let us pass through**: Because of this refusal, Israel fought a battle recorded in Numbers 21. Israel simply asked for safe passage through the land of the Amorites, but they were refused.
>
> b. **The LORD your God hardened his spirit and made his heart obstinate, that He might deliver him into your hand**: God worked behind the scenes in hardening the heart of Sihon, the king of the Amorites.
>
>> i. It was right for God to do this because the Creator has the right to do whatever He pleases with His creatures. But it was also right because of the *way* God did it. God did not persuade a reluctant Sihon to act against Israel; God simply let Sihon's heart take the evil way it wanted to go. God did not change Sihon's heart from good to bad but hardened it in its malice towards Israel.

ii. "Both Pharaoh and Sihon were unaffected by the demands of God which came through God's servants. Neither would bend his will to the will of God and each refusal produced a further hardening of the heart. Thus the demands of God, once rejected, became a hardening influence on Sihon's heart, so that he was unable to respond favourably to Israel's request." (Thompson)

c. **That He might deliver him into your hand**: This explains why God hardened the heart of King Sihon. God led Sihon into the destructive course that his heart desired so that the land of the Amorites became the possession and inheritance of Israel (**that you may inherit his land**). God would not allow Israel to take the land of the Edomites, Moabites, or Ammonites, but He did grant them the land of the Amorites.

d. **Utterly destroyed the men, women, and little ones of every city; we left none remaining**: The war against the Amorites was one of the unique wars of judgment God told Israel to fight. In it, Israel was not just to defeat the Amorites on the field of battle, but to bring judgment against their whole society. The Amorites were among the people that God had long before appointed for judgment (Genesis 15:16) if they did not repent.

i. **We took all his cities**: "This outcome is, of course, in line with Moses' own policy outlined later in Deuteronomy, a code of conduct that specified that cities, houses, wells, vineyards, and olive groves—all would become Israel's without their expending any labor at all in their construction (Deuteronomy 6:10–11; cf. 19:1)." (Merrill)

ii. Thompson on the destruction of all things: "It affirms the lordship of Yahweh over Israel and over his purposes for her in history, but also his judgment on wicked nations. In the Holy War Yahweh accomplished purposes both of redemption and of judgment.... However, the application of the principle in the Christian age is very different."

e. **There was not one city too strong for us**: Thirty-eight years before, Israel refused to go into the Promised Land because they felt that they were over-matched militarily. Here, when they began to enter the land by faith, God showed them how it *could* have been 38 years before – if they had only believed Him.

i. **There was not one city too strong for us** is literally, "there was not one city too high for us." The high walls of the Canaanite cities had intimidated Israel 38 years before (see Deuteronomy 1:28). But walking in faith, even high walls were obstacles that could be overcome in the strength of the LORD.

Deuteronomy 3 – Moses Remembers the March to Canaan, and the Appointment of Joshua

A. Moses remembers the defeat of Bashan.

1. (1-2) God commands Israel to attack Bashan.

"Then we turned and went up the road to Bashan; and Og king of Bashan came out against us, he and all his people, to battle at Edrei. And the LORD said to me, 'Do not fear him, for I have delivered him and all his people and his land into your hand; you shall do to him as you did to Sihon king of the Amorites, who dwelt at Heshbon.'"

> a. **Then we turned and went up the road to Bashan**: As Israel drew closer to the Promised Land, moving westward towards the Jordan River, they passed through the land of **Og**, king of Bashan.
>
>> i. "*Bashan* was the area to the north and north-east of Galilee, an area rich in forests and renowned for its pastures and its high hills, inhabited today by the Druze people." (Thompson)
>
> b. **Do not fear him, for I have delivered him and all his people and his land into your hand**: God specifically commanded Moses and all Israel to **not fear** King Og, despite his size (Deuteronomy 3:11). God would give Israel the same victory that He had given them against the Amorites (Numbers 21:31-32).

2. (3-11) Israel defeats Bashan.

"So the LORD our God also delivered into our hands Og king of Bashan, with all his people, and we attacked him until he had no survivors remaining. And we took all his cities at that time; there was not a city which we did not take from them: sixty cities, all the region of Argob, the kingdom of Og in Bashan. All these cities *were* fortified with high walls, gates, and bars, besides a great many rural towns. And we utterly destroyed them, as we did to Sihon king of Heshbon, utterly destroying the men, women, and children of every city. But all the livestock and the spoil of the cities we took as booty for ourselves.

"And at that time we took the land from the hand of the two kings of the Amorites who *were* on this side of the Jordan, from the River Arnon to Mount Hermon (the Sidonians call Hermon Sirion, and the Amorites call it Senir), all the cities of the plain, all Gilead, and all Bashan, as far as Salcah and Edrei, cities of the kingdom of Og in Bashan.

"For only Og king of Bashan remained of the remnant of the giants. Indeed his bedstead *was* an iron bedstead. (*Is* it not in Rabbah of the people of Ammon?) Nine cubits *is* its length and four cubits its width, according to the standard cubit.

a. **And we took all his cities at that time…sixty cities**: The conquest of King Og of Bashan brought Israel even more territory to occupy on the eastern side of the Jordan River. This victory showed them that they could, through the power of God, overcome the Canaanites they would confront on the west side of the Jordan River.

i. **Sixty cities**: "The term 'city,' however, need not imply that these were places with large populations. While some cities had thousands of inhabitants, others had only a few hundred." (Kalland)

b. **Only Og king of Bashan remained of the remnant of the giants**: Apparently, Og was the last of the *Rephaim* in his area, on the east side of the Jordan River.

i. The repeated references to the *Rephaim* in these first three chapters show that Israel, when trusting in God, was able to defeat this race of fearsome warriors. It also shows that some 40 years before this, Israel's fear of these men (recorded in Numbers 13:32-33) was unfounded. The reasons stated by Israel at Kadesh Barnea recorded in Numbers 13 were exposed as mere excuses considering the victories the next generation experienced by faith.

c. **Indeed his bedstead was an iron bedstead**: Og's **bedstead** was 14 feet by 6 feet in modern measurements (4 meters by 2 meters). Some commentators believe this describes his burial sarcophagus. Whether this was his bed or his coffin, this shows Og's large size.

i. "Allowing the bedstead to have been one cubit longer than Og, which is certainly sufficient, and allowing the cubit to be about *eighteen* inches long, for this is perhaps the average of *the cubit of a man*, then Og was *twelve feet high*. This may be deemed extraordinary, and perhaps almost incredible, and therefore many commentators have, according to their fancy, *lengthened* the *bedstead* and *shortened* the *man*, making the former one-third longer than the person who lay on it, that they might reduce Og to *six* cubits; but even in this way they make him at least *nine feet high*." (Clarke)

ii. **Is it not in Rabbah**: "Its unusual construction and size made it a museum piece, one, the historian said, that was still on exhibit in the Ammonite city Rabbah in his own time." (Merrill)

B. Moses remembers the tribes that settled on the east side of the Jordan River.

1. (12-17) The division of the land conquered on the east side of the Jordan River among the tribes of Reuben, Gad, and half the tribe of Manasseh.

"And this land, *which* we possessed at that time, from Aroer, which *is* by the River Arnon, and half the mountains of Gilead and its cities, I gave to the Reubenites and the Gadites. The rest of Gilead, and all Bashan, the kingdom of Og, I gave to half the tribe of Manasseh. (All the region of Argob, with all Bashan, was called the land of the giants. Jair the son of Manasseh took all the region of Argob, as far as the border of the Geshurites and the Maachathites, and called Bashan after his own name, Havoth Jair, to this day.)

"Also I gave Gilead to Machir. And to the Reubenites and the Gadites I gave from Gilead as far as the River Arnon, the middle of the river as *the* border, as far as the River Jabbok, the border of the people of Ammon; the plain also, with the Jordan as *the* border, from Chinnereth as far as the east side of the Sea of the Arabah (the Salt Sea), below the slopes of Pisgah.

a. **And this land, which we possessed at that time**: Israel had conquered significant areas of land on the eastern side of the Jordan River. The tribes of Reuben and Gad asked for this territory (Numbers 32:1-5), and it was divided between them and half the tribe of Manasseh (Numbers 32:33).

b. **I gave**: The repetition of these words emphasizes that the land belonged to God, and He distributed it as He willed.

2. (18-20) The command for the tribes living east of the Jordan to assist the rest of Israel in the conquest of Canaan.

"Then I commanded you at that time, saying: 'The LORD your God has given you this land to possess. All you men of valor shall cross over armed before your brethren, the children of Israel. But your wives, your little ones, and your livestock (I know that you have much livestock) shall stay in your cities which I have given you, until the LORD has given rest to your brethren as to you, and they also possess the land which

the LORD your God is giving them beyond the Jordan. Then each of you may return to his possession which I have given you.'

> a. **Then I commanded you at that time**: Moses remembered the agreement of the two and one-half tribes recorded in Numbers 32:17-33. God agreed to give Reuben, Gad, and half the tribe of Manasseh this land only on the condition that they would send their **men of valor** over the Jordan as part of the army of the united tribes of Israel.
>
> b. **Then each of you may return to his possession**: Joshua 22:1-9 describes the honorable fulfillment of the promise made by the tribes living east of the Jordan. They fought with the other tribes for at least seven years, conquering the main centers of Canaanite power.

C. Moses remembers the appointment of Joshua.

1. (21-22) Moses encourages Joshua.

"And I commanded Joshua at that time, saying, 'Your eyes have seen all that the LORD your God has done to these two kings; so will the LORD do to all the kingdoms through which you pass. You must not fear them, for the LORD your God Himself fights for you.'

> a. **And I commanded Joshua at that time**: Joshua had a gigantic job to do – to bring a whole nation into a land where they would not be welcome, and where they must fight to possess what God had rightfully given to them.
>
> b. **You must not fear them**: This command was based on a promise – **the LORD your God Himself fights for you**. With God fighting for Israel, as He had done before against **these two kings** (Sihon of the Amorites and Og of Bashan), Israel could trust Him completely. Remembering God's past faithfulness would be one key to Joshua's trust in God for the needs of the present and the future. The same principle is helpful for believers today.
>
> > i. "Once more in the language of holy war he said, 'Do not be afraid,' for he is the 'fighting one' who wages war on their behalf." (Kalland)
> >
> > ii. "We must be careful to recognize that it does not so much mean that God was on their side, as that they were on the side of God. God would not have fought for them, if their cause had been unrighteous. It was because in their warfare they were carrying out His will, that He fought for them…. In no conflict have we any right to ask or expect that God will fight for us, save as we know we are with Him." (Morgan)

2. (23-29) Moses remembers his plea for permission to enter the Promised Land.

"Then I pleaded with the LORD at that time, saying: 'O Lord GOD, You have begun to show Your servant Your greatness and Your mighty hand, for what god *is there* in heaven or on earth who can do *anything* like Your works and Your mighty *deeds*? I pray, let me cross over and see the good land beyond the Jordan, those pleasant mountains, and Lebanon.'

"But the LORD was angry with me on your account, and would not listen to me. So the LORD said to me: 'Enough of that! Speak no more to Me of this matter. Go up to the top of Pisgah, and lift your eyes toward the west, the north, the south, and the east; behold *it* with your eyes, for you shall not cross over this Jordan. But command Joshua, and encourage him and strengthen him; for he shall go over before this people, and he shall cause them to inherit the land which you will see.'

"So we stayed in the valley opposite Beth Peor.

> a. **Then I pleaded with the LORD.... let me cross over and see**: Moses sinned in the wilderness at Meribah, where he so seriously misrepresented God that the LORD said Moses would be denied entry into the Promised Land (Numbers 20:10-13). Yet, Moses knew God was rich in mercy and forgiveness. He knew there was no harm in asking God to relent from His previous judgment and allow him to set his foot in Canaan, the fulfillment of his long labor in leading Israel.
>
> > i. "The verb *besought* [**pleaded**] is a strong one, meaning 'entreat', 'implore favour', 'make supplication'." (Thompson)
> >
> > ii. Moses lived the first 40 years of his life confident in his own ability to deliver Israel. He spent the next 40 years of his life having that confidence demolished as he tended his father-in-law's sheep. He spent the last 40 years of his life as God's instrument to lead and deliver Israel. Yet, because of his sin of misrepresenting God at Meribah (Numbers 20:10-13), he would never see Israel come into Canaan. No wonder Moses **pleaded with the LORD**.
>
> b. **Enough of that! Speak no more to Me of this matter**: God did not want to hear the appeal of Moses on this matter. God would not change His response to the sin of Moses (Numbers 20:10-13). The sin of Moses was judged more severely because of his position as a leader, and as a man who had received and taught God's word (James 3:1).
>
> > i. According to James 3:1, it is right for teachers and leaders to be judged by a stricter standard, though it is unrighteous to hold teachers and leaders to a perfect standard. It was true the people's conduct was worse than the conduct of Moses, but this was irrelevant.

ii. In his sin at Meribah (Numbers 20:10-13), Moses marred a beautiful picture of the redemptive work of Jesus Christ, displayed through the rock which provided water in the wilderness. The New Testament makes it clear this water-providing and life-giving Rock was a picture of Jesus (1 Corinthians 10:4). Jesus, being struck once, provided life for all who would drink of Him (John 7:37). But it was unnecessary – and unrighteous – that Jesus would be struck again, much less again twice, because the Son of God needed only to suffer once (Hebrews 10:10-12). Jesus can now be approached with words of faith (Romans 10:8-10), as Moses should have spoken faith-filled words to bring life-giving water to the nation of Israel. In some sense, Moses spoiled this picture of the work of Jesus Christ.

iii. Ginzberg relates a rabbinic legend that blood and water flowed from the rock that Moses struck instead of speaking to it. "The sign He gave him was to make known to him that, before the water came, blood would flow from the rock at Meribah, when Moses should strike it after uttering the hasty, impatient words that were destined to bring death down upon him."

c. **Speak no more to Me of this matter**: Moses was a great man of intercession – perhaps one of the greatest in the Bible. Yet, God would say "no" even to Moses in prayer. God will sometimes say no even to His mightiest intercessors (Jeremiah 15:1).

d. **Go up to the top of Pisgah**: This was the place where Moses could see Canaan from a distance, and then die – and where the book of Deuteronomy will end.

i. "This eminence, whose modern name, most likely, is Ras es-Siyaghah, lies just north of Mount Nebo and about ten miles east of the Jordan River where it flows into the Dead Sea. From this elevation and vantage point it is possible to take in all of Canaan from Hermon in the north to Beersheba in the south and all the way west to the Mediterranean. Moses waited to ascend the mountain until the time came for him to die (Deuteronomy 34:1–5), thus making this view of the land of promise the last act of his long life." (Kalland)

e. **But command Joshua, and encourage him and strengthen him**: Even though he would not enter Canaan, Moses was responsible for doing all he could to help his successor, Joshua, to excel. This is a godly example for leaders among God's people today, who should always **encourage** and **strengthen** the leaders of the next generation.

i. Moses had the heart of a true shepherd. He knew that his ministry was not centered on himself and his own satisfaction, but on God and His people.

ii. "In fact, Moses' death is not recorded until chapter 34, so that the whole book of Deuteronomy is framed between the announcement of Moses' impending death and the announcement of his actual death. The book is thus, in a sense, the spiritual testament of Moses, Israel's great Lawgiver." (Thompson)

f. **He shall cause them to inherit the land which you will see**: Joshua would lead Israel into the land, not Moses. Yet Moses, at Pisgah, **will see** the Promised Land, with the assurance of God's promise that Israel would possess the land.

i. "We are to pray without ceasing; always praying, never fainting; asking, seeking, knocking. But there are some subjects concerning which God says, 'Speak no more unto Me of this.' In some cases these topics have to do with others, but more often with ourselves, as in the case of the apostle Paul (2 Corinthians 12:9).... If He does not give the exact thing you ask, He will give the Pisgah view and more grace." (Meyer)

ii. "He surely has no reason to complain who is taken from earthly felicity to heavenly glory. In this act God showed to Moses both his goodness and severity." (Clarke)

Deuteronomy 4 – A Call to Obedience

A. Moses challenges the nation to obedience.

1. (1-4) Moses challenges Israel to learn from the example of Baal-Peor.

"Now, O Israel, listen to the statutes and the judgments which I teach you to observe, that you may live, and go in and possess the land which the LORD God of your fathers is giving you. You shall not add to the word which I command you, nor take from it, that you may keep the commandments of the LORD your God which I command you. Your eyes have seen what the LORD did at Baal Peor; for the LORD your God has destroyed from among you all the men who followed Baal of Peor. But you who held fast to the LORD your God *are* alive today, every one of you.

>a. **Now, O Israel, listen**: Moses had reminded Israel of their many rebellions against God in the wilderness (Deuteronomy 1:19-46). Now, as they were ready to enter the Promised Land, Moses wanted them to think about their need for present obedience in consideration of their past rebellions.

>>i. One of Satan's more effective strategies is to make believers remember what they should forget and forget what they should remember. If God's people don't remember their past sins and rebellions against God, they can easily repeat them, falling into the same sinful patterns and traps.

>b. **That you may live**: In the larger sense, spiritual life and death depended on Israel's obedience. Yet also in the more immediate sense, physical life and death depended on their obedience. Israel was about to attack a strong people and displace them from the Promised Land. If Israel didn't have the blessing of the LORD upon them, they would soon suffer great losses and be expelled from Canaan.

i. Israel's first military loss in the Promised Land (Joshua 7) came specifically because they had disobeyed God. A battle was lost, and 36 men died at Ai because one man in Israel (Achan) did not obey the command of the LORD.

c. **You shall not add to the word which I command you, nor take from it**: This is an important principle regarding God's word. God's people are not to **add to** it (in the sense of making the traditions and opinions of men equal to the law of God), nor are they to **take from it** (by bad teaching, explaining away passages, or declaring some biblical authors to be unreliable or uninspired). This idea is repeated in Revelation 22:18-19.

d. **Your eyes have seen what the LORD did at Baal Peor**: At **Baal Peor**, Israel sinned by committing both sexual and spiritual immorality with the women of Moab and Midian (Numbers 25:1-9). This catastrophe resulted in the death of several thousand under God's judgment and had happened within a few months before Moses spoke the words of Deuteronomy to Israel.

i. Moses warned those **alive today**, those who held faithful and did not fall under God's judgment at Baal Peor, that they must continue in that faithfulness.

2. (5-8) Moses speaks of Israel as a great nation, with a great God and His great law.

"Surely I have taught you statutes and judgments, just as the LORD my God commanded me, that you should act according *to them* in the land which you go to possess. Therefore be careful to observe *them*; for this *is* your wisdom and your understanding in the sight of the peoples who will hear all these statutes, and say, 'Surely this great nation *is* a wise and understanding people.'

"For what great nation *is there* that has God *so* near to it, as the LORD our God *is* to us, for whatever *reason* we may call upon Him? And what great nation *is there* that has *such* statutes and righteous judgments as are in all this law which I set before you this day?

a. **Surely I have taught you statutes and judgments**: An important part of the leadership of Moses was to teach Israel God's law and how it applied to their everyday life. Obedience to God's law in the **land** that they would **possess** was essential to them being blessed and flourishing in the land.

b. **Surely this great nation is a wise and understanding people**: This is what Israel's neighbors would say about an Israel that was blessed and flourishing because of their obedience to God's law. God's intention was that through Israel's obedience to the covenant, He would exalt them among the nations and make them a witness. This was so that foreigners, like the queen of Sheba who visited Solomon at the height of his glory, would see that the Lord God of Israel was indeed the Lord God (1 Kings 10).

c. **For what great nation is there that has God so near to it**: By most measures, Israel was not a **great nation**, as they were not especially large in territory or in population. Yet as they were obedient to the covenant, they would enjoy the blessings God promised and avoid the curses He warned them of (Leviticus 26, Deuteronomy 27-28). This would make them a **great nation**.

> i. Another reason Israel was such a **great nation** was that they had received God's word, God's law (**statutes and righteous judgments as are in all this law**). God committed His oracles, His word – to Israel (Romans 3:2).
>
> ii. This was a gift not only to Israel, but to all humanity. "Almost all the nations in the earth showed that they had formed this opinion of the Jews, by borrowing from them the principal part of their civil code. Take away what *Asia* and *Europe*, whether *ancient* or *modern*, have borrowed from the *Mosaic laws*, and you leave little behind that can be called excellent." (Clarke)

3. (9-14) Moses challenges Israel to learn from the example at Mount Sinai (Horeb).

Only take heed to yourself, and diligently keep yourself, lest you forget the things your eyes have seen, and lest they depart from your heart all the days of your life. And teach them to your children and your grandchildren, *especially concerning* **the day you stood before the Lord your God in Horeb, when the Lord said to me, 'Gather the people to Me, and I will let them hear My words, that they may learn to fear Me all the days they live on the earth, and** *that* **they may teach their children.'**

"Then you came near and stood at the foot of the mountain, and the mountain burned with fire to the midst of heaven, with darkness, cloud, and thick darkness. And the Lord spoke to you out of the midst of the fire. You heard the sound of the words, but saw no form; *you* **only** *heard* **a voice. So He declared to you His covenant which He commanded you to perform, the Ten Commandments; and He wrote them on two tablets of stone. And the Lord commanded me at that time to teach you statutes and judgments, that you might observe them in the land which you cross over to possess.**

a. **Only take heed to yourself**: Moses warned Israel to remember what they had seen, experienced, and learned in the wilderness years. This could refer to both the great miracles of God's goodness and provision, and to the judgments God carried out against the unbelieving and complaining among the people of Israel.

b. **The things your eyes have seen**: God strongly tied the faith of Israel to historical events; to things that actually happened at a real time and a real place. Israel's faith was not fundamentally based on speculative theologies, myths, legends, or philosophies; but on the real, historical acts of God.

> i. This pattern continues and is even strengthened in the New Testament. The faith of the Christian is not based on speculative theologies, myths, legends, or philosophies; but on the real, historical acts of Jesus Christ, especially upon His death and resurrection (1 Corinthians 15:13-20).

c. **Teach them to your children and your grandchildren**: Israel was commanded, **take heed to yourself**. But they were not to think only of themselves; they were also to teach their **children** and **grandchildren**.

> i. The goal of this training was that future generations would **learn to fear** the LORD **all the days they live**. "The 'fear of the Lord' is one of the dominating thoughts of the Old Testament. It is to be recognized as the proper response of a man to God. It is God-given and enables a man to reverence God's person, to obey his commandments and to hate evil (Jer. 32:40; Heb. 5:7)." (Thompson)

d. **Especially concerning the day**: The teaching of their children had to include Israel's experience with God at **Horeb** (Mount Sinai) – an experience some 38 years before the events of Deuteronomy, an event most of those present knew only as children, if at all (Exodus 19:17-20:1)

> i. At Horeb, the nation of Israel heard God speak (**I will let them hear My words**). This was part of the experience that they were to pass down to their children and grandchildren.

> ii. **Two tablets of stone**: "It probably is best to see these two tablets as duplicates, with each containing all ten commandments. This would reflect the custom whereby each party to the covenant would have a copy of the document for his own archives and future reference." (Merrill)

e. **He declared to you His covenant**: At Mount Sinai, Israel received God's law, and they also entered into a covenant with Yahweh (Exodus 24:1-8). This covenant would include the promises of blessing on an obedient Israel and promises to curse a disobedient Israel (Leviticus 26).

i. The law applied to Israel in the wilderness but was ultimately given to them for life **in the land** of Canaan.

ii. **His covenant**: "This is the first explicit occurrence in Deuteronomy of *berit*, the fundamental term for expressing the covenant idea and relationship. It appears over three hundred times in the Old Testament, including some twenty-eight times in Deuteronomy, and can apply generically to covenants of all kinds—conditional or unconditional, bilateral or unilateral, royal grant, or suzerain-vassal—or to just an element of covenant, as here." (Merrill)

4. (15-20) Israel's experience at Mount Sinai was a warning against idolatry.

"Take careful heed to yourselves, for you saw no form when the LORD spoke to you at Horeb out of the midst of the fire, lest you act corruptly and make for yourselves a carved image in the form of any figure: the likeness of male or female, the likeness of any animal that *is* on the earth or the likeness of any winged bird that flies in the air, the likeness of anything that creeps on the ground or the likeness of any fish that *is* in the water beneath the earth. And *take heed*, lest you lift your eyes to heaven, and *when* you see the sun, the moon, and the stars, all the host of heaven, you feel driven to worship them and serve them, which the LORD your God has given to all the peoples under the whole heaven as a heritage. But the LORD has taken you and brought you out of the iron furnace, out of Egypt, to be His people, an inheritance, as you are this day.

a. **You heard the sound of the words, but saw no form; you only heard a voice**: The commands at Horeb had to be obeyed. Because they saw no form of God, therefore God commanded that they must never make an image to represent Him.

i. "Howsoever God chose to appear or manifest himself, he took care never to assume any describable form. He would have no *image worship*, because he is a SPIRIT, and they who worship him *must worship him in Spirit and in truth*." (Clarke)

ii. Israel was forbidden to worship any figure or image in the **likeness of male or female**. Man is made in the image of God but is not God. Worship belongs to God alone, and not to any man or any woman, either in person or in likeness.

iii. Israel was forbidden to worship the creation of God. There is no **animal**, **bird**, **sun**, **moon**, or **stars** that are fittingly worshipped. This is worshipping the creature rather than the Creator (Romans 1:25).

b. **The Lord has taken you and brought you out of the iron furnace**: Because God had delivered Israel, He had a claim to their devotion and allegiance. God does not deliver His people so that they can do as they please, but so that they can do as pleases Him. All humanity is obligated to honor and obey God as Creator; God's people have the additional obligation to honor and obey God as their redeemer, He who **brought** them **out of the iron furnace**.

> i. "Bringing Israel out of Egypt was like bringing her out of an iron-smelting furnace—the heavy bondage of Egypt with its accompanying difficulties and tensions being likened to the hottest fire then known." (Kalland)
>
> ii. "For the Lord to be able to humiliate that great empire by rescuing an impotent slave people from its grasp was ample witness to his incomparability." (Merrill)

5. (21-24) Moses challenges Israel to learn from the example of his own failure.

Furthermore the Lord was angry with me for your sakes, and swore that I would not cross over the Jordan, and that I would not enter the good land which the Lord your God is giving you as an inheritance. But I must die in this land, I must not cross over the Jordan; but you shall cross over and possess that good land. Take heed to yourselves, lest you forget the covenant of the Lord your God which He made with you, and make for yourselves a carved image in the form of anything which the Lord your God has forbidden you. For the Lord your God *is* a consuming fire, a jealous God.

a. **The Lord was angry with me for your sakes**: It was for the sake of Israel that God disciplined Moses, not allowing him to enter the Promised Land. Israel needed to see that no man, not even Moses, was above God's law. They also had to understand that it was indeed better that Joshua lead them into the Promised Land instead of Moses.

b. **I must die in this land…but you shall cross over and possess that good land**: Moses humbly acknowledged his sin and failure before Israel back at Meribah (Numbers 20:2-13). Moses also understood that Israel would succeed in taking Canaan without him. God's work among Israel would not end with the death of Moses. God would use Joshua to lead Israel to **possess that good land**.

> i. Moses knew that he was replaceable. God's workers come and go, but God's work goes on. If a work ends with the death of the worker, it may be fairly questioned whether it was a real work of God.

c. **Take heed to yourselves, lest you forget the covenant of the LORD**: Israel's success in possessing the Promised Land did not depend primarily on Joshua's skill as a leader (though God used Joshua's wisdom and skill as a leader). It depended more on Israel's faithfulness to the **covenant** they made with God and their rejection of idolatry (**a carved image**).

d. **For the LORD your God is a consuming fire**: Moses' idea was simply, "If God did not spare me when I sinned against Him, don't think He will spare you if you turn to other gods. God is a **consuming fire**, and we must take Him and obedience to Him seriously." This idea is quoted in Hebrews 12:29.

i. **A jealous God**: "The term *jealous* (*qanna*) does not connote the same as the English word, but rather an active zealousness for righteousness which arose from Yahweh's holiness. Because of this Yahweh would not countenance Israel's allegiance to any other God." (Thompson)

B. Moses warns the nation about the danger of disobedience.

1. (25-28) The price of serving other gods: exile among the nations.

"When you beget children and grandchildren and have grown old in the land, and act corruptly and make a carved image in the form of anything, and do evil in the sight of the LORD your God to provoke Him to anger, I call heaven and earth to witness against you this day, that you will soon utterly perish from the land which you cross over the Jordan to possess; you will not prolong *your* days in it, but will be utterly destroyed. And the LORD will scatter you among the peoples, and you will be left few in number among the nations where the LORD will drive you. And there you will serve gods, the work of men's hands, wood and stone, which neither see nor hear nor eat nor smell.

a. **I call heaven and earth to witness against you this day**: Moses considered Israel after being in the land for many generations, having **grown old in the land**. If then they started to worship a **carved image** or an idol, creation itself would testify against them. They would **provoke** God to **anger** and be **destroyed** in the land God promised to give them.

b. **And the LORD will scatter you among the peoples**: God gave Israel the Promised Land, but not unconditionally. If they persisted in idol worship, God would remove them from the land and scatter them among the nations.

i. This was exactly what happened some 550 years later, at the time of the Babylonian exile of Judah. However, God's judgment against Israel, His scattering of them among the peoples, would not be forever. God would bring them back to the land, as a testimony to His enduring promise to Israel (Jeremiah 31:34-37).

c. **There you will serve gods, the work of men's hands…which neither see nor hear nor eat nor smell**: If Israel was scattered in exile, they would then get their fill of idols. God would put them in places filled with idols.

2. (29-31) God's mercy to exiled Israel.

But from there you will seek the LORD your God, and you will find *Him* if you seek Him with all your heart and with all your soul. When you are in distress, and all these things come upon you in the latter days, when you turn to the LORD your God and obey His voice (for the LORD your God *is* a merciful God), He will not forsake you nor destroy you, nor forget the covenant of your fathers which He swore to them.

a. **From there you will seek the LORD your God, and you will find Him**: God would not totally abandon Israel in exile. When they were ready to turn back to the LORD, He would be ready to receive them.

i. "Even in the predicament of exile God may be sought and found. One feature of Yahweh's covenant with Israel in contrast with the secular treaties was that a rebel might *return* ('repent') to Yahweh and be forgiven and thus have the prospect of beginning a new life of obedience." (Thompson)

b. **If you seek Him with all your heart and with all your soul**: However, if Israel was to find the LORD, they had to seek Him with **all** their heart and **all** their soul.

i. In this context, to seek God with the **heart** has the idea of passionately seeking Him, seeking Him out of true commitment and devotion to the LORD. Seeking God with the **soul** has the idea of seeking God with the mind, will, and emotions; the surrender of one's whole being to God.

c. **When you turn to the LORD your God and obey His voice**: Turning to God would lead Israel to **obey His voice**. The true, sincere seeking of God will lead a man or woman to obey God. If Israel turned to God in obedience, God promised to remember His **covenant** with Israel and restore them.

i. "The Lord here encourages sinners to turn to himself, and find abundant grace. He encourages sinners who had violated his plainest commandments, who had made idols, and so had corrupted themselves, and had consequently been visited with captivity, and other chastisements — he invites them to turn from their evil ways, and seek his face." (Spurgeon)

ii. Spurgeon noted these verses provide:
- A time mentioned (the present, **from there**).
- A way appointed (**seek the LORD**, and He alone).
- An encouragement given (**He will not forsake you**).

3. (32-40) The reasons for serving God.

"For ask now concerning the days that are past, which were before you, since the day that God created man on the earth, and *ask* from one end of heaven to the other, whether *any* great *thing* like this has happened, or *anything* like it has been heard. Did *any* people *ever* hear the voice of God speaking out of the midst of the fire, as you have heard, and live? Or did God *ever* try to go *and* take for Himself a nation from the midst of *another* nation, by trials, by signs, by wonders, by war, by a mighty hand and an outstretched arm, and by great terrors, according to all that the LORD your God did for you in Egypt before your eyes? To you it was shown, that you might know that the LORD Himself *is* God; *there is* none other besides Him. Out of heaven He let you hear His voice, that He might instruct you; on earth He showed you His great fire, and you heard His words out of the midst of the fire. And because He loved your fathers, therefore He chose their descendants after them; and He brought you out of Egypt with His Presence, with His mighty power, driving out from before you nations greater and mightier than you, to bring you in, to give you their land *as* an inheritance, as *it is* this day. Therefore know this day, and consider *it* in your heart, that the LORD Himself *is* God in heaven above and on the earth beneath; *there is* no other. You shall therefore keep His statutes and His commandments which I command you today, that it may go well with you and with your children after you, and that you may prolong *your* days in the land which the LORD your God is giving you for all time."

a. **For ask now**: Moses asked Israel to carefully think about the **days that are past** and consider if God had ever dealt with any other nation the way He had dealt with Israel. Israel had a special place in the plan of God, and they needed to remember this. Israel was a uniquely blessed people, with a unique role in the unfolding plan of God.

i. Israel is a truly chosen people, but in a significant sense, not chosen for salvation. John the Baptist rightly warned the Jews that being a descendant of Abraham did not guarantee their salvation (Matthew 3:9). Israel was chosen to have a special role in God's unfolding plan of the ages, to receive and preserve God's revelation in the Hebrew Scriptures, to be God's light to the nations, to receive unique blessings from God, and (most importantly) to be the people that would bring forth God's Messiah, the Savior of the World.

b. To you it was shown, that you might know that the Lord Himself is God: Israel could *know* that the Lord was God, because of all the amazing things God did in the life of their nation. These included hearing the **voice of God, trials, signs, wonders, war,** and God's **mighty hand**. All these were given to testify to Israel that Yahweh – the Lord – is God.

i. Clarke on verse 34: "In this verse Moses enumerates *seven* different means used by the Almighty in effecting Israel's deliverance."

c. The Lord Himself is God in heaven above and on the earth beneath, there is no other: This was a logical, rational response to hearing what Israel heard, seeing what they saw, and experiencing what they experienced.

i. "The nations of the earth might indeed have their mythic and epic traditions about the intervention of their gods on behalf of their ancestors or even themselves, but none of these can compare in the least to the act of delivering a disorganized, dispirited, militarily inexperienced horde of slaves from the dominion of the mightiest power on earth." (Merrill)

ii. **In heaven above and on the earth beneath** is another way of saying that God is everywhere. "Where is God? Or rather, where is not God? He is higher than heaven, lower than hell, broader than the sea, longer than the earth.... He is nowhere, and yet everywhere; far from no place, and yet not contained in any place." (Trapp)

d. You shall therefore keep His statutes and His commandments: Considering who God is, and all He did for Israel, obedience to His commands made *perfect sense*. It was simply what should be done. We are fools to disobey such a God of love and power.

i. The Lord gives man the invitation: *Come now, and let us reason together, says the Lord* (Isaiah 1:18). When we consider the options, serving God is the only option. We often think that it is difficult to serve the Lord, but we would be in an even worse place without Him. It has been said, "Democracy is the worst form of government ever created, except for all the others." One could also say, "Serving God is the hardest way to live, except for all the other ways."

4. (41-43) Moses sets apart cities of refuge in the land east of the Jordan River.

Then Moses set apart three cities on this side of the Jordan, toward the rising of the sun, that the manslayer might flee there, who kills his neighbor unintentionally, without having hated him in time past, and that by fleeing to one of these cities he might live: Bezer in the

wilderness on the plateau for the Reubenites, Ramoth in Gilead for the Gadites, and Golan in Bashan for the Manassites.

> a. **Then Moses set apart three cities on this side of the Jordan**: This was part of the commanded preparation for entering the Promised Land. God commanded that three cities of refuge be readied on each side of the Jordan River (Numbers 35:14), and here, the three cities on the east side of the Jordan were appointed.
>
>> i. These verses are something of an appendix or an addition at the end of the first sermon Moses gave to Israel on the plains of Moab. They conclude this first of three sections of Deuteronomy.
>
> b. **Three cities on this side of the Jordan**: Moses could not appoint all six cities of refuge, because they had not yet taken the land on the western side of the Jordan River. Still, though he could not obey all of God's command to appoint six cities of refuge, he did what he could – and appointed the three on the east of the Jordan.
>
>> i. "Hence let us learn that, even when we cannot at once entirely carry out what God commands us to do, we are still to be by no means idle. For nothing but sheer laziness stands in our way, unless we speedily commence at God's command what it is His will to finish." (Calvin)

5. (44-49) Introduction to the second sermon of Moses to Israel.

Now this *is* the law which Moses set before the children of Israel. These *are* the testimonies, the statutes, and the judgments which Moses spoke to the children of Israel after they came out of Egypt, on this side of the Jordan, in the valley opposite Beth Peor, in the land of Sihon king of the Amorites, who dwelt at Heshbon, whom Moses and the children of Israel defeated after they came out of Egypt. And they took possession of his land and the land of Og king of Bashan, two kings of the Amorites, who *were* on this side of the Jordan, toward the rising of the sun, from Aroer, which *is* on the bank of the River Arnon, even to Mount Sion (that is, Hermon), and all the plain on the east side of the Jordan as far as the Sea of the Arabah, below the slopes of Pisgah.

> a. **This is the law which Moses set before the children of Israel**: This begins the second major section of Deuteronomy, the start of the second sermon of Moses to Israel. This is the longest of the three sermons of Deuteronomy, lasting all the way through the end of chapter 26.
>
>> i. With Israel on the threshold of the Promised Land, they needed to be instructed again in the law God gave them some 38 years before at Mount Sinai. As Israel camped on the plains of Moab, Moses declared

and explained the Law of God to the new generation before he died and Joshua became the new leader of Israel.

b. **On this side of the Jordan**: If Israel was going to take the Promised Land, they had to be trained in God's word. They would not conquer Canaan by a do-it-yourself spirituality, but only by obedience to the eternal word of God. The same is true for believers today who will never walk in the abundant life God has for them apart from doing it by His word.

i. **Mount Sion**: "An alternative name is given for Mount Hermon, *Sion*, probably the same as Sirion in 3:9 and Psalm 29:6. It is otherwise unknown." (Thompson)

Deuteronomy 5 – Moses Reminds Israel of their Covenant with God at Sinai

A. Moses reminds Israel of their experience at Mount Sinai.

1. (1-3) The present reality of God's covenant with Israel.

And Moses called all Israel, and said to them: "Hear, O Israel, the statutes and judgments which I speak in your hearing today, that you may learn them and be careful to observe them. The LORD our God made a covenant with us in Horeb. The LORD did not make this covenant with our fathers, but with us, those who *are* here today, all of us who *are* alive.

> a. **Moses called all Israel**: After the brief introduction (Deuteronomy 4:44-49), Moses gathered Israel for the second and longest of the three sermons that make up the book of Deuteronomy.
>
> b. **Hear, O Israel**: Israel was bound to the covenant they agreed to in Exodus 24:1-8, yet the covenant was made with the previous generation which died in the wilderness. The present generation had to understand and embrace the covenant if they were to enjoy the blessings of the covenant.
>
> c. **Made a covenant**: Literally, this is to "cut a covenant." The idea of "cutting" is associated with covenant because covenants were normally sealed with sacrifice – the cutting of a sacrificial victim.
>
> d. **The LORD did not make this covenant with our fathers, but with us**: In fact, the covenant was originally made with the previous generation, and Moses did not deny this. But as Moses spoke to the generation that would conquer Canaan, he emphasized that this was *their* covenant. It was a covenant of the living, not of the dead. It was a present reality, not a historical relic.

i. "The fact is emphasized that the Horeb event was not simply an event of the past which concerned Israel's ancestors only, but was the concern of Israel in every age. The original Israel held within it all later Israelites." (Thompson)

ii. There is a sense in which ethnic Israel today is still under the old covenant, first agreed to at Mount Sinai, and agreed again here a generation later (on the plains of Moab), and in some sense with every generation since.

- The old covenant is not a path to salvation – all that is fulfilled in the new covenant, through the person and work of Jesus Christ.
- The old covenant seems to mark God's continued dealings with the Jewish people, especially in the blessing and cursing aspects that were broader parts of the covenant (Leviticus 26, Deuteronomy 27-28). They are bound as a people that God has selected and promised to use for an important role in His unfolding plan of the ages.
- The Jewish people continue to be uniquely blessed in some ways and at some times, and uniquely cursed in some ways and at some times. This is an outworking of the covenant they made with God at Mount Sinai and renewed here in Deuteronomy.
- Any Jewish person in Christ is not under the old covenant; they are clearly and wonderfully under the new covenant.

2. (4-5) God's revelation of Himself to Israel at Mount Sinai.

The LORD talked with you face to face on the mountain from the midst of the fire. I stood between the LORD and you at that time, to declare to you the word of the LORD; for you were afraid because of the fire, and you did not go up the mountain. *He* **said:**

a. **The LORD talked with you face to face**: When God gave His law and made a covenant with Israel, He began with a dramatic revelation of Himself. God manifested His presence at Sinai with fire, smoke, lightning, and the sound of a trumpet (Exodus 19:16-19, 20:18). They audibly heard God's voice from heaven (Exodus 20:1, 20:19, 20:22). This close communication with Israel was described with the figure of speech, **face to face**.

i. The use of this phrase in relation to God's revelation of Himself to Israel at Mount Sinai gives understanding to the use of the phrase **face to face** in other places. Deuteronomy 4:12 specifically says that Israel *saw no form; you only heard a voice.* Yet they had a remarkably transparent communication with God, so the figure of speech **face to face** applies.

ii. Therefore, when Exodus 33:11 says *So the LORD spoke to Moses face to face, as a man speaks to his friend,* it uses this figure of speech. It doesn't mean that Moses literally saw the face of God, which no man can see and live (Exodus 33:20). Exodus 33:11 means Moses had free and unhindered communication with the LORD.

iii. "*Face to face* seems to mean 'in person,' that is, in the immediacy of personal contact." (Thompson)

b. **I stood between the LORD and you at that time**: Israel could not bear such free and unhindered communication with the LORD, so they asked Moses to speak to God on their behalf (Exodus 20:19).

B. Moses reminds Israel of the Ten Commandments God spoke at Mount Sinai.

1. (6-7) The first commandment, forbidding idolatry.

'I *am* the LORD your God who brought you out of the land of Egypt, out of the house of bondage.
'You shall have no other gods before Me.

a. **I am the LORD your God**: In the ancient world (including Egypt), men worshipped many gods. Here Yahweh (**the LORD**), the covenant God of Israel, set Himself apart from any of the other supposed deities.

i. As Moses recounted the giving of the Ten Commandments to Israel at Mount Sinai, he used *almost* the exact words as in the account recorded in Exodus 20.

ii. "In this repetition of the law some things are transposed, and some words are changed, haply to confute that superstitious opinion of the Jews, who were ready to dream of miraculous mysteries in every letter." (Trapp)

b. **Who brought you out of the land of Egypt, out of the house of bondage**: Before God commanded anything, He declared who He was and what He had done for Israel. The foundation was clear: because of who God was and what He had done for His people, Yahweh had the right to command them – and God's people had the obligation to obey Him.

i. Yet, the Ten Commandments were never given with the thought that one might earn righteousness or heaven by obeying them all perfectly or adequately. At Sinai, God also provided for Israel's failure to keep the law, giving them the institution of sacrifice for the atonement of sin. Every sacrifice pointed to the perfect sacrifice offered by Jesus on the cross.

ii. These Ten Commandments can also be summarized as Jesus did, expressing the essence of the law is to love God with your whole being, and to love your neighbor as yourself (Matthew 22:35-40). This simplification doesn't eliminate the Ten Commandments; it fulfills them, showing us the heart and desire of God for His people. The problem is that we haven't kept the two commandments either, much less the ten.

iii. Jesus Christ was the only one to ever keep the law perfectly – either in the ten or the two. He never needed to sacrifice for His own sin, so could be the perfect sacrifice for sin. Wonderfully, His obedience is credited to those who put their love and trust in Him (Romans 8:2-3).

iv. For the believer under the new covenant, God's law is a tutor (Galatians 3:22-25). Before God's plan of salvation in Jesus Christ was fully evident, God's people were *kept under guard by the law* – both in the sense of being bound by the law, but also held in protective custody. The law, through its revelation of God's character and its exposure of sin, prepares people to come to Jesus – but after coming to Jesus in repentance and faith and receiving God's gift through the new covenant, believers no longer live under the law as a tutor (though they remember the lessons taught to them).

v. From the perspective of the entire Bible, it can be said that the law of God has three great purposes and uses:

- It is a guardrail, keeping humanity on a moral path.
- It is a mirror, showing man his moral failure and need for a savior.
- It is a guide, showing the heart and desire of God for His people.

iv. Thompson on the Ten Commandments in the New Testament: "Jesus referred to them on various occasions (Matt. 5:21, 27, 33; Mark 12:29–31; Luke 10:27; 18:20) and they lie behind many statements in the Epistles (Rom. 2:21, 22; Gal. 5:19f.; Eph. 4:28; 5:3; Heb. 4:9; Jas 2:11, etc.)."

c. **You shall have no other gods before Me**: The first commandment logically flows from understanding who God is and what He has done for His people. Nothing is to come **before** God and He is the only God we worship and serve.

i. In the days of ancient Israel, there was a great temptation to worship the gods of materialism (Baal, the god of weather and financial success) and sex (Ashtoreth, the goddess of sex, romance, and reproduction), or any number of other local deities. We are tempted to worship the same gods, but without the old-fashioned names and images.

ii. "Other gods must not be brought into Yahweh's company, for he exists alone as Israel's God." (Merrill)

c. **No other gods before Me**: This did not imply that it was allowed to have other gods if they lined up behind the true God. Instead, the idea is that there are to be no other gods before the sight of the true God in our lives. **Before Me** is literally, "to My face." God would allow no rival gods. He alone must be worshipped.

i. Failure to obey this commandment is called *idolatry*. We are to flee idolatry (1 Corinthians 10:14). Those lives marked by habitual idolatry will not inherit the kingdom of God (1 Corinthians 6:9-10, Ephesians 5:5, Revelation 21:8, 22:15). Idolatry is a work of the flesh (Galatians 5:19-21), which marks our old life instead of the new (1 Peter 4:3), and we are not to associate with those who call themselves Christians who are idolaters (1 Corinthians 5:11).

2. (8-10) The second commandment, forbidding images used for idolatry.

'You shall not make for yourself a carved image—any likeness *of anything* **that** *is* **in heaven above, or that** *is* **in the earth beneath, or that** *is* **in the water under the earth; you shall not bow down to them nor serve them. For I, the** LORD **your God,** *am* **a jealous God, visiting the iniquity of the fathers upon the children to the third and fourth** *generations* **of those who hate Me, but showing mercy to thousands, to those who love Me and keep My commandments.**

a. **You shall not make for yourself a carved image**: The second commandment also prohibited idolatry regarding false gods. In addition, it prohibited the representation of the true God, Yahweh, with any **carved** or created **image** for the purpose of worship.

b. **Any likeness of anything that is in heaven above, or that is in the earth beneath**: In that day as well as in our own, worship was tied closely with images – idealized images, or even images in the mind of man. God does not allow the making of any images for worship.

i. The second commandment didn't forbid making an image of something for artistic purposes. God Himself commanded Israel to make images of cherubim (Exodus 25:18, 26:31). It forbade the making of images as an aid or a help to worship.

ii. "To countenance its *image worship*, the *Roman Catholic Church* has left the whole of this second commandment out of the decalogue, and thus lost one whole commandment out of the *ten*; but to keep up the *number* they have divided the *tenth* into *two*." (Clarke)

iii. John 4:24 explains the rationale behind the second commandment: *God is Spirit, and those who worship Him must worship in spirit and truth*. The use of images and other material things as a focus or "help" to worship denies who God is (*Spirit*) and how we must worship Him (*in spirit and truth*).

c. **For I, the L**ORD **your God, am a jealous God**: God is **jealous** in the sense that He will not accept being merely added to our lives; He insists on being supreme and He does this out of love.

i. "'Zealous' might be a better translation in modern English, since 'jealousy' has acquired an exclusively bad meaning." (Cole, commentary on Exodus 20)

d. **Visiting the iniquity of the fathers upon the children to the third and fourth generations of those who hate Me**: This does not mean God punishes us directly for the sins of our ancestors. The important words are **of those who hate Me**. If the descendants love God, they will not have the iniquity of the fathers visited on them.

i. "'This necessarily implies – IF *the children walk in the steps of their fathers*; for no man can be condemned by Divine justice for a crime of which he was never guilty." (Clarke)

ii. Yet, the focus here is on idolatry, and this refers to judgment on a *national* scale – nations that forsake the LORD will be judged, and that judgment will have effects throughout generations.

3. (11) The third commandment, forbidding the taking of God's name in vain.

'You shall not take the name of the LORD **your God in vain, for the L**ORD **will not hold *him* guiltless who takes His name in vain.**

a. **You shall not take the name of the L**ORD **your God in vain**: In ancient Near Eastern sorcery, it was common to use the name of a god in incantations. This was prohibited by this command, and there are at least three ways this command is commonly disobeyed.

- *Profanity*: Using the name of God in blasphemy and cursing.
- *Frivolity*: Using the name of God in a superficial, stupid way.
- *Hypocrisy*: Claiming the name of God but acting in a way that disgraces Him.

i. Jesus communicated the idea of this command in the disciples' prayer when He taught us to have regard for the holiness of God's name (*Hallowed be Your name*, Matthew 6:9).

b. **For the LORD will not hold him guiltless who takes His name in vain**: The strength of this command has led to strange traditions among the Jewish people. Some go to extreme lengths in attempting to fulfill this command, refusing to even write out the name of God, in the fear that the paper might be destroyed, and the name of God be written **in vain**.

i. "In the ancient world and in the thought of Israel the *name* was held to be part of the one who bore it and its use in the case of a deity was thought to bring the power of the deity to bear on a particular situation. Clearly a believing man might invoke the name of Yahweh, but the careless use of his name was forbidden." (Thompson)

4. (12-15) The fourth commandment, to keep the Sabbath.

'Observe the Sabbath day, to keep it holy, as the LORD your God commanded you. Six days you shall labor and do all your work, but the seventh day *is* the Sabbath of the LORD your God. *In it* you shall do no work: you, nor your son, nor your daughter, nor your male servant, nor your female servant, nor your ox, nor your donkey, nor any of your cattle, nor your stranger who *is* within your gates, that your male servant and your female servant may rest as well as you. And remember that you were a slave in the land of Egypt, and the LORD your God brought you out from there by a mighty hand and by an outstretched arm; therefore the LORD your God commanded you to keep the Sabbath day.

a. **Observe the Sabbath day, to keep it holy**: The command is to respect the seventh day (Saturday) as a day of rest (**you shall do no work**). This rest was for all of Israel – for the **son** and the **servant** and the **stranger** – even including **cattle**.

i. This is an important principle that might be too easily passed over. Here God declared the essential humanity and dignity of women, slaves, and strangers, and said they had the same right to a day of rest as the free Israelite man. This was a radical concept in the ancient world.

ii. The explanation Moses gave of the law here in Deuteronomy set special stress on the truth that the Sabbath was for the foreign-born slaves among Israel. Deuteronomy 5:15 (**remember that you were a slave in the land of Egypt**) is not recorded in Exodus 20.

b. **Remember that you were a slave in the land of Egypt**: This is the reason Moses gives for Israel's Sabbath observance, while in the Exodus giving of the Ten Commandments the reason is rooted in the days of creation (Exodus 20:11). Both aspects are true; Sabbath marks God's rest from His work of creation, and it celebrates redemption.

i. "It is arresting to observe that concerning the Sabbath the ground of the appeal is no longer God's resting during creation but the people's position as redeemed from Egypt's bondage." (Morgan)

ii. This progressive understanding of the meaning of the Sabbath continues in the New Testament concept of the Sabbath. The New Testament explains the Sabbath as an expression of the believer's rest in the finished work of Jesus Christ on their behalf (Hebrews 4:1-7), and a commemoration of God's greatest work of deliverance and redemption through the resurrection of Jesus on the first day of the week.

c. **To keep it holy**: God commanded Israel – and all humanity – to make sure that there was a *sacred time* in their life, a *separated* time of rest.

i. In their traditions, the Jewish people came to carefully quantify what they thought could and could not be done on the Sabbath day, to **keep it holy**. For example, in Luke 6:1-2, in the mind of the Jewish leaders, the disciples were guilty of four violations of the Sabbath every time they took a bite of grain out in the field, because they reaped, threshed, winnowed, and prepared food.

ii. Ancient Rabbis taught that on the Sabbath, a man could not carry something in his right hand or in his left hand, across his chest or on his shoulder. But he could carry something with the back of his hand, his foot, his elbow, or in his ear, his hair, or in the hem of his shirt, or in his shoe or sandal. Also, on the Sabbath Israelites were forbidden to tie a knot - except, a woman could tie a knot in her girdle. So, if a bucket of water had to be raised from a well, an Israelite could not tie a rope to the bucket, but a woman could tie her girdle to the bucket and pull it up from the well.

iii. In observant Jewish homes today, one cannot turn on a light, a stove, or a switch on the Sabbath. It is forbidden to drive a certain distance or to make a telephone call – all carefully regulated by traditions seeking to spell out the law exactly.

d. **Six days you shall labor**: God established the pattern for the Sabbath at the time of creation. When He rested from His works on the seventh day (Exodus 20:11), God made the seventh day a day of rest from all our works (Genesis 2:3). It's as if God said, *having too much to do isn't an excuse for not taking the rest you need – I created the universe and found time to rest from My work.*

i. When God told them to **observe the Sabbath**, He told them to *remember the rest*. "The term 'Sabbath' is derived from the Hebrew verb 'to rest or cease from work.'" (Kaiser) The most important purpose of the Sabbath was to serve as a preview picture of the rest we have in Jesus.

ii. Like everything in the Bible, we understand this with the perspective of the whole Bible, not this single passage. With this understanding, we see that there is a real sense in which Jesus fulfilled the purpose and plan of the Sabbath *for* us and *in* us (Hebrews 4:9-11) – He is our rest. When we remember His finished work we **observe the Sabbath**, we *observe the rest*.

iii. Therefore, the whole of Scripture makes it clear that under the new covenant, no one is under obligation to observe a Sabbath day (Colossians 2:16-17 and Galatians 4:9-11). Galatians 4:10 tells us that Christians are not bound to observe *days and months and seasons and years*. The rest we enter as Christians is something to experience every day, not just one day a week – the rest of knowing we don't have to work to save ourselves, but our salvation is accomplished in Jesus (Hebrews 4:9-10).

iv. The Sabbath commanded here and observed by Israel was a *shadow of things to come, but the substance is of Christ* (Colossians 2:16-17). In the new covenant the idea isn't that there is *no* Sabbath, but that *every day* is a day of Sabbath rest in the finished work of God. Since the shadow of the Sabbath is fulfilled in Jesus, we are free to keep any particular day – or no day – as a Sabbath after the custom of ancient Israel.

v. Yet we dare not ignore the importance of a day of rest – God has built us so that we *need* one. Like a car that needs regular maintenance, we need regular rest – or we will not wear well. Some people are like high-mileage cars that haven't been maintained well, and it shows.

vi. Some Christians are also dogmatic about observing Saturday as the Sabbath as opposed to Sunday. But because we are free to regard all days as given by God, it makes no difference. But in some ways, Sunday is more appropriate; being the day Jesus rose from the dead (Mark 16:9), and first met with His disciples (John 20:19), and a day when Christians gathered for fellowship (Acts 20:7 and 1 Corinthians

16:2). Under the law, men worked towards God's rest; but after Jesus' finished work on the cross, the believer enters rest and goes from that rest out to work.

vii. But we are also commanded to *work* six days (**six days you shall labor**). "He who idles his time away in the *six* days is equally culpable in the sight of God as he who works on the *seventh*." (Clarke) Many Christians should give more "leisure time" to the work of the LORD. Every Christian should have a *deliberate* way to serve God and advance the kingdom of Jesus Christ.

5. (16) The fifth commandment, to honor father and mother.

'Honor your father and your mother, as the LORD your God has commanded you, that your days may be long, and that it may be well with you in the land which the LORD your God is giving you.

a. **Honor your father and your mother**: This command is *wise* and *good* because honor for parents is an essential building block for the stability and health of all society. If the younger generations are constantly at war with older generations, the foundations of society will be destroyed.

i. To **honor** one's parents includes to *prize* them, to *care* for them, and to *show respect* or *reverence* to them. The command is given to children whatever their age.

ii. Jesus used the way the Pharisees interpreted this commandment as an example of how one might keep the law with a limited interpretation yet violate the spirit of the commandment (Matthew 15:3-6).

b. **That your days may be long**: In Ephesians 6:2 Paul repeated this command, emphasizing the *promise* stated here, **that your days may be long**. Rebellion is costly, and many have paid a high price personally for their rebellion against their parents.

6. (17) The sixth commandment, forbidding murder.

'You shall not murder.

a. **You shall not murder**: Some people wonder how God can approve both capital punishment (Exodus 19:12) and this prohibition of murder. In Hebrew as well as in English there is a distinction between *to kill* and *to murder*. As opposed to killing, **murder** is the taking of life without legal justification (execution after due process) or moral justification (killing in defense).

i. The distinction between killing and **murder** is clear in the laws regarding the cities of refuge (Numbers 35:9-34, Deuteronomy 4:41-43).

ii. "The attempt to invoke this law as an argument for pacifism or for the abolition of the death penalty is based on a misunderstanding of verse 17." (Thompson)

b. **You shall not murder**: Jesus carefully explained the heart of this commandment. He showed that it also prohibits us from *hating* someone else (Matthew 5:21-26), because we can wish someone dead in our hearts, yet never have the nerve to commit the deed. Someone may not kill due to a lack of courage or initiative, yet his or her heart is filled with hatred.

7. (18) The seventh commandment, forbidding adultery.

'You shall not commit adultery.

a. **You shall not commit adultery**: Clearly, the *act itself* is condemned. God allows no justification for the ways that many often seek to justify extra-marital sex. It is not to be done, and when it is done it is sin and it causes damage.

i. Because there are different punishments for adultery (Deuteronomy 22:22) and the seduction of a virgin woman (Exodus 22:16-17, Deuteronomy 22:23-29), adultery is distinguished from pre-marital sex in the Old Testament. Each is wrong, but wrong in different ways.

ii. Merrill explains why there is not specific mention of other sexual sins in the Ten Commandments: "Elsewhere such matters as fornication (Num 25:1), prostitution (Deut 22:21), and homosexuality (Judg 19:22; Lev 18:22; Deut 23:17–18) receive attention and are soundly condemned. Adultery, however, implies unfaithfulness, covenant breaking, and so is an apt analogue to covenant infidelity on a higher plane – the divine-human."

b. **You shall not commit adultery**: The New Testament clearly condemns adultery: *Now the works of the flesh are evident, which are: adultery, fornication, uncleanness, lewdness* (Galatians 5:19). The act is condemned, but not *only* the act itself.

i. More than the act itself, Jesus carefully explained the *heart* of this commandment. It prohibits us from looking *at a woman to lust for her*, where we commit adultery in our heart or mind, yet may not have the courage or opportunity to do the act (Matthew 5:27-30). We aren't innocent just because we don't have the opportunity to sin the way we really want to.

8. (19) The eighth commandment, forbidding stealing.

'You shall not steal.

a. **You shall not steal**: This command is another important foundation for human society, establishing the right to personal property. God has clearly entrusted certain possessions to certain individuals, and other people or states are not permitted to take that property without due process of law.

i. "Both here and elsewhere all thievery is condemned in the OT as well as in the NT. The right to personal property is basic to the whole Mosaic economy. The word *ganah* ('to steal') reoccurs in Deuteronomy only in 24:7 in relation to kidnapping – a particularly serious violation of the eighth commandment, because it resulted in slavery." (Kalland)

b. **You shall not steal**: We can also steal from God. Of course, this demands we honor God with our financial resources, so we are not guilty of robbing Him (Malachi 3:8-10). But we can also rob God by refusing to give Him ourselves for obedience and His service, because He bought us and owns us: *knowing that you were not redeemed with corruptible things, like silver or gold...but with the precious blood of Christ* (1 Peter 1:18-19).

c. **You shall not steal**: Ephesians 4:28 gives the solution to stealing. *Let him who stole steal no longer, but rather let him labor, working with his hands what is good, that he may have something to give him who has need.*

9. (20) The ninth commandment, forbidding lying, especially as legal testimony.

'You shall not bear false witness against your neighbor.

a. **You shall not bear false witness against your neighbor**: The primary sense of this command has to do with the legal process. Yet it is common to speak in an *informal* court, where what we say is taken seriously and truth or error matters for us and for others.

i. In an extended sense, we can break the ninth commandment through slander, tale-bearing, creating false impressions, by silence, by questioning the motives behind someone's actions, or even by flattery.

ii. "Slander...is a lie invented and spread with intent to do harm. That is the worst form of injury a person can do to another. Compared to one who does this, a gangster is a gentleman, and a murderer is kind, because he ends life in a moment with a stroke and with little pain. But the man guilty of slander ruins a reputation which may never be regained, and causes lifelong suffering." (Redpath)

iii. "Talebearing...is repeating a report about a person without careful investigation. Many, many times I have known what it is to suffer with that. To repeat a story which brings discredit and dishonor to another person without making sure of the facts, is breaking this commandment.... How many people, especially Christian people, revel in this, and delight in working havoc by telling tales about others. To excuse the action by saying they believed the report to be true, or that there was no intention to malign, is no justification." (Redpath)

iv. Inappropriate *silence* may also break this command. "When someone utters a falsity about another and a third person is present who knows that statement to be untrue but, for reasons of fear or being disliked, remains quiet, that third person is as guilty of breaking this law as if he had told a lie." (Redpath)

v. "If one has evidence of a public charge against anyone and withholds that evidence, 'he will be held responsible' (Lev 5:1). Upholding the truth was important in Israel." (Kalland)

b. **You shall not bear false witness against your neighbor**: The New Testament puts it simply. *Do not lie to one another, since you have put off the old man with his deeds* (Colossians 3:9). Lying and false representations belong to the old man, not to the new life believers have in Jesus Christ.

i. "How very strange that we have ever come to think that Christian maturity is shown by the ability to speak our minds, whereas it is really expressed in controlling our tongues." (Redpath)

ii. "What a startling revelation it would be if a tape recording could be played of all that every church member has said about his fellow members in one week!" (Redpath)

iii. Satan always has an interest in encouraging lies (John 8:44; Acts 5:3), and Jesus Himself was the victim of *false witness* (Mark 14:57). In some ways, we might say this was the sin that sent Jesus to the cross.

10. (21) The tenth commandment, forbidding covetousness of all kinds.

'You shall not covet your neighbor's wife; and you shall not desire your neighbor's house, his field, his male servant, his female servant, his ox, his donkey, or anything that *is* your neighbor's.'

a. **You shall not covet**: All the first nine commands focus more on things that are done, actions that are performed. The tenth command deals with the heart and its desires.

i. "The remarkable thing about this tenth and final statute is that it raises the issue of sin and disobedience from the level of mere act to that of attitude, thought, and desire." (Merrill)

ii. Literally, the word for **covet** here means, "to pant after." Covetousness works like this: the eyes look upon an object, the mind admires it, the will goes over to it, and the body moves in to possess it. Just because the final step has not yet been taken does not mean one is not in the process of coveting in the immediate moment.

b. **Your neighbor's wife...house...field**: Covetousness can be expressed towards all sorts of things; it is the itch to have and to possess what someone else has. It speaks of dissatisfaction with what we have and jealousy towards those who have something "better."

i. Hebrews 13:5 puts it well: *Let your conduct be without covetousness; be content with such things as you have. For He Himself has said, "I will never leave you nor forsake you."*

ii. This last commandment is closely connected with the first commandment against idolatry: *For this you know, that no...covetous man, who is an idolater, has any inheritance in the kingdom of Christ and God* (Ephesians 5:5).

iii. Jesus gave a special warning about covetousness, which explained the core philosophy of the covetous heart: *And He said to them, "Take heed and beware of covetousness, for one's life does not consist in the abundance of the things he possesses."* (Luke 12:15)

iv. Compared to the Exodus 20 giving of the Ten Commandments, here Moses added **his field** to the items that one must not covet. Moses had their inheritance of land in Canaan on his mind.

v. "The prohibition against coveting a neighbor's land would have no meaning if family rights in marriage ties, domestic tranquility, and property ownership did not exist." (Kalland)

C. The response of Israel and the response of God at Mount Sinai.

1. (22-27) The response of Israel: fear and desire to separate from God.

"These words the LORD spoke to all your assembly, in the mountain from the midst of the fire, the cloud, and the thick darkness, with a loud voice; and He added no more. And He wrote them on two tablets of stone and gave them to me.

"So it was, when you heard the voice from the midst of the darkness, while the mountain was burning with fire, that you came near to me, all the heads of your tribes and your elders. And you said: 'Surely the LORD our God has shown us His glory and His greatness, and we have heard His voice from the midst of the fire. We have seen this day that God speaks with man; yet he *still* lives. Now therefore, why should we die? For this great fire will consume us; if we hear the voice of the LORD our God anymore, then we shall die. For who *is there* of all flesh who has heard the voice of the living God speaking from the midst of the fire,

as we *have*, and lived? You go near and hear all that the LORD our God may say, and tell us all that the LORD our God says to you, and we will hear and do *it*.'

    a. **In the mountain from the midst of the fire, the cloud, and the thick darkness, with a loud voice**: The whole scene was indeed awesome. The **LORD spoke**, there was **fire**, a **cloud**, **thick darkness**, a **loud voice**; and it all made such an impression on Israel that they asked Moses to not have God speak to them so directly anymore (Exodus 20:19).

        i. **Why should we die? .... if we hear the voice of the LORD our God anymore, then we shall die** makes it plain. The Mount Sinai experience was not one of sweet fellowship with God. The message of Mount Sinai was not "come to Me," but "stay away, for I am holy, and you are not."

        ii. This is the message of the writer to the Hebrews in Hebrews 12:18-24: We, under the new covenant, *have not* come to Mount Sinai and to the message "stay away." We have come to Mount Zion, where God's message is "come unto Me."

        iii. **Two tablets**: "The fact that they were inscribed on two stone tablets (4:13) suggests to many scholars that some of the commandments were contained on one tablet and the rest on the second. Others, however, maintain, in line with covenant practice, that all ten were engraved on each. That is, they were duplicates with each party to the covenant retaining a copy for his own archives." (Merrill)

    b. **Tell us all that the LORD our God says to you, and we will hear and do it**: Though perhaps Israel was too confident in their ability to obey God, they had a desire to **hear** and **do** what God said.

        i. "And indeed it is still the work of the law to scare men, and to drive them to seek for a Mediator." (Trapp)

2. (28-33) God responds with hopeful pleasure in Israel.

"Then the LORD heard the voice of your words when you spoke to me, and the LORD said to me: 'I have heard the voice of the words of this people which they have spoken to you. They are right *in* all that they have spoken. Oh, that they had such a heart in them that they would fear Me and always keep all My commandments, that it might be well with them and with their children forever! Go and say to them, "Return to your tents." But as for you, stand here by Me, and I will speak to you all the commandments, the statutes, and the judgments which you shall teach them, that they may observe *them* in the land which I am giving them to possess.'

Therefore you shall be careful to do as the Lord your God has commanded you; you shall not turn aside to the right hand or to the left. You shall walk in all the ways which the Lord your God has commanded you, that you may live and *that it may be* well with you, and *that* you may prolong *your* days in the land which you shall possess.

a. **They are right in all that they have spoken**: God was pleased with Israel's response. Their response was evidence that they took Him seriously.

b. **Oh, that they had such a heart**: The sense is that God was pleased by what He saw in Israel, but desired that Israel would *keep* the same attitude of heart.

i. "Here is a sigh from the Divine heart. It recalls the tears of the Lord Jesus over Jerusalem…. God wants the heart." (Meyer)

ii. **Such a heart**: "The deepest fact therein, and the one most powerful in producing results, is not that of the intelligence or the mind; it is that of the desire or heart. A man becomes that which he really desires." (Morgan)

c. **That it might be well with them and their children forever**: This was God's motive in calling for Israel's obedience – **that it might be well** with them. Every command of God is rooted in love for His people, not a mere desire for control, or the desire to inflict harm on His people.

i. "The best interests of his people are deep in the heart of God. This view of divine compassion shows how the Lord's love focuses on what is best for his people." (Kalland)

d. **Therefore you shall be careful to do as the Lord your God has commanded you**: Knowing the glory of God (as revealed at Mount Sinai) and the love of God (as revealed by His desire **that it might be well with them**), gave them even more reason to obey God.

i. When God's people have trouble obeying God, they often either forget His glory, or they forget His love for them. Sometimes they forget both.

Deuteronomy 6 – Moses Reminds Israel of the Commandment and the Warning

A. The Commandment: The essence of God's law.

1. (1-3) Remember the commandment before entering Canaan.

"**Now this *is* the commandment, *and these are* the statutes and judgments which the L**ORD** your God has commanded to teach you, that you may observe *them* in the land which you are crossing over to possess, that you may fear the L**ORD** your God, to keep all His statutes and His commandments which I command you, you and your son and your grandson, all the days of your life, and that your days may be prolonged. Therefore hear, O Israel, and be careful to observe *it*, that it may be well with you, and that you may multiply greatly as the L**ORD** God of your fathers has promised you—'a land flowing with milk and honey.'**

a. **Now this is the commandment**: The Hebrew is emphatic here. Moses called attention to the **Commandment**. In the following verses, God reduced the law to one ruling principle – one commandment that encompassed all the commandments.

b. **That you may observe them**: God did not give His commandments to Israel only for their education or to satisfy their curiosity. God gave His commandments so that they would be observed and obeyed. This was especially important when they came into **the land** of Canaan.

i. "It is this doing of them that is the hard part of the work. It is not easy always to teach them; a man needs the Spirit of God if he is to teach them aright, but practice is harder than preaching. May God grant us grace, whenever we hear his Word, to do it!" (Spurgeon)

c. **That your days may be prolonged.... that it may be well with you**: Israel's fate rested on their obedience to this one great commandment. If they obeyed the commandment, their life would be long and filled with blessing. If they did not obey, they could expect to be cursed by God.

    i. "God does not give long life to all his people; yet obedience to God is the most probable way of securing long life." (Spurgeon)

d. **A land flowing with milk and honey**: This is an often-repeated figure of speech describing the agricultural abundance of Canaan. It appears at least 14 times in Exodus, Leviticus, Numbers, and Deuteronomy. According to Thompson, this was a phrase also used in Egyptian literature to describe Canaan.

    i. Many think the **honey** mentioned here is date honey, not that gathered from bees.

2. (4-5) The great commandment: **Love the LORD your God.**

"Hear, O Israel: The LORD our God, the LORD *is* one! You shall love the LORD your God with all your heart, with all your soul, and with all your strength.

a. **Hear, O Israel**: Among the Jewish people, these words are known as the *Shema* ("hear" in Hebrew). It is the classic Hebrew confession of faith, describing who God is and what the duty of His people is towards Him.

    i. Jesus specifically mentioned the Shema (Matthew 22:37), and its core truth was also in Paul's mind (Romans 3:30, 1 Corinthians 8:6, Ephesians 4:6, 1 Timothy 2:5). James challenged believers (nearly all from a Jewish background) that their confession that God was one was *not* enough (James 2:19).

    ii. "So much so did the centrality of this confession find root in the Jewish consciousness that to this very day the observant Jew will recite the Shema at least twice daily." (Merrill)

b. **The LORD our God, the LORD is one**: This is the essential truth about God. He is a person and not a vague pantheistic force. Being **one**, He cannot be represented by contradictory images. Since **the LORD our God** is **one**, He is not Baal or Ashtoreth – He is the LORD God, and they are not.

    i. In the mind of many Jewish people, this verse alone disqualified the New Testament teaching that Jesus is God, and the New Testament teaching of the Trinity – that there is one God, existing in three Persons. According to Clarke, at some times and places, as Jewish synagogues said the *Shema* together, and when the word **one** (*echad*) was said, they loudly and strongly repeated that one word for several minutes, as if it were a rebuke to Christians with their belief in the Trinity.

ii. Christians must come to a renewed understanding of the unity of God. They must appreciate the fact that **the LORD is one**, not three, as 1 Corinthians 8:6 says: *yet for us there is one God*. Christians worship *one* God, existing in *three* Persons, not three separate gods.

iii. Yet, the statement **the LORD is one** certainly does not contradict the truth of the Trinity. In fact, it establishes that truth. The Hebrew word used here for **one** is *echad*, which speaks most literally of a compound unity, rather than the Hebrew word *yacheed*, which speaks of an absolute unity or singularity (Genesis 22:2, Psalm 25:16).

iv. The very first use of *echad* in the Bible is in Genesis 1:5: *So the evening and the morning were the first day*. This context shows a unity (one day) with the idea of plurality (made up of evening and morning).

- Genesis 2:24 uses *echad* in saying *the two shall become* one *flesh*. Again, the idea of a unity (one flesh), made from a plurality (the two).
- In Exodus 26:6 and 11, fifty gold clasps are used to hold the curtains together, so the tent would be *one* (*echad*). This is another unity (one covering) made up of a plurality (the many parts that made up the one covering, joined by the gold clasps).
- In Ezekiel 37:17 the LORD told Ezekiel to join two sticks (prophetically representing Ephraim/Israel and Judah) into *one* (*echad*), speaking again of a unity (one stick) made up of a plurality (the two sticks).

v. Largely, *echad* does not have the exclusive idea of an absolute singularity. The concept of the Trinity – that there is one God in three Persons – works well with the term *echad*.

c. **The LORD our God**: In addition, even the term referring to **God** in this line suggests the plurality of Deity. The Hebrew word is *Elohim* (**God**), and grammatically, it is a plural word used as if it were singular – the verbs and pronouns used with it are generally in the plural except when it is used in reference to Yahweh (the **LORD**), the covenant God of Israel.

i. Rabbi Simeon ben Joachi, commenting on the word *Elohim*: "Come and see the mystery of the word Elohim; there are *three degrees*, and each degree by itself *alone*, and yet notwithstanding they are all *one*, and *joined together* in *one*, and are not divided from each other." Adam Clarke adds: "He must be strangely prejudiced indeed who cannot see that the doctrine of a Trinity, and of a Trinity in unity, is expressed in the above words."

ii. Leupold quoting Luther on the word *Elohim*: "But we have clear testimony that Moses aimed to indicate the Trinity or the three persons in the one divine nature."

d. **Love the Lord your God with all your heart, with all your soul, and with all your strength**: Knowing who God is allows His people to act towards Him rightly. This is one way that believers give God His due.

i. God wants complete love from His people. This love is appropriate because He loved first and loved completely: *We love Him because He first loved us* (1 John 4:19).

ii. What God most wants from humanity is **love**. It is easy to think that God is more interested in many other things: time, money, effort, will, submission, and so forth. But what God really wants from humanity is their love. When people really love the Lord with all the heart, soul, and mind, then all else is freely given to the Lord. If one starts by giving to God all the rest – money, time, effort, will, and so forth – without giving Him love, then all is wasted – and perhaps, all is lost. "Israel's obedience was not to spring from a barren legalism based on necessity and duty. It was to arise from a relationship based on love." (Thompson)

iii. "Does not this show what is the very nature of God? God is love, for he commands us to love him. There was never an earthly prince or king whom I have heard of in whose statute-book it was written, 'Thou shalt love the king.' No; it is only in the statute-book of him who is the Lord of life and love that we read such a command as this. To my mind it seems a very blessed privilege for us to be permitted to love One so great as God is." (Spurgeon)

iv. Jesus called this *the great commandment* (Matthew 22:37-39). Jesus added that the second commandment, *you shall love your neighbor as yourself,* was *like* this first, great commandment. When God's people love the Lord their God with all their heart, soul, and mind, they will then find the ability to love their neighbor as themselves.

3. (6-9) The continual reminder of the law.

"And these words which I command you today shall be in your heart. You shall teach them diligently to your children, and shall talk of them when you sit in your house, when you walk by the way, when you lie down, and when you rise up. You shall bind them as a sign on your hand, and they shall be as frontlets between your eyes. You shall write them on the doorposts of your house and on your gates.

a. **These words which I command you today shall be in your heart**: This great command must first live in the **heart**. Then it must be communicated to the **children**, the next generation. This great commandment should be a topic of conversation and should always be prominent – as near as the hand, forehead, or the door posts and gates of the home.

b. **Teach them diligently to your children**: The people of God were not only commanded to **teach** their children, but to do it **diligently**. They are commanded to take on the sometimes-difficult task of teaching their children the truth about God and His works. Pastors, Sunday-school teachers, and other Christian workers have their roles, but never replace the role and responsibility of the parent to teach their children, and to do it diligently.

i. "God's thought of the children, and care for them, is evidenced throughout all the enactments of the Law, and indeed in all the ceremonies of worship." (Morgan)

ii. "However much we may love and appreciate the Sunday-school system, — and we cannot love it too much, — I hope we shall never forget that the first duty towards the child belongs to the parent. Fathers and mothers are the most natural agents for God to use in the salvation of their children." (Spurgeon)

iii. "God's testimonies must be taught to our children, and the utmost diligence must be used to make them understand them. This is a most difficult task; and it requires much patience, much prudence, much judgment, and much piety in the parents, to enable them to do this good, this most important work, in the best and most effectual manner." (Clarke)

c. **You shall bind them as a sign on your hand**: The first use of this concept for Israel was that the celebration of Passover would be a sign on their hand and a memorial between their eyes (Exodus 13:9, 16). This puts the phrase in symbolic context, meaning here that the truth of Israel's deliverance from Egypt was to be as familiar and prominent to them as a sign on the hand and head. Here, the context is also symbolic. The commandments of God were to be as familiar and prominent to Israel as a sign on the hand or head.

i. "In the larger sense they are to be committed to memory as the idiom 'upon your hearts' (v. 6) makes clear." (Merrill)

ii. By the time of Jesus, the Jewish people used this passage as the basis for their practice of wearing phylacteries. A phylactery is a small box holding parchment with Scripture passages written on it, and the box is held to the forehead or hand with leather straps.

iii. Jesus condemned the abuse of the wearing of phylacteries among the Pharisees; they would sometimes make their phylactery boxes large and ostentatious to show off their supposedly greater spirituality (Matthew 23:5).

iv. In the end times, there will be a Satanic imitation of this practice, when the number of the Antichrist will be applied to either the hand or forehead of all who will take it (Revelation 13:16).

d. **You shall write them on the doorposts of your house**: Like the command to bind the commandments as a sign on the hands and head, this is given in a symbolic sense, pointing to the kind of prominence and attention that should be given to the word of God among believers.

i. **Write** has the sense of *engrave*. "The image is that of the engraver of a monument who takes hammer and chisel in hand and with painstaking care etches a text into the face of a solid slab of granite. The sheer labor of such a task is daunting indeed, but once done the message is there to stay." (Merrill)

ii. This command leads to the Jewish practice of the *mezuzah*. This is a small container nailed to a doorpost, with the container holding a passage of Scripture.

iii. "I could almost wish that this were literally fulfilled much more often than it is. I was charmed, in many a Swiss village, to see a text of Scripture carved on the door-post. A text hung up in your houses may often speak when you are silent. We cannot do anything that shall be superfluous in the way of making known the Word of God." (Spurgeon)

B. The danger of disobedience.

1. (10-12) The danger of leaving God in times of prosperity.

"So it shall be, when the LORD your God brings you into the land of which He swore to your fathers, to Abraham, Isaac, and Jacob, to give you large and beautiful cities which you did not build, houses full of all good things, which you did not fill, hewn-out wells which you did not dig, vineyards and olive trees which you did not plant—when you have eaten and are full—*then* beware, lest you forget the LORD who brought you out of the land of Egypt, from the house of bondage.

a. **To give you large and beautiful cities which you did not build**: God planned to bring Israel into an abundant, prepared land. In this abundant blessing God had for Israel, there was an inherent danger: That they would **forget the Lord who brought** them **out of the land of Egypt**.

> i. In the conquest of Canaan, the cities and farms were largely spared and became the inheritance of Israel. "The conquest did not result in major destruction of towns and properties so therefore did not leave archaeologically definable evidence. Any attempt to date the conquest must therefore rest on some basis other than the presence or absence of evidence of destruction." (Merrill)

b. **Lest you forget the Lord**: Israel's inheritance of Canaan, with its houses built, fields prepared, vineyards and olive trees flourishing, and cisterns dug, was something like winning the lottery. God warned Israel, "When you receive all this abundance, don't **forget** Me."

> i. In future generations, Israel would often **forget** the Lord. A tragic cycle would be repeated throughout the history of Israel, especially in the time of the judges. God would bless an obedient Israel and they would prosper; they would begin to set their heart on the blessings instead of the Lord who blessed them; God would allow chastisement to turn Israel's focus back upon Him; Israel would repent and obey again, and God would again bless an obedient Israel and they would prosper.
>
> ii. Believers often fail to appreciate the danger of success and prosperity. Success and prosperity are often seen as *theoretical* dangers, without appreciating how they may be real and present dangers to the believer.
>
> iii. When times are good, it is much easier to **forget the Lord who brought you out...from the house of bondage**. When there are no adverse circumstances compelling the remembrance of God, "We are no sooner grown rich, but we are apt to utter that ugly word, This I may thank myself for." (Trapp)
>
> iv. "Our blessings come from sources that are beyond our own industry and skill; they are the fruits of the holy inventiveness of God, and the splendour and fullness of his thoughtfulness towards his poor children. Let us not forget him, since evidently he never forgets us." (Spurgeon)

2. (13-19) How to avoid apostasy in times of prosperity: honoring the Lord in everything we do.

You shall fear the Lord your God and serve Him, and shall take oaths in His name. You shall not go after other gods, the gods of the peoples who *are* **all around you (for the Lord your God** *is* **a jealous God among you), lest the anger of the Lord your God be aroused against you and destroy you from the face of the earth.**

"You shall not tempt the LORD your God as you tempted *Him* in Massah. You shall diligently keep the commandments of the LORD your God, His testimonies, and His statutes which He has commanded you. And you shall do *what is* right and good in the sight of the LORD, that it may be well with you, and that you may go in and possess the good land of which the LORD swore to your fathers, to cast out all your enemies from before you, as the LORD has spoken."

a. **You shall fear the LORD your God and serve Him**: The idea of the **fear of the LORD** is more of an awe-filled respect, an inner dislike at the idea of offending a great, loving God who has done so much for His people.

i. "The derived sensation of standing in awe of God and then of holding him in utmost reverence and respect is, however, essential to the understanding of 'fearing God' especially in Deuteronomy." (Kalland)

ii. This is the passage of Scripture Jesus quoted back to Satan, when tempted by the devil to avoid the cross and win back the world if He would only bow down and worship Satan. Jesus rightly replied, based on the truth **You shall fear the LORD your God and serve Him**; that it was only right to fear, and worship, and serve Yahweh as God – and it was wrong to bow down to Satan, no matter what might be given Him in return (Matthew 4:8-10).

b. **And shall take oaths in His name**: although the concept of the oath in God's name can certainly be abused (as Jesus pointed out in Matthew 5:33-37), there is a permissible use of oaths by those who follow God. This is seen in the truth that God Himself uses oaths (Hebrews 6:13). Here, Israel was told, "you are to swear an oath only in the name of the LORD, not in the name of any other god." Making oaths in the name of any other god would be showing honor and allegiance to that false god.

c. **You shall not tempt the LORD your God as you tempted Him at Massah**: In Exodus 17:1-7, Israel tempted the LORD by doubting His love and concern for them. This was tempting or testing God regarding His love for Israel, something that was not only high-handed against the LORD (because man has no right to test the Almighty) but also disregarding His previous, and constant demonstrations of love and care for Israel (by demanding that God prove His love for them now by giving them what they wanted).

i. Whenever man denies God's love, or demands He do something, man is testing God as if He must answer to man's standards, and man is tempting God to judge him. "To *test* God is to impose conditions on him and to make his response to the people's demand in the hour of crisis the condition of their continuing to follow him." (Thompson)

ii. This was the passage of Scripture which Jesus quoted back to Satan in the wilderness, when tempted to make God the Father prove His love for the Son by spectacularly protecting Jesus if He should jump off the pinnacle of the temple (Matthew 4:5-7). Jesus knew it was wrong to demand this sort of "proof" from His Father, since every day was proof of God the Father's love for the Son.

d. **And you shall do what is right...that it may be well with you**: This theme is repeated once again. Under the old covenant, Israel's blessing was based on their obedience. When they obeyed, they would be blessed; when they disobeyed, they would be cursed.

i. This is not the source of blessing in the new covenant. In the new covenant, we are blessed by faith in Jesus since He fulfills the law in our place (Romans 8:3-4). The watchwords for blessing under the old covenant were *earning* and *deserving*; under the new covenant, blessing is based on *believing* and *receiving*.

ii. The new covenant system works because when we receive the new covenant, God sends with it an inner transformation, where the law of God and the desire to do His will is now written on the heart of the believer. The inner transformation promised by the new covenant helps to protect against the abuse of God's grace.

iii. Under the new covenant there is no *judgment* from God for the disobedience of His people because all the judgment the believer deserved was put on Jesus at the cross. However, there may be *correction* from the hand of a loving God the Father (not in the sense of making believers pay for their sin, but in the sense of training them to not continue in sin), and there are the *natural consequences* of disobedience, which God has not promised to shield the believer from.

iv. Christians who fear the "freedom" of a new covenant relationship with God must ask this question: did Israel come to greater obedience to God through the old covenant? Does the system of earning and deserving blessing make us truly godlier than the system of believing and receiving? Actually, the old covenant leaves one either in total desperation (where they may then look to Jesus), or in a dangerous confidence in one's own works to make them righteous before God.

3. (20-25) How to avoid apostasy in times of prosperity: Teach your children to understand and honor the LORD.

"When your son asks you in time to come, saying, 'What *is the meaning of* the testimonies, the statutes, and the judgments which the Lord our God has commanded you?' then you shall say to your son: 'We were slaves of Pharaoh in Egypt, and the Lord brought us out of Egypt with a mighty hand; and the Lord showed signs and wonders before our eyes, great and severe, against Egypt, Pharaoh, and all his household. Then He brought us out from there, that He might bring us in, to give us the land of which He swore to our fathers. And the Lord commanded us to observe all these statutes, to fear the Lord our God, for our good always, that He might preserve us alive, as *it is* this day. Then it will be righteousness for us, if we are careful to observe all these commandments before the Lord our God, as He has commanded us.'

> a. **When your son asks you in time to come**: Often, the apostasy that comes from prosperity afflicts the next generation more than the present. The next generation grows up *expecting* such prosperity and blessing, often without understanding the repentance and walk with God that led to the prosperity.
>
> b. **Then you shall say to your son**: Therefore, it was essential for Israel to teach and warn their children so that the blessings given to one generation would not become a curse to the next generation.
>
>> i. Key to the teaching was the simple recounting of Israel's history – how God saved them from the bondage of Egypt. Parents need to relate to their children how *they* came to a personal relationship with Jesus, so the children understand that *they* must come to the same relationship.
>
> c. **He brought us out from there, that He might bring us in**: This is a wonderful summary of what God did in the exodus. He **brought** Israel **out**, for the purpose to **bring** Israel **in**. Deliverance from Egypt was only the first step and would have been incomplete without the completion of the work of bringing Israel into Canaan.
>
>> i. This is a similar idea to what Paul would later write: *He who has begun a good work in you will complete it until the day of Jesus Christ* (Philippians 1:6).
>
> d. **Then it will be righteousness for us**: The **it** here that **will be righteousness** does not refer merely to obedience to the commands of the law, but faith in and loyalty to God as expressed through the entire covenant. The covenant God made with Israel included a significant priesthood and sacrificial system, which addressed their inevitable failures to keep the law and pointed to the perfect sacrifice God would provide

through the person and work of Jesus Christ, especially His substitutionary sacrifice at the cross and His resurrection.

i. If someone desires to achieve true righteousness through the law, it is simple, though not easy. All they must do is **observe** all the commandments. However, if anyone fails in their obedience, they then need the atonement of a perfect sacrifice – Jesus Christ, the Lamb of God who takes away the sin of the world.

ii. "The commandments were designed, not as a burden to be borne, but as the gracious provision by a beneficent Sovereign of a guide for good living. Thus would Yahweh preserve Israel alive." (Thompson)

Deuteronomy 7 – Commands to Conquer and Obey

A. The command to conquer the Canaanites.

1. (1-5) The command to bring God's judgment to the Canaanites and their culture.

"When the LORD your God brings you into the land which you go to possess, and has cast out many nations before you, the Hittites and the Girgashites and the Amorites and the Canaanites and the Perizzites and the Hivites and the Jebusites, seven nations greater and mightier than you, and when the LORD your God delivers them over to you, you shall conquer them *and* utterly destroy them. You shall make no covenant with them nor show mercy to them. Nor shall you make marriages with them. You shall not give your daughter to their son, nor take their daughter for your son. For they will turn your sons away from following Me, to serve other gods; so the anger of the LORD will be aroused against you and destroy you suddenly. But thus you shall deal with them: you shall destroy their altars, and break down their *sacred* pillars, and cut down their wooden images, and burn their carved images with fire.

> a. **When the LORD your God**: Israel wasn't in the land yet, but Moses still instructed them as if it were a certainty. This was based on the faithful promise of God, but it was also according to God's principle of *preparation*. God prepares us before He brings us into a place.
>
> b. **Greater and mightier than you**: Moses acknowledged that the **seven nations** of the Canaanites were **greater and mightier than** Israel was at the time. But they were not **greater and mightier** than Yahweh, the LORD, the covenant God of Israel. God brought Israel to face a challenge that was impossible in their own strength, but it was entirely possible in Him.
>
>> i. "The seven nations listed did not acknowledge the sovereignty of Yahweh. Moreover they occupied the land which he had given to his

people. Further, they were devotees of other gods whom Yahweh could not tolerate in his presence. They were, therefore, proper subjects for the Holy War." (Thompson)

ii. "However all these peoples came to be in the land, they were trespassers in the eyes of the Lord, for he already had promised Abraham to give the land to him and his descendants (Gen 12:1, 7; 13:17; 15:18). The Lord himself would therefore drive them out and deliver them over (*natan*) to Israel, who would defeat them." (Merrill)

c. **When the LORD your God delivers them over to you**: By phrasing this with the word **when** (instead of "if"), God communicated the certainty of Israel's conquest in Canaan.

d. **You shall conquer them and utterly destroy them**: Yet God would not do all the work of conquest for Israel. The extent of the work would depend on their faithful response to what God would do.

i. By spiritual analogy, believers should seek, in the power and victory of Jesus Christ, to **conquer** and **utterly destroy** whatever robs them of their spiritual inheritance. In this spiritual sense, to whatever extent the believer is active in this battle, to that extent they will "occupy" and live in what God has granted to them.

e. **Utterly destroy them.... nor show mercy to them**: The judgment God called Israel to carry out was unique in the way that it used the people of God as His instrument of judgment. This was a severe judgment, yet within God's right as judge of all the earth. The tribal groups of Canaan were particularly sinful and depraved people, whom God literally gave hundreds of years to repent (Genesis 15:13-16). Deuteronomy 18:9-14 (among other passages) explains the significant spiritual corruption of the Canaanites.

i. Such judgment seems harsh to the modern reader because it *is* harsh. Modern readers must recognize, that at unique times, God has commanded such judgments. They may happen either through an army that God uses or through judgment that He directly brings, as in the destruction of Sodom and Gomorrah (Genesis 19:24-25).

ii. The Canaanites knew the judgment of God was coming against them and were afraid of it (Joshua 2:9-11, 9:24-25). They could have acted in faith like Rahab (Joshua 2) or could have surrendered like the Gibeonites (Joshua 9), or they could have left the area. Most of the Canaanites did not take any of these three options, and those who remained fell under the judgment of God.

iii. "These idolatrous nations were to be utterly destroyed, and all the others also which were contiguous to the boundaries of the promised land, provided they did not renounce their idolatry and receive the true faith: for if they did not, then no covenant was to be made with them on any secular or political consideration whatever; no mercy was to be shown to them, because the cup of their iniquity also was now full; and they must either embrace, heartily embrace, the true religion, or be cut off." (Clarke)

iv. Ezra recorded the words of the prophets who described the land of Canaan like this: *The land which you are entering to possess is an unclean land, with the uncleanness of the peoples of the lands, with their abominations which have filled it from one end to another with their impurity* (Ezra 9:11).

v. "Albright mentions that the Canaanite Baalism was much cruder and more debased than the religions of Egypt and Mesopotamia. His depiction of some of the acts of Canaanite gods and goddesses in *From the Stone Age to Christianity* (Baltimore: Johns Hopkins University Press, 1946, pp. 175–79) clearly bears this out." (Kalland)

f. **Destroy their altars, and break down their sacred pillars, and cut down their wooden images, and burn their carved images**: Israel was to take special care to destroy anything which would lead them to false or foreign worship. Failure to do this would leave corrupting influences that would **turn** Israel's **sons** from **following** the Lord faithfully.

i. This radical, complete destruction was important because of the depraved nature of the worship of the Canaanites, who worshipped male and female gods of sex and who presented their children for human sacrifice.

ii. The **wooden images** were *Asherim*. "Asherah was also the name of the mother goddess of the Canaanite pantheon, the deity responsible for fertility and the productivity of soil, animals, and humankind. She was represented by either an evergreen tree or by a pole that also spoke of perpetual life. The cult carried on in their name was of the most sensual and sordid type, one practiced in the temples and also under the open sky at high places and in groves of trees. Prominent in its services was sacred prostitution involving priests and priestesses who represented the male and female deities." (Merrill)

iii. "For Israel, separation from those who did not acknowledge Yahweh was a matter of life or death, for her own faith contrasted so greatly with that of her neighbours that any risk of having it watered down in any way was to be avoided. Israel herself was set apart for Yahweh's exclusive use." (Thompson)

2. (6-8) Israel should conquer completely in grateful response to God's love for them.

"For you *are* a holy people to the Lord your God; the Lord your God has chosen you to be a people for Himself, a special treasure above all the peoples on the face of the earth. The Lord did not set His love on you nor choose you because you were more in number than any other people, for you were the least of all peoples; but because the Lord loves you, and because He would keep the oath which He swore to your fathers, the Lord has brought you out with a mighty hand, and redeemed you from the house of bondage, from the hand of Pharaoh king of Egypt.

a. **For you are a holy people to the Lord your God**: Israel was **holy** in their *standing* before God before they were holy in their *conduct*. They were set apart to God by His choosing (**God has chosen you to be a people for Himself**) and were *then* called to live as chosen people.

b. **The Lord did not set His love on you nor choose you because you were more in number**: God's choice of Israel meant the Lord **set His love on** them. According to the nature of God's love, this was not because Israel was inherently more worthy of this love than other peoples. The reasons for God's great love were found in the Lord, not in Israel.

i. "Why God loved them is not stated in the Pentateuch, but the focus of thought is obvious—it is the character of God rather than any excellence in the people that accounts for the choice." (Kalland)

c. **The Lord has brought you out with a mighty hand**: Knowing God's love for them and His work of redemption, delivering Israel from Egypt, Israel had a strong obligation to obey God, even in the difficult work of bringing God's judgment on Canaan.

i. This is the great motivation for obedience among the people of God: knowing and walking in the love of God. When believers really trust in God's love and live with that belief as a conscious fact, obedience is a natural result. God's people are also motivated to conquer anything that would damage that relationship of love.

3. (9-11) Conquer them completely because you serve a God of justice.

"Therefore know that the Lord your God, He *is* God, the faithful God who keeps covenant and mercy for a thousand generations with those who love Him and keep His commandments; and He repays those who hate Him to their face, to destroy them. He will not be slack with him who hates Him; He will repay him to his face. Therefore you shall keep

the commandment, the statutes, and the judgments which I command you today, to observe them.

> a. **He repays those who hate Him to their face**: Over many generations the Canaanites had demonstrated their hatred for God. Now, using Israel as His instrument, God would appoint the Canaanites to judgment.
>
>> i. "Such covenant disloyalty deserves recompense, one described here (literally) as 'repay to their face.' This expression occurs only here and probably means that the judgment would not be reserved for unborn generations but would fall immediately upon those who had sinned in this manner, right there and then." (Merrill)
>
> b. **Therefore you shall keep the commandment**: Knowing God's faithfulness to those who love Him and the certainty of judgment against those who hate Him, God's people are motivated to be loyal to God's covenant with them and to **keep the commandment** of God.

B. Blessing on an obedient Israel.

1. (12-16) Abundant blessings for obedience.

"Then it shall come to pass, because you listen to these judgments, and keep and do them, that the LORD your God will keep with you the covenant and the mercy which He swore to your fathers. And He will love you and bless you and multiply you; He will also bless the fruit of your womb and the fruit of your land, your grain and your new wine and your oil, the increase of your cattle and the offspring of your flock, in the land of which He swore to your fathers to give you. You shall be blessed above all peoples; there shall not be a male or female barren among you or among your livestock. And the LORD will take away from you all sickness, and will afflict you with none of the terrible diseases of Egypt which you have known, but will lay *them* on all those who hate you. Also you shall destroy all the peoples whom the LORD your God delivers over to you; your eye shall have no pity on them; nor shall you serve their gods, for that *will be* a snare to you.

> a. **He will love you and bless you and multiply you**: An essential part of the covenant God made with Israel at Mount Sinai and renewed on the plains of Moab was the *choice* given to Israel (Leviticus 26, Deuteronomy 27-28). Under this covenant, God promised to bless an obedient Israel in astounding, remarkable ways, making them **blessed above all peoples**.
>
> b. **None of the terrible diseases of Egypt**: As in Exodus 15:26, this was God's promise to an obedient Israel. In many ways, their physical health was directly connected to their obedience. Dr. S.I. McMillen in his book *None of These Diseases* noted that many of God's laws to Israel had a

direct impact on their hygiene and health. Practices such as circumcision, quarantine, washing in running water, and eating kosher food made a substantial difference in keeping Israel free from disease.

i. Beyond the direct medical implications, obedience also means we are at peace with God – and free from a tremendous amount of stress and anxiety in life. This has an obvious benefit to the health of any person.

ii. **Terrible diseases of Egypt**: "Is literally the 'evil, bad, distressing, malignant, or horrible diseases of Egypt.' Ancient and modern sources confirm that some virulent and malignant diseases, such as elephantiasis, ophthalmia, and dysentery, were common in Egypt (Pliny the Elder, *Historia Naturalis* 26:1)." (Kalland)

2. (17-24) Have confidence in God's strength.

"If you should say in your heart, 'These nations are greater than I; how can I dispossess them?'— you shall not be afraid of them, *but* you shall remember well what the LORD your God did to Pharaoh and to all Egypt: the great trials which your eyes saw, the signs and the wonders, the mighty hand and the outstretched arm, by which the LORD your God brought you out. So shall the LORD your God do to all the peoples of whom you are afraid. Moreover the LORD your God will send the hornet among them until those who are left, who hide themselves from you, are destroyed. You shall not be terrified of them; for the LORD your God, the great and awesome God, *is* among you. And the LORD your God will drive out those nations before you little by little; you will be unable to destroy them at once, lest the beasts of the field become *too numerous* for you. But the LORD your God will deliver them over to you, and will inflict defeat upon them until they are destroyed. And He will deliver their kings into your hand, and you will destroy their name from under heaven; no one shall be able to stand against you until you have destroyed them.

a. **You shall not be afraid of them, but you shall remember well what the LORD your God did**: Israel's remembrance of God's past faithfulness would give them hope for their current and future challenges.

b. **Remember well what the LORD your God did to Pharaoh and to all Egypt**: In facing present and future challenges, Israel was to remember that God had already demonstrated His power and victory in delivering Israel from Egypt. The exodus became the central act of redemption in the Old Testament, constantly referred to as the ultimate display of God's love and power for His people.

i. In the new covenant, we have a greater act of redemption – the victory won by Jesus in His sacrificial death and glorious resurrection. These become the new centers of God's redemptive work, which God's people must constantly keep in mind to meet present and future challenges.

ii. **God will send the hornet among them**: "The *hornets* which God would send represented some powerful agency which he would use in the overthrow of Israel's enemies (cf. Exod. 23:28; Josh. 24:12). The exact connotation of the term is disputed. The phrase may be intended in a fairly literal sense and refer to swarms of stinging insects that might assist the people of Israel in their attacks on the enemy." (Thompson)

c. **You will be unable to destroy them at once**: God would go before Israel and fight for them (**the great and awesome God, is among you**) but He would not drive all the enemies out at once. Perhaps Israel wanted the land all cleared out before them, but God knew it was not best for the land or for them.

i. As it turned out, under Joshua's leadership it took Israel some seven years to conquer the main strongholds of Canaanite power (Joshua 11:18). After that, it was the responsibility of the individual tribes to possess what God had granted them, driving out remaining pockets of Canaanites.

d. **Lest the beasts of the field become too numerous for you**: The way easiest for Israel was for God to clear all Israel's enemies out at once. But the easy way had consequences Israel could not see or appreciate.

e. **Little by little**: Sometimes to our frustration, this is the way God will work in the life of the believer. Victory comes **little by little**, though God's people might wish it happened all at once. God wants His people to grow in the process of possessing all He has for them in the Promised Land.

i. Doing it all at once might seem easier and better but will have consequences that cannot be seen or appreciated. God cares that His people grow, and so He often causes them to grow **little by little**. A squash can grow almost overnight; an oak tree takes a long time.

3. (25-26) Israel must not share in the abominations of the Canaanites.

You shall burn the carved images of their gods with fire; you shall not covet the silver or gold *that is* on them, nor take *it* for yourselves, lest you be snared by it; for it *is* an abomination to the LORD **your God. Nor shall you bring an abomination into your house, lest you be doomed to**

destruction like it. You shall utterly detest it and utterly abhor it, for it *is* an accursed thing.

    a. **Burn the carved images**: Israel was not to spare any of the idols or objects used in the worship of the Canaanite gods. They could become **snared** by such abominations.

        i. **The silver or gold that is on them**: "Some of the ancient idols were plated over with gold, and God saw that the value of the metal and the excellence of the workmanship might be an inducement for the Israelites to *preserve* them; and this might lead, remotely at least, to idolatry. As the idols were accursed, all those who had them, or any thing appertaining to them, were accursed also." (Clarke)

    b. **An accursed thing**: The conquest of Jericho was only a few weeks away from the sermons Moses gave in the book of Deuteronomy. In the destruction of Jericho, Joshua specifically commanded Israel to destroy any **accursed thing** (Joshua 6:18). One man failed to do this and was severely judged (Joshua 7:15).

        i. **Nor shall you bring an abomination into your house**: "So reprehensible are these objects that they contaminate those who use them or who even bring them into their homes (v. 26). Indeed, they render them to the same judgment as was appropriate to the objects themselves, namely, total eradication." (Merrill)

Deuteronomy 8 – A Warning Against Pride

A. God's work of building humility in Israel during the wilderness years.

1. (1-2) God humbled and tested Israel.

"Every commandment which I command you today you must be careful to observe, that you may live and multiply, and go in and possess the land of which the Lord swore to your fathers. And you shall remember that the Lord your God led you all the way these forty years in the wilderness, to humble you *and* test you, to know what *was* in your heart, whether you would keep His commandments or not.

a. **Every commandment…you must be careful to observe**: God called Israel to complete obedience. This obedience was based on remembering what the Lord had done among them for forty years in the wilderness.

b. **To humble you**: God *humbled* Israel. By God's direction, they had to depend completely on Him. There was nothing else and no one else to provide, guide, and protect them.

i. As God continues to deal with His people through the generations, He often humbles them. It is important for the believer to learn contentment and even joy in a humble, dependent place.

ii. "The snow-drift covers many a muckhill; so doth prosperity many a rotten heart." (Trapp)

c. **And test you**: God *tested* Israel. One purpose of the testing was **to know** what was in their **heart**, and if they would be obedient even in humble, dependent seasons. It was not because God didn't know their hearts, but because *they* didn't know their hearts. Believers must constantly be corrected for their overestimation of themselves.

i. "It is important that we recognize that the meaning of this passage is not that God might know them, but that they might come to know themselves. God knows man perfectly. The important thing is that man should come to know himself." (Morgan)

2. (3-5) God's education of Israel in the wilderness.

So He humbled you, allowed you to hunger, and fed you with manna which you did not know nor did your fathers know, that He might make you know that man shall not live by bread alone; but man lives by every *word* that proceeds from the mouth of the LORD. Your garments did not wear out on you, nor did your foot swell these forty years. You should know in your heart that as a man chastens his son, *so* the LORD your God chastens you.

   a. **So He humbled you**: All of God's education begins here. Some never even make it past this first essential step. If believers are not humble and not teachable, there is then no point to the rest of any of God's education.

   b. **Allowed you to hunger, and fed you with manna**: One aspect of God's humbling work in Israel was to compel them to obvious, total dependence on the LORD. Israel had to rely on God beyond their own knowledge (**which you did not know**), and beyond their own ability.

      i. F.B. Meyer observed that God allows several types of hunger in the life of His people, to teach them. He may allow a hunger for love, a hunger for recognition, or a hunger for comfort and ease. "These seasons of hunger are necessary for the discipline of life. But, thank God, He is able to satisfy us; and out of His riches in glory in Christ Jesus He can and will fulfill every need of ours." (Meyer)

      ii. Yet, God did not teach Israel only through **hunger**; He also taught them as He **fed** them **manna**. "Note carefully that they were not to learn through hunger only, but also through bread. This is very important. We are sometimes prone to think that God only speaks to us through limitation and suffering. It is not so. He speaks through prosperity and through joy. In the day of adversity He certainly speaks, and we generally listen. But He also is intending to teach us in the day of abounding gladness. Let us listen then also." (Morgan)

   c. **That He might make you know that man shall not live by bread alone**: On the negative side, this was the lesson God wanted them to learn – that true life is found in more than full stomachs and material things. On the positive side, they had to learn that **man lives by every word that proceeds from the mouth of the LORD**. Many today still live by **bread alone**, living only for material things, for what can be bought, sold, earned, or possessed materially.

i. This statement is a command, but it is also a simple statement of fact: **man shall not live by bread alone**. A person may exist by material things alone, but they will not *live*. The one who considers only the material yet thinks they have life is something like the living dead.

ii. Some people don't **live** by God's word because they only *fight* with God's word: "The worst implement with which you can knock a man down, is the Bible; it is intended for us to live upon,—not to be the weapon of our controversies, but our daily food, upon which we rejoice to live." (Spurgeon)

iii. Believers live by every **word** that proceeds from the mouth of God, not by every feeling or experience. "You have never received spiritual life by your own feelings. It was when you believed God's Word that you lived; and you will never get an increase of spiritual life, and grow in grace, by your own feelings or your own doings. It must still be by your believing the promises and feeding on the Word." (Spurgeon)

iv. It is the word of God that is our food and substance, and not our own dreams or imaginations. If someone is more excited about some dream or vision than about God's word, then something is wrong. *The prophet who has a dream, let him tell a dream; And he who has My word, let him speak My word faithfully. What is the chaff to the wheat?" says the* LORD. (Jeremiah 23:28)

v. God's people must live by **every** word: "In places where they cut diamonds, they sweep up the dust, because the very dust of diamonds is valuable; and in the Word of God, all the truth is so precious that the very tiniest truth, if there be such a thing, is still diamond dust, and is unspeakably precious." (Spurgeon)

vi. We may find life in every word that proceeds from the mouth of the LORD. "Oh, keep to the Word, my brothers! Keep to it as God's Word, and as coming out of his mouth. Suck it down into your soul; you cannot have too much of it. Feed on it day and night, for thus will God make you to live the life that is life indeed." (Spurgeon)

- Like bread, we need the word of God to live.
- Like bread, we need the word of God for growth.
- Like bread, we need the word of God for strength.

d. **Man shall not live by bread alone**: This was the passage of Scripture that Jesus quoted to Satan in the wilderness, when He was tempted to make bread out of stones to feed Himself after a long period of fasting (Matthew 4:3-4). Jesus knew that there was more to life than food, and that His Spirit-led and Scripture-dependent fasting brought Him life that miraculous bread, in that circumstance, could not. Jesus therefore refused to use divine power for something that was, in that situation, unnecessary and self-focused instead of focused on His God and Father.

> i. "Our glorious David took this smooth and shining stone out of the clear and silvery brook of Scripture, and threw it at Goliath's head, an example to us to meet temptations with the weapons of Scripture, not with the words or traditions of men." (Spurgeon)
>
> ii. When Jesus appealed to the word of God (Matthew 4:4), He appealed to its *written* form, not as a myth or oral tradition. It was the divinely inspired written word that Jesus considered to be the word of God.
>
> iii. In some sense, the time Jesus spent fasting in the wilderness (Matthew 4:1-2) was a time He also was **humbled**, compelled in His humanity to even greater dependence upon God the Father. Israel did not always respond to God well in their seasons of greater humility and dependence, but Jesus always did.
>
> iv. Food is a gift from God, to be gratefully received as it is sanctified with the word of God and prayer (1 Timothy 4:4-5). Yet, the Scriptures are direct in their rebuke of those who serve their stomach (Romans 16:18), in the sense that the satisfaction of their stomach is an idol they serve (Philippians 3:19).

e. **Your garments did not wear out**: God did more than miraculously provide Israel with manna and water. He also preserved their **garments** and brought health to their well-traveled feet. The remarkable, gracious, generous provision of God to Israel in the wilderness was undeniable proof of His great love for them. It meant that when God chastened Israel, He did it with the goal of instruction and training, not as a mere demonstration of wrath.

> i. Ginzberg related strange and mythical legends from the rabbis about these **garments**: "During their forty years' march they had no need of change of raiment. The robe of purple which the angels clothed each one among them at their exodus from Egypt remained ever new; and as a snail's shell grows with it, so did their garments grow with them. Fire could not injure these garments, and though they wore the same things throughout forty years, still they were not annoyed by vermin."

3. (6-10) Blessings in the land for Israel.

"Therefore you shall keep the commandments of the LORD your God, to walk in His ways and to fear Him. For the LORD your God is bringing you into a good land, a land of brooks of water, of fountains and springs,

that flow out of valleys and hills; a land of wheat and barley, of vines and fig trees and pomegranates, a land of olive oil and honey; a land in which you will eat bread without scarcity, in which you will lack nothing; a land whose stones *are* iron and out of whose hills you can dig copper. When you have eaten and are full, then you shall bless the LORD your God for the good land which He has given you.

> a. **Therefore you shall keep the commandments of the LORD your God**: If Israel would put their focus on *every word that proceeds from the mouth of the LORD* (Deuteronomy 8:3). then the LORD would take care of all the material things – and bring them into a materially abundant land supplied with water, flourishing with agriculture, and containing precious natural resources.
>
> > i. God is not against material things – except when they come between Him and us. God wanted to materially bless a spiritually obedient Israel. This is the simple principle Jesus would later explain: *seek first the kingdom of God and His righteousness, and all these things shall be added to you* (Matthew 6:33).
> >
> > ii. "The reference to *iron* and *copper* in the hills is remarkably exact. Ancient copper mines and smelters have been discovered in recent years in the Arabah below the Dead Sea, and geological survey has demonstrated the presence of ores of copper and iron in the nearby hills." (Thompson)
>
> b. **Then you shall bless the LORD your God for the good land which He has given you**: Israel's proper response to such gracious provision from God was worship and gratitude. They were to **bless the LORD** for receiving what they did not earn or deserve.
>
> > i. "No more graphically beautiful landscape of Canaan exists than in the word picture Moses painted here." (Merrill)

B. A warning against pride.

1. (11-17) The danger of pride in the blessed life.

"Beware that you do not forget the LORD your God by not keeping His commandments, His judgments, and His statutes which I command you today, lest—*when* you have eaten and are full, and have built beautiful houses and dwell *in them*; and *when* your herds and your flocks multiply, and your silver and your gold are multiplied, and all that you have is multiplied; when your heart is lifted up, and you forget the LORD your God who brought you out of the land of Egypt, from the house of bondage; who led you through that great and terrible wilderness, *in which were* fiery serpents and scorpions and thirsty land where there

was no water; who brought water for you out of the flinty rock; who fed you in the wilderness with manna, which your fathers did not know, that He might humble you and that He might test you, to do you good in the end—then you say in your heart, 'My power and the might of my hand have gained me this wealth.'

> a. **Beware that you do not forget the LORD your God by not keeping His commandments**: When everything is fine and life is filled with abundance, the heart is easily lifted up in pride. It is easy to forget the LORD Himself and to forget it was all His gracious gift.
>
>> i. "The very blessing and abundance of the land, however, would tend to lull its inhabitants into a sense of complacency and self-sufficiency." (Merrill)
>>
>> ii. "Solomon's wealth did him more hurt than ever his wisdom did him good." (Trapp)
>>
>> iii. **Fiery serpents**: "Serpents whose bite occasioned a most violent inflammation, accompanied with an unquenchable *thirst*, and which terminated in death. See on Numbers 21:6." (Clarke)
>
> b. **My power and the might of my hand have gained me this wealth**: The proud claim that one's own **power** and **might** is the true source of one's wealth is more commonly believed in the heart than said with the lips. Some people who claim to give glory and thanks to God believe in their heart that it was their own work.
>
>> i. "Such a claim is an arrogant elevation of self to the status of God." (Thompson)

2. (18) The correcting principle against pride in the blessed life.

"**And you shall remember the LORD your God, for *it is* He who gives you power to get wealth, that He may establish His covenant which He swore to your fathers, as *it is* this day.**

> a. **Remember the LORD your God**: In times of abundance, it is easy to forget the LORD, or to at least no longer seek Him with the urgency seen in times of great need.
>
> b. **It is He who gives you power to get wealth**: Man naturally focuses on their own hard work and brilliance. Yet God gives the body, the brain, and the talent. It is all of God.
>
> c. **That He may establish His covenant**: In the case of Israel, God blessed them according to and for the sake of **His covenant**. This would ultimately further *His* eternal purpose. Therefore, the people of God have no fundamental right to use their material blessing to further selfish purposes.

Allowing for legitimate and appropriate enjoyment of God's blessing, resources should be used to advance the kingdom of God.

3. (19-20) The penalty of pride in the blessed life.

Then it shall be, if you by any means forget the LORD your God, and follow other gods, and serve them and worship them, I testify against you this day that you shall surely perish. As the nations which the LORD destroys before you, so you shall perish, because you would not be obedient to the voice of the LORD your God.

a. **If you by any means forget the LORD**: Moses understood that forgetting God might have many causes, coming by several different **means**. Here, the context points to a proud, blessed, materially abundant Israel forgetting God. Worse, they might **follow other gods** and **worship** them.

b. **I testify against you this day that you shall surely perish**: Moses loved Israel, but he loved God more. Without hesitation, he would take the witness stand against a disobedient, proud Israel – and warn them before God that they will **surely perish** because of their pride and disobedience.

c. **As the nations which the LORD destroys before you, so shall you perish**: Israel would be tempted to look at the nations being judged in front of them, and to think, "We're better than them, so we are safe. God would never deal with us that way." But God would deal with them that way if they rose up in pride against Him. In His judgment, God did eventually use other nations to drive Israel out of the land, until He restored them from exile.

d. **So you shall perish**: Proud self-reliance would lead Israel to destruction, and the same is true for the people of God since.

i. In some sense, pride is the most Satanic of sins because it was by pride that Satan himself fell. Satan prizes a proud believer over the most notorious sinner because he looks at the proud believer and says, "Now *there's* a man just like me!"

ii. Pride of *face* is obnoxious; pride of *race* is vulgar; but the worst pride is the pride of *grace*.

Deuteronomy 9 – The Battles Ahead and the Failures Behind

A. Considering the battles ahead.

1. (1-2) The difficulty of the battles ahead.

"Hear, O Israel: You *are* to cross over the Jordan today, and go in to dispossess nations greater and mightier than yourself, cities great and fortified up to heaven, a people great and tall, the descendants of the Anakim, whom you know, and *of whom* you heard *it said,* 'Who can stand before the descendants of Anak?'"

> a. **You are to cross over the Jordan today**: Israel was on the threshold of the Promised Land, and was only a few weeks from the miracle God would use for the crossing of the river (Joshua 3).
>
>> i. "This was spoken about the *eleventh* month of the *fortieth* year of their journeying, and it was on the first month of the following year they passed over; and during this interim Moses died." (Clarke)
>
> b. **Go in to dispossess nations greater and mightier than yourself**: God was leading Israel into a challenge beyond their ability to meet. It was a test that they could only meet if they trusted in God.
>
> c. **Cities great and fortified up to heaven**: This was the same report Israel heard 38 years before when the 12 spies went through Canaan. They came back saying, *the cities are fortified and very large* and that the inhabitants were *strong* (Numbers 13:28). When Israel heard this report 38 years earlier, they refused to take Canaan by faith. The new generation would now face the same enemies, trusting God to fulfill His promise.
>
>> i. God did not inspire Israel with a false sense of confidence or excitement. He wanted them to realistically know what the battle ahead would be like. Jesus called His disciples with a similar sense

of realism. Jesus said, *If anyone desires to come after Me, let him deny himself, and take up his cross, and follow Me* (Matthew 16:24). Jesus warned potential disciples of the great cost of following Him.

ii. This was so far beyond the natural ability of Israel that they were compelled to trust God in a radical way. This was not something just beyond their ability, and half-measures of faith were of no use.

2. (3) Why victory is possible with the difficult battles ahead.

Therefore understand today that the Lord your God *is* He who goes over before you *as* a consuming fire. He will destroy them and bring them down before you; so you shall drive them out and destroy them quickly, as the Lord has said to you.

a. **Understand today**: Just as much as Israel had to understand the impossibility of conquering Canaan in their own strength, they were also to understand the *certainty* of victory in the Lord.

b. **The Lord your God is He who goes over before you as a consuming fire. He will destroy them**: God could conquer the Canaanites, and He would fight for Israel. In some battles, God did this directly (Joshua 10:10-11, 14). In other battles, God worked through Joshua and the army of Israel. This is implied in the promise, **you shall drive them out and destroy them quickly**. God was calling Israel to be *workers together with Him* (2 Corinthians 6:1).

i. "Almost in the same breath, Moses said that Israel would drive out the inhabitants (v.3) and that the Lord would have driven them out, indicative again that Israel's abilities were from the Lord. At best they were the Lord's instruments." (Kalland)

c. **Destroy them quickly**: God did not want the Israelites to show mercy to the Canaanites. He wanted Israel to be a unique army of judgment against the Canaanites and their culture, which was so depraved that it deserved this kind of judgment.

i. Archaeologist William F. Albright, in his book *From the Stone Age to Christianity*, describes what the primary focus of Canaanite religion was: sex. The featured idols recovered by archaeologists are hundreds of nude female forms in sexually suggestive poses, as well as male idols associated with homosexual cults. (*From the Stone Age to Christianity*, pages 232-235)

ii. "Thus the Canaanites, with their orgiastic nature-worship, their cult of fertility in the form of serpent symbols and sensuous nudity, and their gross mythology, were replaced by Israel." (Albright, page 281)

3. (4-6) The danger of pride when the LORD gives them victory.

"Do not think in your heart, after the LORD your God has cast them out before you, saying, 'Because of my righteousness the LORD has brought me in to possess this land'; but *it is* **because of the wickedness of these nations** *that* **the LORD is driving them out from before you.** *It is* **not because of your righteousness or the uprightness of your heart** *that* **you go in to possess their land, but because of the wickedness of these nations** *that* **the LORD your God drives them out from before you, and that He may fulfill the word which the LORD swore to your fathers, to Abraham, Isaac, and Jacob. Therefore understand that the LORD your God is not giving you this good land to possess because of your righteousness, for you** *are* **a stiff-necked people.**

a. **Do not think in your heart**: Israel's temptation to pride would first appear in their thoughts. Before men speak proud words, they think proud thoughts. Therefore, Israel must not think in their heart that it was because of their **righteousness** that the LORD gave them the land. Instead, it was because of the **wickedness** of the Canaanite nations.

i. The same principle is true regarding the salvation of God's people by grace through faith in the person and work of Jesus Christ. Believers must never think that they have gained their right standing before God because of their own **righteousness**.

ii. John Trapp recorded several sayings or proverbs of the ancient world that reflect man's desire to *earn* his own righteousness and justification before God. "I will not have heaven for nothing" said one, and another said, "Give me heaven, for Thou owe it to me." The same idea is expressed in an old Roman Catholic teaching that dying men should pray, "LORD, join my righteousness with Christ's righteousness" as if the two together could accomplish something. Instead, God's people must look to the righteousness of Jesus alone.

iii. "In these words, another peril…is revealed, that, namely, of interpreting His goodness to them as resulting from their own righteousness. In the case of these very people, in process of time this was the particular sin that wrought their undoing. They came to look with contempt upon others, a sure sign of self-righteous pride." (Morgan)

b. **For you are a stiff-necked people**: The idea is that Israel, like a rebellious domestic animal used to pull things, would stiffen its neck against the yoke God would put upon it. They would not submit to God's direction in their lives.

i. "Stiff-necked' is a metaphor for stubbornness, one suggesting unwillingness to submit to the yoke of God's sovereignty." (Merrill)

B. The stiff-necked character of Israel was demonstrated in their past failures.

1. (7) A call to remember their past rebellions.

"Remember! Do not forget how you provoked the Lord your God to wrath in the wilderness. From the day that you departed from the land of Egypt until you came to this place, you have been rebellious against the Lord.

a. **Do not forget**: God's purpose in reminding Israel of their rebellions against Him was not to discourage them or to make them feel defeated. The purpose was so that they would recognize their own weakness, and trust in Him. They needed to remember that the entire exodus journey had been marked by times of rebellion.

b. **You have been rebellious against the Lord**: Remembering their past rebellions against God and the painful consequences that followed could help Israel live out a poverty of spirit that Jesus said was an important foundation for a life of blessing (Matthew 5:3).

2. (8-21) Remembering the rebellion at Mount Horeb.

Also in Horeb you provoked the Lord to wrath, so that the Lord was angry *enough* with you to have destroyed you. When I went up into the mountain to receive the tablets of stone, the tablets of the covenant which the Lord made with you, then I stayed on the mountain forty days and forty nights. I neither ate bread nor drank water. Then the Lord delivered to me two tablets of stone written with the finger of God, and on them *were* all the words which the Lord had spoken to you on the mountain from the midst of the fire in the day of the assembly. And it came to pass, at the end of forty days and forty nights, *that* the Lord gave me the two tablets of stone, the tablets of the covenant.

"Then the Lord said to me, 'Arise, go down quickly from here, for your people whom you brought out of Egypt have acted corruptly; they have quickly turned aside from the way which I commanded them; they have made themselves a molded image.'

"Furthermore the Lord spoke to me, saying, 'I have seen this people, and indeed they are a stiff-necked people. Let Me alone, that I may destroy them and blot out their name from under heaven; and I will make of you a nation mightier and greater than they.'

"So I turned and came down from the mountain, and the mountain burned with fire; and the two tablets of the covenant *were* in my two hands. And I looked, and behold, you had sinned against the LORD your God—had made for yourselves a molded calf! You had turned aside quickly from the way which the LORD had commanded you. Then I took the two tablets and threw them out of my two hands and broke them before your eyes. And I fell down before the LORD, as at the first, forty days and forty nights; I neither ate bread nor drank water, because of all your sin which you committed in doing wickedly in the sight of the LORD, to provoke Him to anger. For I was afraid of the anger and hot displeasure with which the LORD was angry with you, to destroy you. But the LORD listened to me at that time also. And the LORD was very angry with Aaron *and* would have destroyed him; so I prayed for Aaron also at the same time. Then I took your sin, the calf which you had made, and burned it with fire and crushed it *and* ground *it* very small, until it was as fine as dust; and I threw its dust into the brook that descended from the mountain.

a. **Also in Horeb you provoked the LORD to wrath**: This recalls the events at Mount Sinai, where Israel worshipped a golden calf when Moses was gone a long time on Mount Sinai, receiving the law from the LORD (Exodus 32).

i. **I stayed on the mountain forty days and forty nights. I neither ate bread nor drank water**: "This clearly miraculous sojourn gives tangible support to Moses' own observation that 'man does not live on bread alone but on every word that comes from the mouth of the Lord' (Deut 8:3)." (Merrill)

b. **Written with the finger of God**: The original tablets of the law Moses received on Mount Sinai were written by God Himself (Exodus 32:16) and contained the Ten Commandments. God spoke the Ten Commandments to Israel **on the mountain from the midst of the fire** (Exodus 20:1, 18-19).

i. "The *tables of stone* or *tables of the covenant* were the 'documents' on which the covenant was recorded. This was in the manner of the Near Eastern treaties where the treaties were recorded on *tablets*." (Thompson)

c. **I will make of you a nation mightier and greater than they**: God told Moses of His desire to wipe out Israel in judgment, and to start over again with a new nation, descended from Moses himself.

d. **The mountain burned with fire**: The burning fires on Mount Sinai were physical representations of the glory of God and His holy presence. The mountain began to burn when Israel first came to Mount Sinai (Exodus 9:18). Those fires had burned for 40 days straight, and they were burning *at the very time* Israel made a golden **calf** and began to worship it.

> i. **Made for yourselves a molded calf**: "The animal was not intended as an object of worship but as a symbol of the deity. In some examples in the ancient Near East animals appear alone, but the context suggests that they symbolize a deity. The attempt to symbolize Yahweh's presence among his people by a golden calf could only lead to deep confusion." (Thompson)

e. **I took the two tablets and threw them out of my two hands and broke them before your eyes**: In anger at the rebellion of Israel against Yahweh, Moses broke the tablets that were written on by the finger of God (Exodus 32:19).

> i. "Not by an unbridled passion, but in zeal for God's honour, and by direction of God's Spirit, to signify to the people, that the covenant between God and them contained in those tables was broken and made void, and they were now quite cast out of God's favour, and could expect nothing from him but fiery indignation and severe justice." (Poole)

f. **For I was afraid**: The Hebrew word here is a rare word, translated in the Septuagint by the strong word *ekphobos*, which means "exceedingly frightened" or "stricken with terror." When Moses saw the sin of Israel and knew the holiness of God, he was *very* **afraid** for the sake of the people of Israel.

g. **I prayed for Aaron also**: Aaron's sin, detailed in Exodus 32:1-6, was so bad, that he surely would have been destroyed in judgment by the LORD – except Moses prayed for him. Moses was a man with prevailing power in prayer, and a man who loved his brother Aaron.

> i. "Moses' intercession for Aaron is not mentioned in Exodus.... even Israel's High Priest had to be snatched from judgment, according to Deuteronomy." (Thompson)

h. **Burned it with fire and crushed it and ground it very small**: Moses burnt the idol, ground it up, and sprinkled it in the people's drinking water (Exodus 32:20) for at least three reasons.

- To show this god was nothing and could be destroyed easily.
- To completely obliterate the idol.
- To make the people suffer an immediate consequence of their sin.

3. (22-24) Parenthesis: remembering the rebellions at Taberah, Massah, Kibroth Hattaavah, and Kadesh Barnea.

"Also at Taberah and Massah and Kibroth Hattaavah you provoked the Lord to wrath. Likewise, when the Lord sent you from Kadesh Barnea, saying, 'Go up and possess the land which I have given you,' then you rebelled against the commandment of the Lord your God, and you did not believe Him nor obey His voice. You have been rebellious against the Lord from the day that I knew you.

a. **Also at Taberah**: The name **Taberah** means "burning," and this refers to events recorded in Numbers 11:1-3. When the people of Israel first left Mount Sinai to head towards Kadesh Barnea and the Promised Land, they immediately complained, and God sent fires of judgment against them at a place they called **Taberah** because of the burning fires of God's judgment.

b. **And Massah**: Exodus 17:7 describes the naming of a place called **Massah**, which means "tempted," because there Israel provoked the Lord by doubting His loving care and concern for them in the wilderness.

c. **Kibroth Hattaavah**: The name means "graves of craving" and was the place where Israel longed for meat instead of manna, and God gave them meat. However, miraculously provided meat became plagued in the mouths of those with greedy and discontented hearts (described in Numbers 11:31-34).

d. **When the Lord sent you from Kadesh Barnea**: Moses briefly remembered the rebellion at **Kadesh Barnea**, where Israel doubted God's love for them and refused to enter the Promised Land by faith – rebelling against the Lord (Numbers 13, 14).

e. **You did not believe Him nor obey His voice**: Israel's disobedience to God began with unbelief, the failure to **believe Him**. They did not believe God loved them and was mighty enough to bring them into the Promised Land. Taken together, the events and places mentioned in these verses show Israel's long history of rebellion against God in the wilderness (**from the day that I knew you**).

 i. "In every case Israel questioned God's plan for her life. They neither believed his promises nor obeyed his commands." (Thompson)

 ii. "Catalogues should be kept of our sins, and oft perused, yea, though they be pardoned, that we may renew our repentance, and keep our souls humble, supple, and soluble." (Trapp)

4. (25-29) Moses' prayer of intercession for Israel when they rebelled at Mount Horeb.

"Thus I prostrated myself before the LORD; forty days and forty nights I kept prostrating myself, because the LORD had said He would destroy you. Therefore I prayed to the LORD, and said: 'O Lord GOD, do not destroy Your people and Your inheritance whom You have redeemed through Your greatness, whom You have brought out of Egypt with a mighty hand. Remember Your servants, Abraham, Isaac, and Jacob; do not look on the stubbornness of this people, or on their wickedness or their sin, lest the land from which You brought us should say, "Because the LORD was not able to bring them to the land which He promised them, and because He hated them, He has brought them out to kill them in the wilderness." Yet they *are* Your people and Your inheritance, whom You brought out by Your mighty power and by Your outstretched arm.'

> a. **Therefore I prayed to the LORD**: This great prayer of intercession from Moses is described more fully in Exodus 32:11-14. Moses asked for mercy upon Israel because of God's past faithfulness to them (**whom You have redeemed**).
>
>> i. "His work as an intercessor was outstanding. Indeed, the biblical picture is that, had it not been for Moses' selfless intercession and God's merciful forbearance, the nation would have been destroyed." (Thompson)
>>
>> ii. "This prayer of Moses (vv.19–20) is one of the most critical interventions in Israel's history (Exod 32:9–14). Another prayer of the same dimension was Samuel's at Mizpah (1 Sam 7:5, 8–9). The Lord reminded Jeremiah of these extraordinarily efficacious prayers when he told him that his heart would not go out to Judah in the last days of the empire (Jer 15:1)." (Kalland)
>
> b. **Remember Your servants Abraham, Isaac, and Jacob**: Moses asked for mercy upon Israel because of God's past faithfulness to the patriarchs.
>
>> i. "As if he had said: 'These are their descendants, and the covenant was made with those patriarchs in behalf of these.' God bestows many blessings on comparatively worthless persons, either for the sake of their pious ancestors, or on account of the religious people with whom they are connected." (Clarke)
>
> c. **Lest the land from which You brought us should say, "Because the LORD was not able"**: Moses asked for mercy upon Israel because of concern for the glory of God's own name and His reputation among the nations.
>
> d. **Your people…Your inheritance…You brought out…Your mighty power…Your outstretched arm**: Moses asked for mercy upon Israel

because they were God's people. In many ways, Moses could speak to God referring to Israel as belonging to Him.

i. We can seek the mercy and power of God through prayer by praying with the same heart and by pleading the same reasons before the Lord. Prayer on solid reasons like these is far more effective than merely casting wishes up towards heaven. We can pray with confidence:

- Because of God's past faithfulness to us.
- Because of His past faithfulness to our forefathers.
- Because of His own glory and reputation among the nations.
- Because we are His people.

ii. Keeping these things in mind is also a way to refine our prayers. When we pray only for the things consistent with God's glory, we have our hearts set on the right things.

Deuteronomy 10 – Israel's Restoration After the Golden Calf

A. God's plan of recovery for Israel after the rebellion at Mount Sinai.

1. (1-5) Israel must return to the word of God, so God commanded the giving of the new tablets of the law.

"At that time the LORD said to me, 'Hew for yourself two tablets of stone like the first, and come up to Me on the mountain and make yourself an ark of wood. And I will write on the tablets the words that were on the first tablets, which you broke; and you shall put them in the ark.'

"So I made an ark of acacia wood, hewed two tablets of stone like the first, and went up the mountain, having the two tablets in my hand. And He wrote on the tablets according to the first writing, the Ten Commandments, which the LORD had spoken to you in the mountain from the midst of the fire in the day of the assembly; and the LORD gave them to me. Then I turned and came down from the mountain, and put the tablets in the ark which I had made; and there they are, just as the LORD commanded me."

    a. **Hew for yourself two tablets of stone like the first**: Moses broke the tablets of the law (Exodus 32:19), not only out of anger, but also as a powerful visual representation of Israel's breaking of the law of God and the covenant He made with them. Now God commanded that they restore the law by making two new tablets of the law.

        i. **Which you broke**: "That breaking of the first tables was natural; and unintentionally, it was symbolic. This is what man has ever done with the law of God." (Morgan)

        ii. In the days of King Josiah repentance and revival came to the people of God when they focused on God's word again (2 Kings 22:8-23:25).

b. **He wrote on the tablets according to the first writing**: God wanted His written word to be the starting point for Israel's restored relationship with Him. Therefore, God gave a second set of tablets, even writing on these with His own hand.

> i. This is a powerful expression of God's restoring grace. "The whole Bible is full of the truth that He finds a way for His banished ones to return, gives to failing man his second chance; writes again the broken law, restores the years the canker-worm has eaten, makes the marred vessel over anew, seeks and saves the lost. Upon the basis of that grace, men may hope, and start anew." (Morgan)

> ii. This is a powerful expression of the inspiration of God's word. Though God did not literally write the Scriptures with His own hand, He did perfectly guide the minds and hands of the writers, so that the Scriptures are "God-breathed" (2 Timothy 3:16). The Bible is given by the inspiration of God and comes, as it were, from His hand through human authors.

> iii. **From the midst of the fire**: "The law was given in fire; it is 'a law of fire' (Deuteronomy 33:2), given by God, who is 'a consuming fire' (Hebrews 12:29), and hath a tribunal of fire (Ezekiel 1:27), and shall plead with transgressors in flames of fire (Isaiah 66:15, 16)." (Trapp)

c. **And put the tablets in the ark which I had made; and there they are**: The tablets of the law were preserved in the ark of the covenant, and no further mention is made of these tablets in the Bible.

> i. "Things which belonged together are here linked together without strict attention to chronological order or the lapse of time. In fact, the whole procedure took some time, for the documents had to be prepared, the ark had to be made, and the tabernacle prepared." (Thompson)

2. (6-9) In order to deal with Israel's sin problem, God established an enduring priesthood.

(Now the children of Israel journeyed from the wells of Bene Jaakan to Moserah, where Aaron died, and where he was buried; and Eleazar his son ministered as priest in his stead. From there they journeyed to Gudgodah, and from Gudgodah to Jotbathah, a land of rivers of water. At that time the LORD separated the tribe of Levi to bear the ark of the covenant of the LORD, to stand before the LORD to minister to Him and to bless in His name, to this day. Therefore Levi has no portion nor inheritance with his brethren; the LORD *is* his inheritance, just as the LORD your God promised him.)

a. **Where Aaron died, and where he was buried; and Eleazar his son ministered as priest in his stead**: This parenthesis speaking about the priesthood demonstrated the need for priestly sacrifice and intercession in restoring a covenant relationship with God after a time of rebellion. Israel needed the sacrifice, intercession, and blessing that the Levites would bring to the nation.

i. The need for a priesthood said to Israel: "You can't do it on your own. You must come to God through a mediator, who will atone for your sin, pray for you, and bless you. You will perish if you refuse your priestly mediator, and trust in your own ability to do these things."

ii. **The children of Israel journeyed**: "It appears that after leaving Kadesh, Israel went toward Edom and then later returned to Kadesh before starting on the last trip around Edom and up onto the plains of Moab. Consequently the order here is the reverse of that in Numbers 33:31–33." (Kalland)

b. **To stand before the LORD to minister to Him and to bless in His name**: Restoring a covenant relationship with God after a time of rebellion must *always* have a focus on the priestly ministry of Jesus the Messiah. This work of Jesus is shown by His atonement for sin at the cross, by His intercession for His people in heaven, and by the blessing that He bestows from heaven.

i. "The phrase *stand before* is an idiom meaning 'wait upon', 'serve'. It is used of many kinds of service in the Old Testament." (Thompson)

ii. "The Levites were noticeably absent until Moses descended from the mountain, and then they became the Lord's ministers of wrath and punishment (Exod 32:25–29). By both election and obedience they demonstrated their qualifications to be the Lord's inheritance (v. 9; cf. Num 18:20, 24)." (Merrill)

3. (10-11) God's command for Israel to rise and journey to Canaan.

"As at the first time, I stayed in the mountain forty days and forty nights; the LORD also heard me at that time, *and* the LORD chose not to destroy you. Then the LORD said to me, 'Arise, begin *your* journey before the people, that they may go in and possess the land which I swore to their fathers to give them.'"

a. **Arise, begin your journey**: Israel's rebellion at Mount Sinai with the golden calf was significant; it was no small matter. Yet God did not end His covenant with Israel or His relationship with them. After they came back to His word and came through His priesthood, it was time to move forward. God had a place to take them, and they had to begin the journey.

b. **That they may go in and possess the land**: Getting right with God after a time of sin and covenant-breaking must *always* lead to continued progress. It does no good to come back to the Bible, come through God's priesthood in Jesus, and then remain stuck in the same place. God wants His people to go forward and make progress with Him.

B. What God required of Israel.

1. (12-13) What the LORD requires of Israel, the covenant nation.

"And now, Israel, what does the LORD your God require of you, but to fear the LORD your God, to walk in all His ways and to love Him, to serve the LORD your God with all your heart and with all your soul, *and* to keep the commandments of the LORD and His statutes which I command you today for your good?

a. **What does the LORD your God require of you**: In His grace, God gave Israel a summary of His commands, His expectations of them under the covenant agreed to on Mount Sinai (Exodus 24:3-8). Though Moses spoke this to Israel on the plains of Moab in the context of covenant renewal, this statement has a general application to all God's people.

i. "In a passage of great beauty, thrilling with earnestness, Moses made a statement summarizing the truth concerning the requirements of God as His people entered the land. The whole revealed the fact that everything depended on their relationship to Him. They were to fear Him, that is reverence; to walk in His ways, that is obedience; to love Him, that is worship; to serve Him, that is co-operation; to keep His commandments, that is fidelity." (Morgan)

b. **Fear the LORD your God**: God requires from His people a reverential honor. This is not a fear that would make God's people avoid Him, but a heart that so honors God that we would be hesitant to offend Him.

c. **To walk in all His ways**: God requires His people to live after the pattern He has set. God's people are to **walk** on His road not their own. Israel was to **walk** in God's **ways**, not in their own ways or in the ways of the Canaanites.

d. **To love Him**: God requires His people to love Him. This means the love He expects isn't a love that just happens spontaneously, but it is a love that comes from a decision to set their affection on Him. It is a love that responds to the love of God that He first gives (1 John 4:19).

i. "That ye *love* him—have confidence in him as your father and friend, have recourse to him in all your necessities, and love him in return for his love." (Clarke)

e. **To serve the LORD your God with all your heart and with all your soul**: God requires His people to serve Him, to do everything in the name of Jesus (Colossians 3:17). Service to God should not be superficial but performed with one's whole being.

f. **To keep the commandments of the LORD and His statutes**: God requires His people to not only know His word, but also to **keep** it. God's people keep His word when they obey it and when they guard the integrity of God's word.

g. **For your good**: Every command of God is given for the **good** of humanity. His commandments are never given merely so God can exercise His power, or so He can feel important. Every command God gives is with the best interest of humanity in mind, even when it is not immediately apparent.

2. (14-15) Why God required this from Israel.

Indeed heaven and the highest heavens belong to the LORD your God, *also* the earth with all that *is* in it. The LORD delighted only in your fathers, to love them; and He chose their descendants after them, you above all peoples, as *it is* this day.

a. **The LORD delighted only in your fathers, to love them**: God requires this conduct from His people because they are His special possession. Though **heaven** and **earth** belong to God, He set His focus and attention on Israel beginning with their fathers.

b. **He chose their descendants after them, you above all peoples, as it is this day**: God's choosing of Israel gave them some privilege, but also great responsibility. Under their covenant with God, Israel had a unique accountability before the LORD.

3. (16) What it takes to fulfill what God requires.

Therefore circumcise the foreskin of your heart, and be stiff-necked no longer.

a. **Therefore circumcise the foreskin of your heart**: All males among Israel had to be circumcised eight days after they were born (Leviticus 12:3). But this minor surgery was only a symbol for the real work of cutting away the flesh that God desired. God wanted Israel to be a spiritual people, trusting and obeying Him, and receiving the same righteousness by faith that Abraham received (Genesis 15:6).

i. The Bible often uses the word *uncircumcised* to refer to people as Gentiles, outside the covenant of God and not in a right relationship with Him (Judges 14:3, 15:18, 1 Samuel 14:6, 17:26, Acts 11:3,

Galatians 2:7). Therefore, the idea of a **foreskin** of the **heart** means that someone could be outwardly a Jew, but not in a right relationship with God in his heart.

ii. This theme would be repeated later in the prophets, such as Jeremiah 4:4 (*Circumcise yourselves to the LORD, and take away the foreskins of your hearts*). This idea is also stated in Leviticus 26:41, Jeremiah 9:26, and Ezekiel 44:7 and 9. When Stephen rebuked the council, he said they were *uncircumcised in heart and ears* (Acts 7:51).

iii. To truly fulfill God's law, it takes more than being given a command and having the intention to keep it. It takes an inner transformation, a transformation that only God can bring.

b. **And be stiff-necked no longer**: The phrase **stiff-necked** was a figure of speech that pictured a farm animal (such as a donkey or an ox) that resisted the will of its master. God called Israel to stop their resistance, and to submit to Him.

4. (17-22) A call to obedience, reverence, and compassion.

For the LORD your God *is* God of gods and Lord of lords, the great God, mighty and awesome, who shows no partiality nor takes a bribe. He administers justice for the fatherless and the widow, and loves the stranger, giving him food and clothing. Therefore love the stranger, for you were strangers in the land of Egypt. You shall fear the LORD your God; you shall serve Him, and to Him you shall hold fast, and take oaths in His name. He *is* your praise, and He *is* your God, who has done for you these great and awesome things which your eyes have seen. Your fathers went down to Egypt with seventy persons, and now the LORD your God has made you as the stars of heaven in multitude.

a. **The LORD your God is God of gods and LORD of lords**: The basis of this brief section of commands is set in the character of God. Yahweh (the **LORD**), the covenant God of Israel, was and is above all gods, both by nature and authority. He is the **great God, mighty and awesome**.

i. "That is, He is the source whence all being and power proceed; every agent is finite but himself; and he can counteract, suspend, or destroy all the actions of all creatures whensoever he pleases. If he determine to save, none can destroy; if he purpose to destroy, none can save. How absolutely necessary to have such a God for our friend!" (Clarke)

ii. **God of gods**: "The designations do not suggest that there are in reality other divine gods or lords over whom God rules. Rather, as God and Lord he is supreme over all. The superlative is based on the idea that other gods are said to exist but does not admit of their reality." (Kalland)

iii. **Mighty**: "The adjective *mighty* (*gibbor*) is commonly used of a warrior, and seems to have overtones of the Holy War in which Yahweh as leader in battle displayed the qualities of a warrior (Ps. 24:8; Isa. 9:6; 10:21; 42:13; Jer. 20:11)." (Thompson)

b. **Who shows no partiality nor takes a bribe**: When God requires His people to show justice, compassion, and reverence, it is because these virtues answer to aspects of God's own character. God compassionately **administers justice** for the disadvantaged, and He **loves the stranger**.

i. Because God **loves the stranger**, believers are to **therefore love the stranger**. "And to show yourselves the friends of God.... Friends are like-minded." (Trapp)

ii. "What God does in the social realm his people are to imitate (cf. Exod 22:22–24). They must be especially sensitive to aliens living among them, particularly since they also had been aliens in Egypt (v. 19)." (Merrill)

c. **Who has done for you these great and awesome things**: The obedience God calls His people to is always set in the context of what He has done for them. Service and obedience to the LORD are grateful responses to His goodness. If there is a lack in obedience and reverence, there is almost always a lack of appreciation for what the LORD has done.

i. One great thing God did for Israel was to cause them to grow into a significant nation. The family of Jacob went to Egypt as about **seventy persons** and over 400 years became a **multitude**.

d. **He is your praise**: This is true of God and for the people of God in at least two senses. First, He is the *object* of praise. Second, He makes His people *praiseworthy*. Any wisdom, beauty, or skill among God's people is not to their praise, but **He is your praise**.

Deuteronomy 11 – Blessing and Curses for Israel

A. Blessing in Israel's past and future.

1. (1-7) Israel must remember the many ways God had already blessed them.

"**Therefore you shall love the** Lord **your God, and keep His charge, His statutes, His judgments, and His commandments always. Know today that** *I do* **not** *speak* **with your children, who have not known and who have not seen the chastening of the** Lord **your God, His greatness and His mighty hand and His outstretched arm—His signs and His acts which He did in the midst of Egypt, to Pharaoh king of Egypt, and to all his land; what He did to the army of Egypt, to their horses and their chariots: how He made the waters of the Red Sea overflow them as they pursued you, and** *how* **the** Lord **has destroyed them to this day; what He did for you in the wilderness until you came to this place; and what He did to Dathan and Abiram the sons of Eliab, the son of Reuben: how the earth opened its mouth and swallowed them up, their households, their tents, and all the substance that** *was* **in their possession, in the midst of all Israel—but your eyes have seen every great act of the** Lord **which He did.**"

> a. **Therefore you shall love the** Lord **your God**: God *commanded* Israel to **love** Him. Love is not a matter left entirely up to the impulses or feelings of God's people. People choose to love the Lord or to not love Him.
>
>> i. Additionally, this is a reminder of what the Lord really wants from His people – their **love**. We could give God a hundred other things, but none of it really matters unless we also give Him our love. As Jesus said to the Ephesian church in Revelation 2:4: *I have this against you, that you have left your first love*. To lose love is to lose everything.
>
> b. **Keep His charge, His statutes, His judgments, and His commandments**: Those who love God will want to please Him, and to honor God as He has revealed in His word. To whatever extent a person

fails to obey God, it can also be said that they are lacking in their love for Him.

i. As Jesus said in John 14:15: *If you love Me, keep My commandments.* Real love for Jesus will be seen in obedience.

c. **Know today that I do not speak with your children, who have not known and who have not seen**: Moses addressed the generation which saw the works of God among Israel, both in blessing and chastening. He spoke to the generation that *should* know and remember.

i. **The LORD has destroyed them to this day**: "It is a documented fact that neither Thutmose IV nor Amenhotep III, the kings of Egypt who succeeded the pharaoh of the exodus, Amenhotep II, were able to field large armies or undertake major military campaigns until after the period suggested by 'until this very day,' that is, about 1400 b.c." (Merrill)

d. **Dathan and Abiram**: These were the two key associates in the rebellion of Korah (Numbers 16), and perhaps the instigators of the rebellion. When Korah, Dathan, and Abiram challenged the leadership of Israel, God vindicated His servant Moses.

e. **Which He did...what He did...how He made...how the LORD destroyed them...what He did for you...what He did...every great act of the LORD which He did**: Moses called Israel to remember what *God* had done in their history. The works of God were more important to think about than the works of men.

i. "A diary should be diligently kept of what God does for us (Psalm 102:18), for the help of our slippery memories, and the stirring up of our dull hearts to a contention in godliness." (Trapp)

ii. Most of history, both social and personal, is concerned with what *man* has done. But God wants His people to look at history and see what *He has done.* There is more to learn and more to benefit when we look at the works of God instead of the works of man.

iii. Because Israel personally experienced so many great works of God, they were highly accountable. "They could not plead either ignorance or lack of personal accountability. What they had experienced should have provided the highest motivation to loving response and obedience." (Merrill)

2. (8-15) A conditional promise of blessing in the land of Canaan.

"Therefore you shall keep every commandment which I command you today, that you may be strong, and go in and possess the land which

you cross over to possess, and that you may prolong *your* days in the land which the LORD swore to give your fathers, to them and their descendants, 'a land flowing with milk and honey.' For the land which you go to possess *is* not like the land of Egypt from which you have come, where you sowed your seed and watered *it* by foot, as a vegetable garden; but the land which you cross over to possess *is* a land of hills and valleys, which drinks water from the rain of heaven, a land for which the LORD your God cares; the eyes of the LORD your God *are* always on it, from the beginning of the year to the very end of the year.

'And it shall be that if you earnestly obey My commandments which I command you today, to love the LORD your God and serve Him with all your heart and with all your soul, then I will give *you* the rain for your land in its season, the early rain and the latter rain, that you may gather in your grain, your new wine, and your oil. And I will send grass in your fields for your livestock, that you may eat and be filled.'

a. **Therefore you shall keep every commandment**: Remembering what God had done for Israel in their past should lead Israel to greater obedience and trust, and this would equip them to take the Promised Land.

b. **A land flowing with milk and honey**: If Israel felt it was a sacrifice to obey God and His commandments, it was a sacrifice well rewarded. God promised them a land which was far superior to Egypt, which did not need to be artificially irrigated, but was watered by rains which God would send upon the obedient nation.

i. Calling Egypt a place where they **watered by foot** refers to the system of artificial irrigation that used foot-driven pumps to lift water from the Nile to nearby fields. Canaan received **water from the rain of heaven** and did not need to use this kind of irrigation.

ii. **Watered by foot**: "The technique referred to is attested in ancient texts and drawings and still exists in parts of Egypt. It consists of networks of ditches, canals, and holding tanks from and into which river water could be 'pumped' by means of a paddlewheel-like device called a *shaduf* in Arabic. This was powered by pedals or similar systems so that one could indeed say that the irrigation was done by foot." (Merrill)

c. **If you earnestly obey My commandments**: God's promise to provide for Israel had a condition. They had to **earnestly obey** all that He commanded. If they made God and His honor their priority, God promised to provide for them. This same principle was later stated by Jesus (Matthew 6:33).

i. The promise of the blessing of rain was important because one of the attractive Canaanite gods was *Baal* – the god who was said to control the weather and rain. Perhaps the Israelites would be tempted to think, "Now that we are in Canaan, if we want rain, we must worship the Canaanite god of rain." But the LORD promised that if they would worship and obey Him, He would supply abundant rain.

d. **The early rain and the latter rain**: The **early rain** fell in October and November and was important to help soften the ground for plowing and preparing the soil for the seed. The **latter rain** fell about April and helped the crops come to final harvest. Both seasons of rain were helpful to successful farming.

i. "By the *first* or *former rain* we are to understand that which fell in Judea about November, when they sowed their seed, and this served to moisten and prepare the ground for the vegetation of the seed. The *latter rain* fell about April, when the corn was well grown up, and served to fill the ears, and render them plump and perfect. Rain rarely fell in Judea at any other seasons than these." (Clarke)

e. **A land for which the LORD your God cares**: God declared His special care for the land of Israel, both then and now. He is the LORD of all the earth (Psalm 24:1) but chose the land we commonly call Israel to be the place where His work of redemption was centered. God said that His **eyes** are **always on** this land, all through the year.

i. "This is an arresting description of the Holy Land, and the place it occupies in the world geographically and historically is equally remarkable…. In light of Biblical reference, and of its own history interpreted by such reference, it is impossible to think of it without reverence. It is the land for which God careth." (Morgan)

3. (16-17) Warning Israel of the danger of turning from God in times of prosperity.

Take heed to yourselves, lest your heart be deceived, and you turn aside and serve other gods and worship them, lest the LORD's anger be aroused against you, and He shut up the heavens so that there be no rain, and the land yield no produce, and you perish quickly from the good land which the LORD is giving you.

a. **Lest your heart be deceived**: God had to warn Israel against the deceptions of prosperity. The person who turns from God in times of prosperity is deceived. They believe they are somehow responsible for the blessings received and they become proud and self-reliant.

b. **He shut up the heavens so that there be no rain**: Just such a judgment came upon Israel in the days of Ahab, the wicked king over Israel in the time Elijah was a prophet (1 Kings 17:1).

    i. The constant need for rain kept Israel in continual dependence on the LORD. It is good for believers to have things that keep them in unbroken dependence on the LORD. God's people should never despise those things or find themselves longing for the day when they will no longer need to depend on God as much.

4. (18-21) Blessing is gained by keeping the word of God always before you.

"Therefore you shall lay up these words of mine in your heart and in your soul, and bind them as a sign on your hand, and they shall be as frontlets between your eyes. You shall teach them to your children, speaking of them when you sit in your house, when you walk by the way, when you lie down, and when you rise up. And you shall write them on the doorposts of your house and on your gates, that your days and the days of your children may be multiplied in the land of which the LORD swore to your fathers to give them, like the days of the heavens above the earth.

a. **Lay up these words of mine in your heart and in your soul**: God called Israel to not only read and know the word of God, but to also *treasure* it. Valuing God's word is a logical response to understanding who God is and how wonderful it is that He speaks through the Bible.

b. **Bind them as a sign on your hand…frontlets between your eyes**: From God's first use of this idea for Israel in reference to Passover (Exodus 13:9, 16), this should be understood as a symbol, meaning to hold a truth or idea in constant prominence. The commandments of God were to be as familiar and prominent to Israel as a sign on the hand or head.

    i. By the time of Jesus, the Jewish people used this passage (and Deuteronomy 6:8) as the basis for their practice of wearing phylacteries. A phylactery is a small box holding parchment with Scripture passages written on it, and the box is held to the forehead or hand with leather straps.

c. **Speaking of them**: God's word was to be the constant topic of their conversation as they sat, walked, came in, or went out. It is fair for believers today to consider how much God's word, His truth, is part of their daily conversation.

    i. **Like the days of the heavens**: "The expression *as long as the heavens are above the earth* is a vivid way of saying 'for ever'. The divine promise sworn to the fathers would never fail for men who obeyed God." (Thompson)

B. The choice of blessing or curses.

1. (22-25) The promise of blessing.

"For if you carefully keep all these commandments which I command you to do—to love the LORD your God, to walk in all His ways, and to hold fast to Him—then the LORD will drive out all these nations from before you, and you will dispossess greater and mightier nations than yourselves. Every place on which the sole of your foot treads shall be yours: from the wilderness and Lebanon, from the river, the River Euphrates, even to the Western Sea, shall be your territory. No man shall be able to stand against you; the LORD your God will put the dread of you and the fear of you upon all the land where you tread, just as He has said to you.

> a. **To love the LORD your God, to walk in all His ways, and to hold fast to Him**: All the commandments are summarized in these three phrases (**love, walk, hold fast**). Each of these speaks of more than a reluctant and compelled obedience; they speak of a real relationship of love between God and His people, with obedience flowing naturally from that relationship.
>
> > i. "Ceremony, ritual, and other professions of religion would count for nothing if this personal relationship with God were to be discounted." (Merrill)
>
> b. **The LORD will drive out…and you will dispossess greater and mightier nations**: God promised to fight the battles for an obedient Israel, and He did (Joshua 10:10-11, 14). There are many people who want God to fight for them, but they have little interest in obeying Him, or in cultivating the deep relationship of love which obedience grows from.
>
> c. **Every place on which the sole of your foot treads**: God repeated this promise to Joshua, just when Israel was about to cross over the Jordan River into Canaan (Joshua 1:3).
>
> > i. "It is worth noting that David and Solomon created an empire that included all this (2 Sam 8:1–14; 1 Kgs 4:21–24), but it is equally significant that the Transjordan was not in the ancient promises even though it was settled by the tribes of Reuben, Gad, and half of Manasseh's tribe (cf. Num 32:33–42), even with God's blessing (Deut 3:18–23)." (Merrill)
>
> d. **No man shall be able to stand against you**: When Israel walked in love with the LORD and was obedient to Him, they were unbeatable. No man

could defeat them. Greater was God who was with them than he who was in the world (1 John 4:4). God sent the Canaanites **fear** and **dread** of Israel (Joshua 2:9).

2. (26-28) The choice: Blessing or cursing?

"Behold, I set before you today a blessing and a curse: the blessing, if you obey the commandments of the LORD your God which I command you today; and the curse, if you do not obey the commandments of the LORD your God, but turn aside from the way which I command you today, to go after other gods which you have not known.

> a. **Behold, I set before you today a blessing and a curse**: The three great elements of the old covenant God made with Israel on Mount Sinai were the law, the sacrifice, and the choice. Israel had a choice – to obey and be blessed or to disobey and be cursed. This aspect of their covenant made a cause-and-effect relationship with God.
>
>> i. It is important to recognize that in Jesus Christ, believers do not have an old covenant relationship with God. They may expect to be blessed, not because of their obedience, but because of their position in Jesus. In the new covenant, the deserved curse was laid upon Jesus Christ (Galatians 3:10-14). Though there may be an inherent curse of consequences in disobedience or even in the correcting hand of God, God does not punish us or curse believers under the new covenant. This is because all that they deserved, past, present, and future, was placed upon Jesus.
>
> b. **I set before you today**: Under this covenant, it was up to Israel. If they wanted to be blessed, as they were in the days of David and Solomon, then they should walk in obedience. But if they disobeyed, they would be cursed as they were in most of the days of the later kings.
>
>> i. A choice was *required*. There was no neutral ground. God wouldn't just leave them alone. It would either be blessing or cursing, and God would glorify Himself through either option.
>
> c. **To go after other gods which you have not known**: Inherent in Israel's disobedience was idolatry. Those who walk in disobedience, exalt themselves against God. They declare that their rules, standards, and desires, are all more important than His. This is idolatry in its most common form.

3. (29-32) Making the choice known to the people.

Now it shall be, when the LORD your God has brought you into the land which you go to possess, that you shall put the blessing on Mount Gerizim and the curse on Mount Ebal. *Are* **they not on the other side of the Jordan, toward the setting sun, in the land of the Canaanites who**

dwell in the plain opposite Gilgal, beside the terebinth trees of Moreh? For you will cross over the Jordan and go in to possess the land which the LORD your God is giving you, and you will possess it and dwell in it. And you shall be careful to observe all the statutes and judgments which I set before you today.

> a. **You shall put the blessing on Mount Gerizim and the curse on Mount Ebal**: The recitation of the blessings on Mount Gerizim and the curse on Mount Ebal will be detailed in later chapters and carried out in Joshua 8:30-35. God wanted this covenant to be known to all Israel because the entire nation was bound by this covenant.
>
>> i. "The covenant which was first entered into at Sinai (Exod. 19:1–8), and now renewed on the plains of Moab (Deuteronomy 29:1), would need to be renewed once Israel crossed the Jordan. That such a ceremony was eventually carried out is clear from Joshua 8:30–35." (Thompson)
>
> b. **Mount Gerizim…Mount Ebal**: The name **Gerizim** is supposed to be associated with fruitful harvests, and the name **Ebal** is supposed to be associated with barrenness. Appropriately, the blessings came from Gerizim and the curses from Ebal.
>
>> i. "*Mount Gerizim* lies to the south and *Mount Ebal* to the north of the valley through which the road passes on the way from Shechem to Samaria. Shechem lay on the shoulder between the two, hence its name (Heb. *sekem* means 'shoulder')." (Thompson)
>>
>> ii. "No doubt they were chosen because of their centrality and natural adaptability for such an event. They are close to each other and are both about 3,000 feet above sea level, Ebal being about 230 feet higher than Gerizim." (Kalland)
>>
>> iii. "That Gerizim *is* very *fruitful*, and that Ebal *is* very *barren*, is the united testimony of all who have travelled in those parts." (Clarke)

Deuteronomy 12 – The Worship God Commands

A. The place of worship.

1. (1-4) The command to destroy Canaanite places of worship.

"These *are* the statutes and judgments which you shall be careful to observe in the land which the LORD God of your fathers is giving you to possess, all the days that you live on the earth. You shall utterly destroy all the places where the nations which you shall dispossess served their gods, on the high mountains and on the hills and under every green tree. And you shall destroy their altars, break their *sacred* pillars, and burn their wooden images with fire; you shall cut down the carved images of their gods and destroy their names from that place. You shall not worship the LORD your God *with* such *things.*

> a. **You shall utterly destroy all the places**: For Israel to honor God with their worship, there had to be **places** where they would refuse to worship. When Israel came into the **land**, they had to destroy the wicked, idolatrous places where the Canaanites worshipped their gods.
>
>> i. The normal practice in the ancient world was to take a nice building such as a temple previously used to worship a prior god, and simply make it a place to worship one's own god. Yahweh, the covenant God of Israel, wanted none of that in His own worship. He commanded that the places of pagan worship be destroyed, and that His people should **not worship** Him **with such things**.
>>
>> ii. The worship of many of those who think of themselves as God's people is corrupted this way. It isn't that they worship too little; they worship too much. They worship the LORD *and* the things of the world. God doesn't want such worship. It is an abomination to Him.
>>
>> iii. Many people could really begin to worship God in Spirit and in truth (John 4:24), if they would only "destroy" in their hearts their

pagan places of worship. Because they give their hearts to so many other things, there is little to give to the Lord.

b. On the high mountains and on the hills and under every green tree: Much of the pagan worship of the Canaanites was a sexualized veneration of fertility and nature. Therefore, their shrines and temples were often in pleasant outdoor settings. God didn't want Israel to adopt this approach of worshipping the creature rather than the Creator (Romans 1:25).

i. "The custom of placing shrines on mountains and hills and under leafy trees is referred to elsewhere in the Old Testament as a common practice of the Canaanites. It was copied by Israel in times of apostasy (1 Kgs 14:23; 2 Kgs 16:4; 17:10; 2 Chr. 28:4; Isa. 57:5; Jer. 2:20; 3:6, 13), making reform necessary." (Thompson)

2. (5-9) The command to worship at God's appointed place.

"But you shall seek the place where the Lord your God chooses, out of all your tribes, to put His name for His dwelling place; and there you shall go. There you shall take your burnt offerings, your sacrifices, your tithes, the heave offerings of your hand, your vowed offerings, your freewill offerings, and the firstborn of your herds and flocks. And there you shall eat before the Lord your God, and you shall rejoice in all to which you have put your hand, you and your households, in which the Lord your God has blessed you.

"You shall not at all do as we are doing here today—every man doing whatever *is* right in his own eyes—for as yet you have not come to the rest and the inheritance which the Lord your God is giving you.

a. **You shall seek the place**: There was a specific **place** God chose where Israel was to worship Him. It wasn't left up to their feelings or preferences. At Mount Sinai, Israel build the tabernacle according to the pattern God gave them. That God-ordained place of sacrifice and worship was carried by Israel to where God guided them. Like the worship of believers today, Israel's worship was based on what pleased God, not on what pleased the worshipper. Worship was a community activity, not only an individual activity.

i. **The place where the Lord your God chooses**: "It has been argued that in pre-monarchic times the central sanctuary moved from place to place, Shechem (Josh. 24:1), Bethel (Judg. 20:18, 26, 27) and Shiloh (Judg. 18:31; 1 Sam. 1:3, 21; 4:3, 4), and that each place became in turn *the place which Yahweh your God will choose*." (Thompson)

b. **There you shall take your burnt offerings, your sacrifices**: The place of worship was to be a place of atonement, confession (which was made when hands were laid on the head of the sacrificial victim), and cleansing.

c. **There you shall take…your tithes**: The place of worship was to be a place of giving. There were other places where an Israelite could give and be generous but giving had to begin at the place of worship God had appointed.

i. Some have thought that because Deuteronomy 12:6 mentions **your tithes**, that this was an *additional* tithe that was commanded of Israel, on top of the tithe commanded in Numbers 18. Some even call this the "festival tithe." But in context, this passage is only speaking of *where* to bring the tithe, not commanding the bringing of an additional tithe.

d. **There you shall eat before the LORD your God, and you shall rejoice**: The place of worship is to be a place of joyful fellowship with God and others.

i. "The particular value of these words is that they reveal the Divine thought of worship. It is an exercise of rejoicing, resulting from blessedness. God blesses men, and in that blessedness they rejoice before Him." (Morgan)

ii. "No one duty is more pressed in both the Testaments, than this of rejoicing in the Lord always." (Trapp)

e. **Not at all do as we are doing here today – every man doing whatever is right in his own eyes**: During their wilderness years and before crossing the Jordan, it seems that each Israelite pretty much conducted their own worship as they pleased. But God was not ultimately pleased with this; worship was not a matter left up to whatever pleased the individual. Real worship is concerned with what pleases God.

i. "Everyone doing 'as he sees fit' (v.8) indicates that the camp life of the desert years was less controlled than the settled life in Canaan under the regimen of the covenant-treaty stipulations was to be. The messages of Deuteronomy were needed as preparation for that new life to come." (Kalland)

ii. Much of what is called worship in today's church really isn't worship. It is self-focused, man-focused, and personal experience-focused instead of being God-focused. Much of today's worship is measured by how the worshipper feels instead of being measured by how God is honored and worshipped.

iii. "Singing should be congregational, but it should never be performed for the credit of the congregation. 'Such remarkable singing! The place is quite renowned for its musical performances!' This is a poor achievement. Our singing should be such that God hears it with pleasure—singing in which there is not so much art as heart, not so much of musical sound as of spiritual emotion." (Spurgeon)

3. (10-14) The joy of real worship in God's appointed place.

But *when* you cross over the Jordan and dwell in the land which the LORD your God is giving you to inherit, and He gives you rest from all your enemies round about, so that you dwell in safety, then there will be the place where the LORD your God chooses to make His name abide. There you shall bring all that I command you: your burnt offerings, your sacrifices, your tithes, the heave offerings of your hand, and all your choice offerings which you vow to the LORD. And you shall rejoice before the LORD your God, you and your sons and your daughters, your male and female servants, and the Levite who *is* within your gates, since he has no portion nor inheritance with you. Take heed to yourself that you do not offer your burnt offerings in every place that you see; but in the place which the LORD chooses, in one of your tribes, there you shall offer your burnt offerings, and there you shall do all that I command you.

a. **There will be the place where the LORD your God chooses**: A particular *place* is important to worship. The man who tells himself, "I can worship God just as well out on the golf course" is a *man doing whatever is right in his own eyes* (Judges 17:6, 21:25) It is fine for anyone to worship God out on the golf course; but there must also be a specific place where one comes to worship with God's people.

i. This goes against the trend of our times. Studies find that among baby-boomers, 70% say that you should attend worship services not out of a sense of duty, but only if it "meets your needs." 80% say you can be a good Christian without attending church. A staggering percentage of those who claim to be evangelical Christians rarely attend church.

b. **And you shall rejoice before the LORD your God**: Worship at God's appointed place should be marked with joy. It is a good thing to come and honor our God and should be done with pleasure and joy.

i. "All Christian duties should be done joyfully; but especially the work of praising the Lord. I have been in congregations where the tune was dolorous to the very last degree; where the time was so dreadfully slow that one wondered whether they would ever be able to sing through the 119 Psalm; whether, to use Watt's expression, eternity would not be too short from them to get through it; and altogether, the spirit of the people has seemed to be so damp, so heavy, so dead, that we might have supposed that they were met to prepare their minds for a hanging rather than for blessing the ever-gracious God." (Spurgeon)

ii. "We ought not to worship God in a half-hearted sort of way; as if it were now our duty to bless God, but we felt it to be a weary business, and we would get it through as quickly as we could, and have done with it; and the sooner the better. No, no; 'All that is within me, bless his holy name.' Come, my heart, wake up, and summon all the powers which wait upon thee! Mechanical worship is easy, but worthless. Come rouse yourself, my brother! Rouse thyself, O my own soul!" (Spurgeon)

c. **And you shall rejoice**: The emphasis on **shall** shows that rejoicing is *commanded*. It is also commanded in the New Testament; *Rejoice always* (1 Thessalonians 5:16); *Rejoice in the Lord always. Again I will say, rejoice!* (Philippians 4:4). If a believer can't rejoice out of feeling like it, they should then rejoice out of being commanded.

i. "No one duty is more pressed in both the Testaments, than this of rejoicing in the Lord always, but specially in his immediate services." (Trapp)

B. The practice of worship.

1. (15-28) Things permitted and prohibited regarding butchering animals, sacrificing animals, and respecting the sanctity of blood.

"However, you may slaughter and eat meat within all your gates, whatever your heart desires, according to the blessing of the LORD your God which He has given you; the unclean and the clean may eat of it, of the gazelle and the deer alike. Only you shall not eat the blood; you shall pour it on the earth like water. You may not eat within your gates the tithe of your grain or your new wine or your oil, of the firstborn of your herd or your flock, of any of your offerings which you vow, of your freewill offerings, or of the heave offering of your hand. But you must eat them before the LORD your God in the place which the LORD your God chooses, you and your son and your daughter, your male servant and your female servant, and the Levite who *is* within your gates; and you shall rejoice before the LORD your God in all to which you put your hands. Take heed to yourself that you do not forsake the Levite as long as you live in your land.

"When the LORD your God enlarges your border as He has promised you, and you say, 'Let me eat meat,' because you long to eat meat, you may eat as much meat as your heart desires. If the place where the LORD

your God chooses to put His name is too far from you, then you may slaughter from your herd and from your flock which the LORD has given you, just as I have commanded you, and you may eat within your gates as much as your heart desires. Just as the gazelle and the deer are eaten, so you may eat them; the unclean and the clean alike may eat them. Only be sure that you do not eat the blood, for the blood *is* the life; you may not eat the life with the meat. You shall not eat it; you shall pour it on the earth like water. You shall not eat it, that it may go well with you and your children after you, when you do *what is* right in the sight of the LORD. Only the holy things which you have, and your vowed offerings, you shall take and go to the place which the LORD chooses. And you shall offer your burnt offerings, the meat and the blood, on the altar of the LORD your God; and the blood of your sacrifices shall be poured out on the altar of the LORD your God, and you shall eat the meat. Observe and obey all these words which I command you, that it may go well with you and your children after you forever, when you do *what is* good and right in the sight of the LORD your God.

a. **You may slaughter and eat meat within all your gates**: In the ancient world, almost every time an animal was butchered it was also sacrificed to a god. Here, the LORD made it clear that not every slaughtered animal was considered a sacrifice to Him. It was permitted to **slaughter and eat meat** apart from sacrifice.

b. **You may not eat within your gates the tithe…the firstborn of your herd…your freewill offerings, or of the heave offering**: In several sacrifices described in the Law of Moses, a portion of the meat was given to the one who brought the offering. As a family, they would enjoy the meat at the tabernacle in a celebration feast. This command instructed Israel that all such sacrifices had to be made and eaten at the tabernacle, and nowhere else.

i. "Sacred meals, such as those set out here, are to be eaten at the central sanctuary and there alone. These are to be shared with the members of the family and with any Levite who may be in the town, in a spirit of happy rejoicing." (Thompson)

ii. "What was sacrifice becomes food. The same Person and facts, apprehended by faith, are, in regard to their bearing on the divine government, the ground of pardon, and in regard to their operation within us, the source of spiritual sustenance. Christ for us is our pardon; Christ in us is our life." (Maclaren)

iii. **Do not forsake the Levite as long as you live in your land**: "These had no inheritance, and were to live by the sanctuary: if therefore the offerings were withheld by which the Levites were supported, they of course must perish. Those who have devoted themselves to the service of God in ministering to the salvation of the souls of men, should certainly be furnished at least with all the *necessaries* of life. Those who withhold this from them sin against their own mercies, and that ordinance of God by which a ministry is established for the salvation of souls." (Clarke)

c. **Only be sure that you do not eat the blood**: Since the blood was the picture of life in any animal or man (**for the blood is the life**), God would not allow Israel to eat meat that had not been properly bled. Instead, it was to be given to God by pouring it out on the earth. This was an illustration of the principle that all life belongs to God.

i. Commentators suggest different reasons *why* God commanded that the blood be poured out **on the earth like water** in honor of the idea that blood represented the life of the creature. Thompson said it was to prevent the blood from being poured out on a pagan altar. Merrill said it was to return it to the earth from which the Creator brought forth life.

2. (29-32) The worship of God must be pure.

"When the LORD **your God cuts off from before you the nations which you go to dispossess, and you displace them and dwell in their land, take heed to yourself that you are not ensnared to follow them, after they are destroyed from before you, and that you do not inquire after their gods, saying, 'How did these nations serve their gods? I also will do likewise.' You shall not worship the L**ORD **your God in that way; for every abomination to the L**ORD **which He hates they have done to their gods; for they burn even their sons and daughters in the fire to their gods.**

"Whatever I command you, be careful to observe it; you shall not add to it nor take away from it.

a. **That you do not inquire after their gods**: When God gave Israel the land, they were commanded to guard against a sinful curiosity (**How did these nations serve their gods?**). An old proverb warns against excessive curiosity: *curiosity killed the cat*. Ungodly curiosity has also killed many spiritual lives.

i. Israel's attraction to the Canaanite gods was especially strange, given that *Yahweh had clearly conquered them* in the days of Joshua. It was strange to worship inferior gods. "Over and over again in Israel's history they showed their proclivity to follow after gods that were defeated and discredited in the face of the Lord's powerful displays of sovereignty." (Merrill)

b. **You shall not worship the LORD your God in that way**: God would not accept just any offering of worship. The LORD had to be worshipped *in Spirit and in truth* (John 4:24)

c. **They burn even their sons and daughters in the fire to their gods**: This referred to the practice of Molech worship, where Canaanites offered up their children by placing them alive on a burning hot statue of Molech, while the sound of beating drums drowned out the screams of the tortured infants.

i. "While all pagan practices were excluded, the sacrifice of children is mentioned specially. This was one of the most ancient religious practices of Syria-Palestine. Already at the beginning of the second millennium BC it seems that infant sacrifice was practised in the land." (Thompson)

ii. Israel had a tragic history of following this horrible god Molech.

- At the least, Solomon sanctioned the worship of Molech, building a temple to this idol (1 Kings 11:7).
- King Ahaz of Judah gave his own son to Molech (2 Kings 16:3).
- One of the great crimes of the northern tribes of Israel was their worship of Molech, leading to the Assyrian captivity (2 Kings 17:17).
- King Manasseh of Judah gave his son to Molech (2 Kings 21:6).
- Up to the days of King Josiah of Judah, Molech worship continued, because he destroyed a place of worship to that idol (2 Kings 23:10).

d. **Whatever I command you, be careful to observe it**: The standard for worship was reflected in God's word – not in human preference or opinion.

Deuteronomy 13 – Keeping the Worship of God Pure

A. Protecting against those who would entice Israel to serve other gods.

1. (1-3) Protecting against the deceiver who comes with miraculous signs.

"If there arises among you a prophet or a dreamer of dreams, and he gives you a sign or a wonder, and the sign or the wonder comes to pass, of which he spoke to you, saying, 'Let us go after other gods'—which you have not known—'and let us serve them,' you shall not listen to the words of that prophet or that dreamer of dreams, for the LORD your God is testing you to know whether you love the LORD your God with all your heart and with all your soul.

a. **If there arises among you**: This section of the long sermon of Moses (Deuteronomy 5:1 to 26:19) deals with threats that could come from within Israel, threats to the faithful worship of Yahweh, the covenant God of Israel.

b. **A dreamer of dreams**: Dreams can come from God (Numbers 12:6, Genesis 37:5-11), or they can be false prophecies (Jeremiah 23:25-26). God's people must be careful to never put too much confidence in claimed revelation from dreams, and any such claim should be tested. False prophets might use dreams to give weight to their message (Deuteronomy 13:1-5, Jeremiah 23:25-28).

i. God may certainly speak through dreams, and many passages of the Bible show this. In the Bible, those to whom God spoke through dreams include the pagan ruler Abimelech (Genesis 20:3), Jacob (Genesis 28:12, 31:11), Laban (Genesis 31:24), a Midianite (Judges 7:13), Solomon (1 Kings 3:5), Nebuchadnezzar (Daniel 2:1), Daniel (Daniel 7:1), Joseph (Matthew 1:20, 2:13, 2:22), and Pilate's wife (Matthew 27:19).

ii. In the Bible, God spoke to unbelievers or pagans in dreams almost twice as many times as He spoke to His people in dreams. We hear many stories today about how God speaks to people in the Muslim world with dreams about Jesus.

iii. It's always important to remember that not every dream is a revelation from God. Dreams can come just because our minds are busy: *A dream comes through much activity.... For in the multitude of dreams and many words there is also vanity* (Ecclesiastes 5:3, 5:7).

iv. People shouldn't look for messages from God anywhere else than the Bible – it is God's voice. Yet believers may recognize that from time to time God will choose an unusual way to communicate, yet never against the Bible or never equal to the Bible's authority or importance.

c. **And he gives you a sign or a wonder**: Moses warned the people that there may arise from among them prophets or workers of signs who could also produce a **sign** or a **wonder**.

i. Deuteronomy 18:22 told Israel what to do with a prophet who spoke a word and it did *not* come to pass. This passage told Israel what to do with a prophet who spoke a word and it came to pass, but they then spoke against what God has already revealed in His word.

d. **And the sign or the wonder comes to pass**: It is possible for a false teacher to "prove" their point through some kind of apparent **sign** or **wonder**. These apparent signs and wonders might be false, tricks used to deceive. Or it is also possible that apparent signs and wonders are works of Satan, performed through agents that may know they are Satan's instruments, or may not be aware of it.

i. "The sign or wonder had to be tested against the message of the prophet, for only when the message was consistent with the whole range of divine revelation could the accompanying miracles be given credibility." (Merrill)

ii. The display of supernatural power – even real supernatural power – does not *prove* that a message comes from God. Those who are immediately convinced at the apparent presence of supernatural power are in danger of being deceived. 2 Thessalonians 2:9 reminds us that the *coming of the lawless one is according to the working of Satan, with all power, signs, and lying wonders.*

iii. This is why Jesus said *and these signs will follow those who believe* (Mark 16:17). Signs are to follow believers, instead of believers following signs.

e. **You shall not listen to the words of that prophet or dreamer of dreams**: One with godly discernment will always carefully examine the *message* of a spiritual leader, instead of looking only to the spiritual experiences which may surround him or her.

i. In considering some of the great prophets of the Old Testament – men such as Elijah and Elisha, who worked many spectacular signs and wonders – if even *they* were to say, **let us go after other gods**, then Israel was to reject them and put them to death. This general attitude carries over into the New Testament when Paul told the Galatian Christians that even if he or an angel from heaven were to preach another gospel, they should be rejected and regarded as accursed by God (Galatians 1:8-9).

ii. It is interesting to consider Elijah's confrontation with the prophets of Baal at Mount Carmel (1 Kings 18:20-40) in this context. According to the commands here in Deuteronomy 13, even if the prophets of Baal were able, in some way, to produce fire from heaven, they should still have been rejected and even executed. Elijah's challenge that the true God could be discerned from a supernatural event was a special exception prompted by a special revelation from God (1 Kings 18:36), not a standing principle.

f. **The LORD your God is testing you to know whether you love the LORD your God with all your heart**: This explains one of God's reasons for allowing such deceivers to exist among His people – to allow the hearts of His people to be tested and proven, to see if they really love the God of truth or are merely seeking a spiritual sign or experience.

i. "And particularly there are many signs, yea, such as men may think to be wonders, which may be wrought by evil spirits, God so permitting it for divers wise and just reasons, not only for the trial of the good, as it here follows, but also for the punishment of ungodly men, who would not receive Divine truths, though attested by many evident and unquestionable miracles, and therefore are most justly exposed to these temptations to believe lies." (Poole)

ii. **God is testing you**: Meyer described three areas where Christians are commonly tested: in Christian service, in their use of money, and in actions regarding doubtful things. "How much happens to us for this reason! God proves us — not that He may learn aught of us which He did not know before, but that He may reveal us to ourselves. We need to know ourselves, that we may be prompted to know and use His infinite resources, and that, in the great consciousness of our frailty and weakness, we may be led to avail ourselves of His grace." (Meyer)

2. (4-5) The penalty for the deceiver who comes with miraculous signs.

You shall walk after the LORD your God and fear Him, and keep His commandments and obey His voice, and you shall serve Him and hold fast to Him. But that prophet or that dreamer of dreams shall be put to death, because he has spoken in order to turn *you* away from the LORD your God, who brought you out of the land of Egypt and redeemed you from the house of bondage, to entice you from the way in which the LORD your God commanded you to walk. So you shall put away the evil from your midst.

a. **You shall walk after the LORD**: Israel was commanded to not let a deceiver succeed in leading them astray. No matter how attractive the deception, they were to keep focused on a faithful **walk** with God according to His truth.

b. **But that prophet or that dreamer of dreams shall be put to death**: Ancient Israel was a unique state. The civil government of Israel was directly appointed by God and charged with maintaining spiritual order as well as civil order. Therefore, heresy and deception were capital crimes and punished by execution. This was how Israel was to **put away the evil** from their **midst**.

i. For many centuries, when the church held significant political influence, it often exercised the death penalty against heretics. The institutional church rarely directly put heretics to death; accused and condemned heretics were normally given over to the civil government for execution. "This power is still in the Christian magistrate, to inflict capital punishment on gross heretics; such as was Servetus at Geneva." (Trapp, mid-1600s)

ii. Under the new covenant, God has not commanded the formation of Christian nations along the same pattern as He did with biblical Israel. Israel was commanded to use capital punishment against heretics. Under the new covenant, neither the church nor the state has the same divine command to execute false teachers. Instead, false teachers should be noted and avoided (Romans 16:17, 2 Thessalonians 3:14-15, 1 Timothy 6:3-5, 2 John 1:10-11). This is how Christians, under the new covenant, are to **put away the evil** from their **midst**.

c. **Who brought you out of the land of Egypt and redeemed you from the house of bondage**: God's authority over Israel was based on the redemption He won for them in rescuing Israel from their slavery in Egypt. This great work demanded Israel's faithful allegiance to Yahweh.

3. (6-11) The penalty for a relative who would lead an Israelite to worship other gods.

"If your brother, the son of your mother, your son or your daughter, the wife of your bosom, or your friend who is as your own soul, secretly entices you, saying, 'Let us go and serve other gods,' which you have not known, neither you nor your fathers, of the gods of the people which *are* all around you, near to you or far off from you, from *one* end of the earth to the *other* end of the earth, you shall not consent to him or listen to him, nor shall your eye pity him, nor shall you spare him or conceal him; but you shall surely kill him; your hand shall be first against him to put him to death, and afterward the hand of all the people. And you shall stone him with stones until he dies, because he sought to entice you away from the LORD your God, who brought you out of the land of Egypt, from the house of bondage. So all Israel shall hear and fear, and not again do such wickedness as this among you.

a. **Brother…your son or your daughter…your wife…your friend**: God commanded Israel that they should not allow their close family relations to lead them to worship other gods. Such influence was to be rejected (they were to not **consent** or even **listen** to such false teachers), and those teachers were also to be executed (**you shall surely kill him**). This was God's command for biblical Israel under the old covenant.

i. By God's command, the relative should be one of the main witnesses against the guilty party (**your hand shall be first against him to put him to death**). This was the "casting of the first stone," the initiation of execution by one of the witnesses to the crime deserving the death penalty.

ii. "The nature of God's covenant with Israel was such that loyalty and love to him were more important than the love of one's family." (Thompson)

iii. This command demonstrates that God never puts ultimate priority on family relationships. If a family member forsakes the LORD, we are never to follow them in their apostasy. Jesus always comes first, as He said in Matthew 10:37: *He who loves father or mother more than Me is not worthy of Me. And he who loves son or daughter more than Me is not worthy of Me.*

b. **Secretly entices you**: God's prohibition of the worship of other gods was so comprehensive that it also included private conversations. The invitation to worship other gods did not have to be public to be of great concern to God's people.

c. **So all Israel shall hear and fear**: If Israel properly addressed the problem of false teachers among them, it would teach the people to properly honor and reverence God. Proper opposition to false teaching would discourage the practice of leading people away from Yahweh and to false gods.

i. "This extreme punishment is expected to produce good results. Though many modern sociologists declare that punishment—especially capital punishment—is no deterrent to crime, the message Moses proclaimed as the Word of God says that it would be a deterrent." (Kalland)

ii. "Unfortunately, the injunction must seldom if ever have been carried out. Over and over again Israel and Judah were unfaithful to the Lord, a pattern of life that brought a series of judgments upon them, culminating in the eventual demise and deportations of the respective kingdoms (cf. 2 Kgs 17:7–23; 24:3)." (Merrill)

B. Protecting the nation against those who would lead them into idolatry.

1. (12-14a) How to deal with reports of a city given over to idolatry.

"If you hear someone in one of your cities, which the LORD your God gives you to dwell in, saying, 'Corrupt men have gone out from among you and enticed the inhabitants of their city, saying, "Let us go and serve other gods"'—which you have not known—then you shall inquire, search out, and ask diligently.

a. **Then you shall inquire**: If reports arose regarding an Israelite city given over to idolatry, there was first to be a careful investigation.

i. **Corrupt men**: "*Children of Belial…lawless men;*—persons *good for nothing* to themselves or others, and capable of nothing but mischief." (Clarke)

b. **Inquire, search out, and ask diligently**: The command to carefully investigate would guard Israel against making harsh, unfounded judgments. Perhaps there were a few idolaters in the city who needed to be punished, but the city as a whole was not given over to idolatry. The matter had to be investigated.

i. Under the leadership of Joshua, Israel wisely followed this practice of carefully investigating charges of apostasy before treating the accused as guilty (Joshua 22:10-34). When the two-and-one-half tribes that settled on the east side of the Jordan were thought to have built an altar to a pagan god, Israel was ready to make war against them according to these commands in Deuteronomy. Yet, their investigation proved the accusation to be unfounded.

2. (14b-18) The penalty for a city given over to idolatry.

And *if it is* indeed true *and* certain *that* such an abomination was committed among you, you shall surely strike the inhabitants of that city with the edge of the sword; utterly destroying it, all that is in it and its livestock—with the edge of the sword. And you shall gather all its plunder into the middle of the street, and completely burn with fire the city and all its plunder, for the Lord your God. It shall be a heap forever; it shall not be built again. So none of the accursed things shall remain in your hand, that the Lord may turn from the fierceness of His anger and show you mercy, have compassion on you and multiply you, just as He swore to your fathers, because you have listened to the voice of the Lord your God, to keep all His commandments which I command you today, to do *what is* right in the eyes of the Lord your God.

> a. **Such an abomination**: The investigation was to determine if an **abomination** was committed among the people of Israel. The word **abomination** here refers to a gross, offensive idolatry. Later in Daniel and in the New Testament, the word is used in the phrase *abomination of desolation*, which refers to the ultimate idolatry of the Antichrist – the establishing of an idolatrous image of himself in the Most Holy Place (2 Thessalonians 2:3-4).
>
>> i. "The term *abominable thing* (*toeba*) is used in the Old Testament for something that is totally displeasing to God and denotes something impure, unclean and totally devoid of holiness (cf. Deuteronomy 7:25, 26; 14:3; 17:1, 4; 18:9; 20:18)." (Thompson)
>
> b. **You shall surely strike the inhabitants of that city with the edge of the sword; utterly destroying it**: If the investigation found that the city was indeed given over to idolatry, it was then to be treated as a Canaanite city. They were to **utterly** destroy the city, including its property. The property was to be given to the Lord by destroying it, a form of "sacred destruction."
>
>> i. The entire community was under judgment, both because of their toleration of the abomination, and their being party to it. "Theirs was a corporate guilt and, as so often in the Old Testament, they were judged corporately." (Thompson)
>>
>> ii. This made certain that no one could profit materially by declaring a city to be given over to idolatry. If this provision were *not* in the Law of Moses one could imagine a city being falsely accused and plundered under a pretended concern for faithfulness to the Lord.

iii. "As God did not permit them to take the spoils of these idolatrous cities, they could be under no temptation to make war upon them....

How few religious wars would there ever have been in the world had they been regulated by this principle: 'Thou shalt neither extend thy territory, nor take any spoils!'" (Clarke)

iv. "The very same punishment which was inflicted upon the cities of the cursed Canaanites, to whom having made themselves equal in sin, it is but fit and just that God should equal them in punishment." (Poole)

c. **It shall be a heap forever; it shall not be built again**: The destroyed town was to be left as **a heap forever**. The mound of ruins would be a testimony to the rest of Israel.

i. The word **heap** is literally *tel*, and the word *tel* is used in Arabic for any ruined site. Throughout Israel today, one will see curious mounds rising from a plain. These *tels* are the heaped up remains of ancient, destroyed cities, covered over with centuries of dust and accumulated dirt.

ii. **Not be built again**: "This doom, which goes contrary to the common practice of rebuilding towns on the ruins of the site, as the stratigraphic remains of tells in the Middle East plainly show, indicates how serious the Lord considered any defection from him." (Kalland)

d. **To do what is right in the eyes of the LORD your God**: This demonstrates that Israelites were never to regard ethnic or national connections greater than their connection to the LORD God; if their fellow countrymen were given over to idolatry, they were not to be spared.

i. The commands of Deuteronomy 13 compel the modern believer to remain faithful to God. If signs or wonders, close relatives, or national or ethnic ties would lead a person to unfaithfulness to Jesus Christ, all of those should be rejected in honor and faithfulness to the LORD.

ii. Morgan described four ways in this section of Deuteronomy that people are seduced from the true worship of God to the worship of idols. These remain a challenge to the people of God.

- Curiosity (Deuteronomy 12:29-32).
- Signs and wonders (Deuteronomy 13:1-5).
- Enticements of human affection (Deuteronomy 13:6-11).
- Failure to discipline, to confront false teaching (Deuteronomy 13:12-18).

Deuteronomy 14 – Living All of Life for the Lord

A. Commands regarding separation from pagan practices.

1. (1) The command to abstain from pagan burial customs.

"You *are* the children of the LORD your God; you shall not cut yourselves nor shave the front of your head for the dead.

> a. **You shall not cut yourselves nor shave the front of your head for the dead**: Among the pagan cultures surrounding Israel, it was common to cut the body or shave the front of one's head, doing it **for the dead** – that is, as a part of pagan burial rituals.
>
>> i. "The cutting of the body and the shaving of the head were common mourning rites in the ancient Near East and are referred to in many places in the Old Testament (Isaiah 3:24; 15:2; 22:12; Jeremiah 16:6; 41:5; Ezekiel 7:18; Amos 8:10; Micah 1:16)." (Thompson)
>>
>> ii. "The mutilation of the body persists still in some countries.... Such practices were forbidden in Israel, both because they hinted at some conformity to pagan practices and also because Israel had a respect for the body as God's creation which was not to be disfigured or misused." (Thompson)
>
> b. **You are the children of the LORD your God**: Among Christians today, there is something wrong if our burial customs mimic the superstitious rituals of the ungodly. Christians should not *sorrow as others who have no hope* (1 Thessalonians 4:13). Believers may certainly mourn the passing of loved ones, but as those who have eternal hope in Jesus, God's people should be different in their mourning.
>
>> i. "It is most probable that the Hebrew people never came to any clear certainty about personal immortality, it was given them to know that their attitude toward death, and so toward sorrow, could not be that of people whose gods were not real. They were the children of the living

God. Therefore there must be nothing of the hopelessness or despair, in the presence of death, or in the sorrow arising from it." (Morgan)

ii. "That the law was not always observed in Israel is clear from Jeremiah 41:5; Ezekiel 7:18; Amos 8:10." (Thompson)

2. (2) The principle behind the commands for separation.

For you *are* a holy people to the LORD your God, and the LORD has chosen you to be a people for Himself, a special treasure above all the peoples who *are* on the face of the earth.

a. **You are a holy people**: The idea behind **holy** is "separate." The people of Israel were a people separate for the LORD. In Jesus, believers are also a holy people: *But you are...a holy nation* (1 Peter 2:9).

b. **The LORD has chosen you to be a people for Himself**: The people of Israel were **chosen** by God, to be His own special people. In Jesus, believers also are a chosen people, special to God: *But you are a chosen generation... His own special people* (1 Peter 2:9).

c. **A special treasure**: The people of Israel were a **special treasure** to God. In Jesus, believers also are a special treasure to God: *His inheritance* (Ephesians 1:18).

d. **Above all the peoples who are on the face of the earth**: Each of these glorious privileges (**holy, chosen, special treasure**) carries with it a special responsibility. If God regarded Israel as something special among the nations, they had to conduct themselves as something special among the nations.

3. (3-21) The command to be separate regarding foods.

"You shall not eat any detestable thing. These *are* the animals which you may eat: the ox, the sheep, the goat, the deer, the gazelle, the roe deer, the wild goat, the mountain goat, the antelope, and the mountain sheep. And you may eat every animal with cloven hooves, having the hoof split into two parts, *and that* chews the cud, among the animals. Nevertheless, of those that chew the cud or have cloven hooves, you shall not eat, *such as* these: the camel, the hare, and the rock hyrax; for they chew the cud but do not have cloven hooves; they *are* unclean for you. Also the swine is unclean for you, because it has cloven hooves, yet *does* not *chew* the cud; you shall not eat their flesh or touch their dead carcasses.

"These you may eat of all that *are* in the waters: you may eat all that have fins and scales. And whatever does not have fins and scales you shall not eat; it *is* unclean for you.

"All clean birds you may eat. But these you shall not eat: the eagle, the vulture, the buzzard, the red kite, the falcon, and the kite after their kinds; every raven after its kind; the ostrich, the short-eared owl, the seagull, and the hawk after their kinds; the little owl, the screech owl, the white owl, the jackdaw, the carrion vulture, the fisher owl, the stork, the heron after its kind, and the hoopoe and the bat.

"Also every creeping thing that flies is unclean for you; they shall not be eaten. "You may eat all clean birds.

"You shall not eat anything that dies *of itself;* you may give it to the alien who *is* within your gates, that he may eat it, or you may sell it to a foreigner; for you *are* a holy people to the LORD your God.

"You shall not boil a young goat in its mother's milk.

a. **These are the animals which you may eat**: Certain animals were considered **detestable** and could not be eaten. Only certain mammals were allowed for food, and the rule was simple. If an animal had a divided hoof (not a single hoof like a horse), and it chewed its cud, then it could be eaten. For example, the camel, the rock hyrax, and the hare all chew the cud, but do not have divided hooves – instead, they have paws – so they are considered unkosher or **detestable** for food. Additionally, the swine has a divided hoof, but does not chew the cud – so it is considered unkosher.

b. **These you may eat of all that are in the waters**: Only certain sea creatures could be eaten, and the rule was simple. Any water creature having both fins and scales was kosher and could be eaten. Therefore, most fishes were considered clean – except a fish like the catfish, which has no scales. Shellfish were unclean because clams, crabs, oysters, and lobster all do not have fins and scales.

c. **All clean birds you may eat**: Only certain birds could be eaten; though there was no rule given to determine if a bird was clean or unclean, the specifically mentioned unclean birds (and flying **creeping things**) are either predators or scavengers; these were considered unclean.

i. These animals fall into one of three categories: *predators* (unclean because they ate both the flesh and the blood of animals), *scavengers* (unclean because they are carriers of disease, and they regularly have contact with dead bodies), or *potentially poisonous or dangerous* foods such as shellfish and the like. Eliminating these from the diet of Israel no doubt had a healthy effect, and one of the reasons for the dietary laws of Israel was to keep Israel healthy!

d. **You shall not eat anything that dies of itself**: If any animal **dies of itself**, then it would not have been properly bled; therefore, it is unkosher.

i. It was important to bleed animals before eating them, because the blood represented the life principle of the animal (Leviticus 17:11), and the life principle belonged to God and God alone. Another reason for dietary laws respecting blood was to project an important symbolism to Israel regarding blood and the principle of the sanctity of life.

e. **You shall not boil a young goat in its mother's milk**: This unusual law was a command to not imitate a common pagan fertility ritual. It illustrated the third principle behind the dietary laws of Israel: They were a statement of separation from the nations and prevented Israel from having easy fellowship (sitting down at a common meal) with Gentiles.

i. This law, because of strange rabbinical interpretations, became the reason why one cannot have a kosher cheeseburger. Observant Jews today will not eat milk and meat at the same meal (or even on the same plates, or using the same utensils or the same pots), because the rabbis insist that the meat in the hamburger may have come from the calf of the cow that gave the milk for the cheese, and the cheese and the meat would "boil" together in one's stomach and be a violation of this command.

ii. "The same law occurs in both Exodus 23:19 and 34:26. It may have in view a Canaanite rite described in an Ugaritic poem, where the injunction is given 'cook a kid in the milk, a lamb in the cream'. The Israelite law is possibly a rejection of this custom." (Thompson)

B. The command of the tithe.

1. (22-23) The command to tithe.

"You shall truly tithe all the increase of your grain that the field produces year by year. And you shall eat before the LORD your God, in the place where He chooses to make His name abide, the tithe of your grain and your new wine and your oil, of the firstborn of your herds and your flocks, that you may learn to fear the LORD your God always.

a. **You shall truly tithe**: The word **truly** is important; since the **tithe** described giving ten percent, God commanded that it truly be ten percent. One might easily imagine Israelites discovering ways to give God less than **truly** ten percent.

b. **All the increase of your grain**: Seemingly, the word **increase** means the grain left over after the seed-grain was taken out. This meant that the tithe was assessed on the *income*, not on the total *assets*.

c. **You shall eat before the LORD**: When the tithe was delivered to the tabernacle (and later, to the temple), a portion of the tithe was enjoyed in a ceremonial meal in the presence of the LORD. The remainder was given to the priest. **New wine** was unfermented grape juice.

> i. "There was always a danger that Canaanite deities might be honoured at harvest time. To avoid this, insistence is here made that any religious ceremonies associated with the harvest and with tithing should be conducted at Yahweh's sanctuary and not at a pagan sanctuary." (Thompson)

d. **That you may learn to fear the LORD your God always**: This was the purpose of tithing; to build an honor and reverence for God. The paraphrase in the Living Bible puts it plainly: *The purpose of tithing is to teach you always to put God first in your lives* (Deuteronomy 14:23b, Living Bible).

2. (24-27) Tithing for those who live at long distances from the tabernacle.

But if the journey is too long for you, so that you are not able to carry *the tithe*, or if the place where the LORD your God chooses to put His name is too far from you, when the LORD your God has blessed you, then you shall exchange *it* for money, take the money in your hand, and go to the place which the LORD your God chooses. And you shall spend that money for whatever your heart desires: for oxen or sheep, for wine or similar drink, for whatever your heart desires; you shall eat there before the LORD your God, and you shall rejoice, you and your household. You shall not forsake the Levite who *is* within your gates, for he has no part nor inheritance with you.

a. **But if the journey is too long for you**: Since the tithe was to be brought to one place for all of Israel, some would be farther than others. And, if someone was far away, they would find it difficult to transport the grain and livestock that the tithe required.

b. **You shall exchange it for money**: If distance prevented the easy transport of the animals, they could exchange their tithe for money, and then use the money to make their tithe when they came to the tabernacle (and later, the temple).

> i. These laws show the common-sense aspect of God's commands. He did not place unreasonable demands on Israel, and made ways for them to more practically obey Him. This led Israel to **rejoice**.

> ii. "This practical and perfectly legitimate way of making pilgrimage manageable continued on into New Testament times and, in fact, lies behind the gospel accounts of Jesus and the moneychangers (Matt 21:12–13; cf. John 2:13–16). Like any other concession of this kind,

it was subject to abuse by those who, like the moneychangers, would profit from the exchange by charging exorbitant rates." (Merrill)

3. (28-29) The third-year tithe.

"At the end of *every* third year you shall bring out the tithe of your produce of that year and store *it* up within your gates. And the Levite, because he has no portion nor inheritance with you, and the stranger and the fatherless and the widow who *are* within your gates, may come and eat and be satisfied, that the LORD your God may bless you in all the work of your hand which you do.

a. **At the end of every third year you shall bring out the tithe of your produce of that year**: Some have said this speaks of another tithe (sometimes called the "poor tithe") to be brought every three years. Yet since it speaks of *the* **tithe**, and since it also went to the Levite and not only to the poor, it is best to understand that this was not an additional tithe, but a command that once every three years the tithe also be available to the poor, not only to the Levite.

i. As Kalland points out: "The Jewish rabbis have usually held that there were three tithes: (1) for the priests and Levites, (2) for the communal meals, (3) every third year for the nonlanded (i.e., the Levites, aliens, fatherless, and widows)." Kalland objects to this rabbinic approach, and accurately observes, "So all the designations of tithes speak of one basic tithe to be put to various uses."

ii. "Every third year, however, the tithe was to be stored in the Israelite's own town or village to provide a charitable fund for the needy, the Levites, the resident aliens, the widows, the orphans, etc." (Thompson)

iii. **The Levite, because he has no portion nor inheritance**: "God chose to make his ministers thus dependent on the people, that they might be induced (among other motives) to labour for their spiritual profiting, that the people, thus blessed under their ministry, might feel it their duty and privilege to support and render them comfortable." (Clarke)

b. **That the LORD your God may bless you in all the work of your hand which you do**: God will bless the giving heart. Ask anyone who gives as the Bible instructs them to give – they are blessed.

i. The New Testament nowhere specifically commands tithing, but it certainly does speak of it in a positive light if it is done with a right heart (Luke 11:42).

ii. It is also important to understand that tithing is not a principle dependent on the Mosaic Law; as Hebrews 7:5-9 explains, tithing was practiced and honored by God before the law of Moses.

iii. What the New Testament does speak with great clarity on is the principle of giving; that giving should be regular, planned, proportional, and private (1 Corinthians 16:1-4); that it must be generous, freely given, and cheerful (2 Corinthians 9).

iv. Since the New Testament doesn't emphasize tithing, one might not be strict on it for Christians (though some Christians do argue against tithing on the basis of self-interest). Yet since giving is to be proportional, we should be giving *some* percentage – and ten percent is a good benchmark – and *starting* place. For some to give ten percent is nowhere near enough; for others, at their present time, five percent may be a massive step of faith.

v. If our question is, "How little can I give and still be pleasing to God?" our heart isn't in the right place at all. We should have the attitude of some early Christians, who essentially said: "We're not under the tithe – we can give *more*!" Giving and financial management is a *spiritual* issue, not just a financial one (Luke 16:11).

vi. "Not getting, but giving, is the way to thrive in the world." (Trapp)

Deuteronomy 15 – Laws Regarding the Poor

A. Laws regarding the poor.

1. (1-6) Release of debts every seventh year.

"At the end of *every* seven years you shall grant a release *of debts*. And this *is* the form of the release: Every creditor who has lent *anything* to his neighbor shall release *it*; he shall not require *it* of his neighbor or his brother, because it is called the Lord's release. Of a foreigner you may require *it*; but you shall give up your claim to what is owed by your brother, except when there may be no poor among you; for the Lord will greatly bless you in the land which the Lord your God is giving you to possess *as* an inheritance—only if you carefully obey the voice of the Lord your God, to observe with care all these commandments which I command you today. For the Lord your God will bless you just as He promised you; you shall lend to many nations, but you shall not borrow; you shall reign over many nations, but they shall not reign over you.

> a. **You shall grant a release of debts**: In Israel, money was always loaned with the understanding that every seventh year, debts would be canceled. As a result, there was no long-term debt in the sense that money was not borrowed, or owed, for more than six years.
>
>> i. Some commentators believe this cancellation of debt was only for one year – that the debts did not need to be paid in the year the land took its Sabbath rest. It is more likely that it refers to a complete cancellation of debt.
>
> b. **It is the Lord's release**: This was an important matter to God; the settling of debts every seven years was **called the Lord's release**. As Israel obeyed this command, there would never be a permanent under-class in Israel. Some might go through a bad period but would have the opportunity to rebuild their lives financially on a regular basis.

i. "No evidence exists that the Mosaic economy in its details was ever fully implemented with its sabbatical years and years of Jubilee." (Kalland)

ii. **Of a foreigner you may require it**: This release of debts was not commanded regarding the foreigners who lived in Israel, who were distinct from those from other nations who had joined Israel. "The *foreigner* (*nokri*) was different from the resident alien (*ger*) who was absorbed into the Israelite community (cf. 14:21a). It was legal to require payment of debts from foreigners during the sabbatical year, for they were not included in the family circle of Israel. The law was designed to relieve poverty in Israel and to regulate relations between members of the covenant community." (Thompson)

c. **When there may be no poor among you**: In ancient Israel, God established an economic system in which no one *had* to be chronically poor. If people would obey the LORD, He would bless them (both sovereignly and as the natural result of their obedience), and there would be little chronic poverty in Israel.

i. However, Deuteronomy 15:11 – just a few verses later – states: *For the poor will never cease from the land.* This is not a contradiction. God established a system where no one *must* be chronically poor, yet He knew that because of disobedience, there would be some chronically poor people in Israel.

ii. God did not unconditionally guarantee prosperity for Israel, either on a national or individual basis. The LORD did guarantee the opportunity for prosperity for an obedient Israel.

d. **You shall lend to many nations**: If Israel obeyed and the individual citizens of Israel enjoyed the blessing of God's prosperity, then they would as a nation be prosperous, and blessed above other nations. They would have the resources to **lend**, instead of having to **borrow**.

2. (7-11) The command to be generous to the poor.

"If there is among you a poor man of your brethren, within any of the gates in your land which the LORD your God is giving you, you shall not harden your heart nor shut your hand from your poor brother, but you shall open your hand wide to him and willingly lend him sufficient for his need, whatever he needs. Beware lest there be a wicked thought in your heart, saying, 'The seventh year, the year of release, is at hand,' and your eye be evil against your poor brother and you give him nothing, and he cry out to the LORD against you, and it become sin among you. You shall surely give to him, and your heart should not be grieved when

you give to him, because for this thing the LORD your God will bless you in all your works and in all to which you put your hand. For the poor will never cease from the land; therefore I command you, saying, 'You shall open your hand wide to your brother, to your poor and your needy, in your land.'

a. **You shall not harden your heart nor shut your hand from your poor brother**: The law of release in the seventh year (Deuteronomy 15:1-6) was never to be used to discourage giving to those in need. The law might discourage *lending* to the poor, therefore God wanted Israel to be generous givers to those in need.

i. "The poor and needy were the special concern of God and the covenant family was expected to ensure the welfare of every member of the family. Hence Israelite law was framed to protect the underprivileged." (Thompson)

ii. **You shall open your hand wide**: "Thy benevolence shall be in proportion to his distress and poverty, and thy ability. Thou shalt have no other rule to regulate thy charity by." (Clarke)

iii. **Lest there be a wicked thought in your heart**: "It is not enough that we abstain from base deeds. The heart must be free from baseness in thought." (Morgan)

iv. **Your eye be evil**: "An evil eye signifies a covetous disposition. See the same form of expression used by our Lord in the same sense, Matt. 6:23.... Covetousness darkens the soul; liberality and benevolence enlighten it." (Clarke)

b. **Of your brethren**: Under God's covenant, the people of ancient Israel had a special responsibility to show generosity to their **brother** who was **poor and needy**, meaning their fellow Israelite, or those in their own community. Generosity to those outside of Israel was good, but there was a priority to help those in the immediate community (**in your land**).

i. Galatians 6:10 reminds believers, *as we have opportunity, let us do good to all, especially to those who are of the household of faith.* Charitable giving is to begin with those brothers and sisters closest to the believer, though it certainly can extend outward from there.

ii. **The poor will never cease**: "With unashamed realism the writer concludes that, in fact, there would always be poor in the land, because Israel would always be disobedient. Hence there would always be opportunities to display generosity towards the poor." (Thompson)

iii. "Perhaps Jesus was thinking of v.11 when he said, 'The poor you will always have with you' (Matt 26:11; Mark 14:7; John 12:8)." (Kalland)

iv. **To your poor and needy**: "See how God calls them, not 'the poor', but 'thy poor' and 'thy needy.' The Church of God should feel a peculiar property in the poor and needy, as if they were handed over, in the love of Christ to his people, that they might care for them." (Spurgeon)

3. (12-15) The command to release slaves every seventh year.

"If your brother, a Hebrew man, or a Hebrew woman, is sold to you and serves you six years, then in the seventh year you shall let him go free from you. And when you send him away free from you, you shall not let him go away empty-handed; you shall supply him liberally from your flock, from your threshing floor, and from your winepress. *From what* **the LORD your God has blessed you with, you shall give to him. You shall remember that you were a slave in the land of Egypt, and the LORD your God redeemed you; therefore I command you this thing today.**

a. **Your brother, a Hebrew…is sold to you and serves you**: These commands have first in mind a fellow Israelite who was **sold** into slavery through either their inability to pay their debts or to provide for themselves (Leviticus 25:39-46).

i. Though it is almost impossible for us to relate to in the modern world, this kind of slavery was necessary and helpful in the ancient world. For most of humanity's history, the poorest people were sometimes confronted with a choice between death by starvation or becoming a slave. In such circumstances, it is hard to call slavery *good*, but it was certainly preferred to the alternative (death).

ii. This does not have in mind what is normally considered the "slave trade," where people were kidnapped and enslaved, which was directly condemned (Exodus 21:16, Deuteronomy 24:7). Later, the prophet Amos rebuked Tyre for their traffic in slaves as a violation of the *covenant of brotherhood* (Amos 1:9-10).

b. **In the seventh year you shall let him go free from you**: Even as debts were to be canceled every seventh year, so were slaves to be freed. The slaves thought of here are those who have had to sell themselves into slavery because of their debt. This made certain that a "bankruptcy" did not harm the people of Israel all their lives. The worst that could happen is they would have to serve someone without pay for six years.

c. **You shall not let him go away empty-handed**: God commanded generosity to the departing slave, giving him something to start with in his new life as a freeman. This would give the slave about to be freed hope and greater incentive to diligently serve his master.

4. (16-18) The law of the bondservant.

And if it happens that he says to you, 'I will not go away from you,' because he loves you and your house, since he prospers with you, then you shall take an awl and thrust *it* through his ear to the door, and he shall be your servant forever. Also to your female servant you shall do likewise. It shall not seem hard to you when you send him away free from you; for he has been worth a double hired servant in serving you six years. Then the LORD your God will bless you in all that you do.

a. **If it happens that he says to you, "I will not go away from you"**: If a slave loved his master, and wanted to continue to serve him, he was not required to leave his master at the seventh year (Exodus 21:5-6).

b. **Because he loves you...you shall take an awl and thrust it through his ear to the door**: The willing slave could stay, and his status was declared by piercing through his ear lobe with an awl at the door of his master's home. In this, he declared his love and devotion to his master – a willing slave, who was free to choose and yet chose his master.

i. It's a remarkable thing to think of this ceremony being carried out. A servant said, "I know I have fulfilled my *obligations* to my master, and I have served what I have owed. Yet I love my master and am so grateful for what he has given that I will gladly obligate myself for life, not out of debt or shame or defeat, but out of love."

ii. Jesus is the great fulfillment of this willing slave. Jesus said prophetically in Psalm 40:6: *My ears You have opened*, it speaks of this "opening" of the ear in the bondservant ceremony. He was the willing bondservant of God the Father.

c. **He shall be your servant forever**: Once agreeing to be a bondservant, that one was committed to their master forever. It was a permanent relationship. In many ways, the follower of Jesus Christ is like a bondservant to their Savior.

i. "Like the sailor driven by the tempest, we have taken the first harbour that offered. But when we have tested the blessed Master, and found Him so sweet and strong, we elect to remain with Him, not for His gifts or even His salvation, but for Himself. We do not wish to go out free; we love Him so dearly that we would rather go anywhere with Him than remain without Him…. This resolve of ours is ratified by Him. He nails our ear to His cross. Through the blood of self-sacrifice, and self-surrender; through our deeper appreciation of the meaning of his cross, as separating us from the old selfish life." (Meyer)

ii. "Come, dear heart, if you find Christ to-night, if you believe in him, and are at liberty, come and have your ear bored. You do not like baptism; come and have your ear bored. You do not like to join the church, and confess Christ. Well, I know that it may be a 'bore' to you; but for all that, come and have your ear bored." (Spurgeon)

d. **Then the LORD your God will bless you**: God promised that Israel's obedience under the old covenant would bring them blessing. It was costly to give liberty to such workers, but it honored God and was right because the bound servant was **worth double** that of a hired servant.

B. The law of the firstborn.

1. (19) The principle of the firstborn.

"All the firstborn males that come from your herd and your flock you shall sanctify to the LORD your God; you shall do no work with the firstborn of your herd, nor shear the firstborn of your flock."

a. **All the firstborn males**: God required that the **firstborn males** be set apart to Him for at least three reasons. First, because Israel was God's firstborn (Exodus 4:22), and this honored that fact. Second, because the firstborn was thought to be the best, and the best was always given to God. Third, it was to be a reminder to all generations of when God redeemed Israel, His firstborn.

b. **Sanctify to the LORD**: This means to "set apart to the LORD"; the firstborn was to be set apart to God. The firstborn animal was not to be used as a domesticated animal would normally be used (**you shall do no work with the firstborn of your herd, not shear the firstborn of your flock**).

2. (20-23) What to do with the giving of the firstborn.

You and your household shall eat *it* **before the LORD your God year by year in the place which the LORD chooses. But if there is a defect in it,** *if it is* **lame or blind** *or has* **any serious defect, you shall not sacrifice it to the LORD your God. You may eat it within your gates; the unclean and the clean** *person* **alike** *may eat it,* **as** *if it were* **a gazelle or a deer. Only you shall not eat its blood; you shall pour it on the ground like water.**

a. **You and your household shall eat it before the LORD your God**: When the firstborn animal was brought to the tabernacle (or later, the temple) and given to the priests for sacrifice to the LORD, a portion of the sacrifice went to the family that brought the animal. It was given so that they could eat a joyful ceremonial meal before the LORD.

b. **If there is a defect in it**: If the firstborn was defective in any way, the animal was given to the priests, but not sacrificed to the LORD. Or, it could also be redeemed for money and the money given to the LORD (Exodus 34:19-20).

> i. "The offering of the firstborn is qualified further by the stipulation that it be as near a perfect specimen as possible (Deuteronomy 15:21). This is not so much because God does not love and accept the flawed and failed but because the offerer must be prepared to part with what is most valuable to him. There is little sacrifice in giving up something that has little or no market value anyway (cf. Lev 22:17–25)." (Merrill)

Deuteronomy 16 – The Three Major Feasts

A. The observance of Passover.

1. (1-2) The sacrifice of the Passover.

"Observe the month of Abib, and keep the Passover to the LORD your God, for in the month of Abib the LORD your God brought you out of Egypt by night. Therefore you shall sacrifice the Passover to the LORD your God, from the flock and the herd, in the place where the LORD chooses to put His name.

> a. **You shall sacrifice the Passover to the LORD...in the place where the LORD chooses to put His name**: At the first Passover, each family in Israel sacrificed the Passover lamb at their home. But when Israel came into the Promised Land, the sacrifice was to be made at the tabernacle (and later, the temple).
>
>> i. The Passover sacrifice could come from the **flock** or the **herd**. At a Passover in the days of Josiah, there are goats and bulls mentioned in reference to sacrifice, not only lambs (2 Chronicles 35:7). At Hezekiah's Passover, bulls are also mentioned in sacrifice (2 Chronicles 30:24). Either God accepted Passover sacrifices other than lambs, or these refer to sacrifices associated with the Feast of Unleavened Bread, or these were "extra" sacrifices in addition to the Passover lambs.
>
> b. **For in the month of Abib the LORD your God brought you out of Egypt by night**: Exodus 12 describes the first Passover, when Israel was delivered from Egypt, and God sent His judgment upon the firstborn of Egypt. God passed over the homes which obediently sacrificed the Passover lamb and applied its blood to the door posts of the home.
>
> c. **Keep the Passover to the LORD**: Prophetically, the feast of **Passover** clearly presents Jesus as the Passover sacrifice (1 Corinthians 5:7), the Lamb

of God who was sacrificed, and whose blood was received and applied, so the wrath of God would pass over those who believe.

2. (3-4) The Feast of Unleavened Bread, associated with Passover.

You shall eat no leavened bread with it; seven days you shall eat unleavened bread with it, *that is,* **the bread of affliction (for you came out of the land of Egypt in haste), that you may remember the day in which you came out of the land of Egypt all the days of your life. And no leaven shall be seen among you in all your territory for seven days, nor shall** *any* **of the meat which you sacrifice the first day at twilight remain overnight until morning.**

a. **For you came out of the land of Egypt in haste**: For the first Passover, the **unleavened bread** was a practical necessity because they left Egypt in such haste there was no time to allow for the dough to rise.

i. "Unleavened bread can be made in less time than leavened bread (and it keeps better); so it is reminiscent of the precipitate nature of their departure from Egypt after the death of the firstborn of the Egyptians." (Kalland)

ii. **That you may remember**: "The value of the passover feast was to educate that conscience and to bring to life for each individual the great fact of national deliverance, compelling the children of each new generation to accept the obligations of a redeemed people." (Thompson)

b. **And no leaven shall be seen among you in all your territory for seven days**: The symbolism of the Feast of Unleavened Bread, following Passover, continued to be important. Leaven was a picture of sin and corruption, because of the way a little leaven would influence a whole lump of dough, and also because of the way leaven would "puff up" the lump – even as pride and sin make a person "puffed up" with self-importance.

i. Significantly, God called them to life an "unleavened" life after their initial deliverance from Egypt. Symbolically, they were being called to pure living in the sight of God.

ii. Some people also suggest that removing all the leaven once a year benefitted the health of Israel. At that time, they normally used a piece of dough from the previous batch to make the bread for that day and did so repeatedly. This could allow harmful bacteria to grow in the dough, therefore it was good to remove all leaven and start all over at least once a year.

iii. The purity of the feast of Unleavened Bread followed upon the blood-deliverance of Passover. The people of God can only walk in purity before the LORD after their blood-deliverance at the cross.

c. **You shall eat no leavened bread with it**: Prophetically, the feast of Unleavened Bread relates to the time of Jesus' burial, after His perfect, sinless sacrifice on the cross, during which He was received by God the Father as holy and complete. Jesus was the *Holy One* who would not *see corruption* (Acts 2:27), perfectly accomplishing our salvation.

i. The burial (or actually, entombment) of Jesus was an essential part of the message of the New Testament church (1 Corinthians 15:3-4).

3. (5-8) Regulations for Passover.

"You may not sacrifice the Passover within any of your gates which the LORD your God gives you; but at the place where the LORD your God chooses to make His name abide, there you shall sacrifice the Passover at twilight, at the going down of the sun, at the time you came out of Egypt. And you shall roast and eat *it* in the place which the LORD your God chooses, and in the morning you shall turn and go to your tents. Six days you shall eat unleavened bread, and on the seventh day there *shall be* a sacred assembly to the LORD your God. You shall do no work *on it*.

a. **At the place where the LORD your God chooses**: This repeats the command previously stated in verses 5-6 of this chapter. The Passover sacrifice was to be offered at God's sanctuary, the tabernacle, and then at the temple that replaced it.

i. This means that when Israel gathered at the tabernacle or temple for Passover, thousands of lambs were sacrificed, one for each household.

b. **At twilight, at the going down of the sun**: This repeats the command stated in Exodus 12:6 and Leviticus 23:5. The Passover lamb for each family was to be killed at this time of day.

c. **Six days you shall eat unleavened bread**: The feast of unleavened bread started immediately after Passover.

B. The observance of the Feast of Weeks (Pentecost).

1. (9-10) The Feast of Weeks.

"You shall count seven weeks for yourself; begin to count the seven weeks from *the time* you begin *to put* the sickle to the grain. Then you shall keep the Feast of Weeks to the LORD your God with the tribute of a freewill offering from your hand, which you shall give as the LORD your God blesses you.

a. **From the time you begin to put the sickle to the grain**: The Feast of Weeks (or Pentecost) was a feast associated with the joy of the start of harvest, during which Israelites brought a **freewill offering** to the LORD, as a demonstration of the thanks in their hearts.

i. "It has a variety of names in the Old Testament, 'the feast (pilgrimage) of weeks' (10; Exod. 34:22), 'the feast of harvest' (Exod. 23:16) and 'the day of the first fruits' (Num. 28:26; cf. Exod. 23:16; 34:22)." (Thompson)

ii. "The phrase 'fifty days' in Leviticus 23:16 in the LXX [Septuagint] led to the designation of the Feast of Weeks as Pentecost." (Kalland)

b. **Which you shall give as the LORD your God blesses you**: The amount each individual Israelite brought as a **freewill offering** was determined by the proportion in which they had been blessed. Those who had been blessed with more were expected to offer more.

2. (11-12) The joy of Pentecost.

You shall rejoice before the LORD your God, you and your son and your daughter, your male servant and your female servant, the Levite who *is* within your gates, the stranger and the fatherless and the widow who *are* among you, at the place where the LORD your God chooses to make His name abide. And you shall remember that you were a slave in Egypt, and you shall be careful to observe these statutes.

a. **You shall rejoice**: There was no ritual of animal sacrifice commanded at Pentecost. Instead, it was a time of joyful thanksgiving for the harvest, and a generous heart-response to God.

i. **Rejoice**: "The offerings of the Israelites were to be eaten with festivity, communicated to their friends with liberality, and bestowed on the poor with great generosity, that they might partake with them in these sacred repasts *with joy before the Lord*." (Clarke)

b. **You shall remember**: The joy of Pentecost was made greater by remembering the bondage Israel had escaped and blessings God had given. This was a blessing to all, especially the **stranger**, the **fatherless**, and the **widow**.

i. "All the members of the community, regardless of their social or economic status, were invited to participate in the festivities. The most disadvantaged among them were, in fact, especially to be welcomed, for Israel must remember their own bondage in Egypt and how the Lord had freed them so that now they could enjoy such blessings." (Merrill)

c. **And you shall remember that you were a slave in Egypt, and you shall be careful to observe these statutes**: Leviticus 23:15-21 describes how, at the feast of Pentecost, Israel was to celebrate by bringing a new grain offering and the waving of two loaves of *leavened* bread to the LORD. Prophetically, this is a powerful picture of the work of God in the new covenant, fulfilled at the day of Pentecost in Acts 2.

i. No atoning sacrifice was necessary because the price had already been paid by Jesus.

ii. With 3,000 having come to faith in Jesus Christ as Messiah and Lord (Acts 2:41), there was a great harvest to God, and great thanksgiving for that harvest.

iii. The response to God on the day of Pentecost was not made out of obligation to a particular law. It was the sincere heart-response of God's people to Him (Acts 2:37).

iv. The church, founded on the day of Pentecost, would include the "leavened bread" of the Gentiles, presented as holy before God, and made holy by the work of Jesus the Messiah.

C. The observance of the Feast of Tabernacles.

1. (13-15) How to observe the Feast of Tabernacles.

"You shall observe the Feast of Tabernacles seven days, when you have gathered from your threshing floor and from your winepress. And you shall rejoice in your feast, you and your son and your daughter, your male servant and your female servant and the Levite, the stranger and the fatherless and the widow, who *are* within your gates. Seven days you shall keep a sacred feast to the LORD your God in the place which the LORD chooses, because the LORD your God will bless you in all your produce and in all the work of your hands, so that you surely rejoice.

a. **You shall observe the Feast of Tabernacles seven days**: This was to happen on the fifteenth day of the Jewish month Tishri (on the Jewish ceremonial calendar). The Feast of Tabernacles was a time to rejoice in God's deliverance and provision for Israel during the time of wilderness wandering; a time when having come into the Promised Land, they could look back with gratitude on all God had done to deliver and provide in the difficult times of the wilderness.

i. "Whereas the Feast of Weeks marked the first of the harvest season for wheat, the Feast of Tabernacles signified its culmination. At the same time, almost all other crops of field and orchard matured by this time and were likewise gathered in (cf. Lev 23:40)." (Merrill)

ii. Leviticus 23:39 says of the Feast of Tabernacles, *on the first day there shall be a sabbath-rest, and on the eighth day a sabbath-rest*. The Feast of Tabernacles began and ended in rest. It was centered on celebration, rest and refreshment, and remembering what God had done. This rest was welcome after the hard work of bringing in the harvest.

iii. "The third feast of the year was in some ways the greatest of all. It is called in Leviticus 23:39 'the feast of Yahweh' and in Ezekiel 45:25 'the feast'.... Thanksgiving for the harvest and festive joy were the keynotes of this festival also (Deuteronomy 16:14; Leviticus 23:40)." (Thompson)

b. **Your male servant and your female servant**: God commanded great *social* good through the Sabbath and in the Feasts. In most other ancient cultures, there were no regular days of rest, and there were no holidays. In His goodness, God *commands* days and weeks of rest, all centered on Him.

c. **Observe the Feast of Tabernacles**: Prophetically, the feast of **Tabernacles** points to the Millennial rest and comfort of God for Israel and all of God's people. From beginning to end, it speaks of peace and rest.

i. The Feast of Tabernacles is specifically said to be celebrated during the Millennium (Zechariah 14:16-19).

2. (16-17) The command to observe each of these three feasts.

"Three times a year all your males shall appear before the LORD **your God in the place which He chooses: at the Feast of Unleavened Bread, at the Feast of Weeks, and at the Feast of Tabernacles; and they shall not appear before the L**ORD **empty-handed. Every man** *shall give* **as he is able, according to the blessing of the L**ORD **your God which He has given you.**

a. **Three times a year all your males shall appear before the L**ORD **your God in the place which He chooses**: This chapter mentions only three (four, if one counts the Feast of Unleavened Bread as a separate feast) of the seven feasts of Israel. Not mentioned in this chapter are the feasts of trumpets, of firstfruits, and the Day of Atonement.

i. **They shall not appear before the L**ORD **empty-handed**: "The observance of each of these feasts was a recognition of what the people owed to God.... in every one of them, they were called upon to bring gifts to God.... Where the full hands of worshippers are the results of hearts full of love, however poor intrinsically our gifts may be, they are very precious to Him." (Morgan)

b. **All your males**: The feasts mentioned in this chapter were the ones which every Jewish man, to the best of His ability, was required to attend at the **place** of God's choosing, where the tabernacle or temple stood and God's altar was present.

> i. Jesus was obedient to this command. He made the trip from Galilee to Jerusalem to be at these feasts (Luke 2:41, John 7:2, 10).
>
> ii. **Males** are specifically said to be required to attend these feasts, but females were not excluded. "The lack of such distinction in gender in the longer festival passages and, indeed, direct reference to female participation (cf. e.g., Deut 16:11, 14) make clear that only the males were required to attend but that females were welcome and, indeed, encouraged to do so." (Merrill)

3. (18-20) The appointment of judges and officers.

"You shall appoint judges and officers in all your gates, which the Lord your God gives you, according to your tribes, and they shall judge the people with just judgment. You shall not pervert justice; you shall not show partiality, nor take a bribe, for a bribe blinds the eyes of the wise and twists the words of the righteous. You shall follow what is altogether just, that you may live and inherit the land which the Lord your God is giving you.

> a. **You shall appoint judges and officers in all your gates**: God knew the importance of just judges and officials to a nation. Therefore, God commanded that they **shall not pervert justice** nor **show partiality**, and not **take a bribe**.
>
> > i. **Judges and officers**: "Judges, *shophetim*, among the Hebrews, were probably the same as our *magistrates* or *justices of the peace*. Officers, *shoterim*, seem to have been the same as our inquest *sergeants, beadles*, &c., whose office it was to go into the houses, shops, &c., and examine *weights, measures*, and the civil conduct of the people." (Clarke)
> >
> > ii. The recognition of judges and officers shows that justice doesn't just spontaneously happen in a community, even with the best laws. There must be men who will carry out the law, using appropriate wisdom, zeal, and mercy to see that the law is honored and fulfilled in both specific command and by principle.
>
> b. **Follow what is altogether just**: In contrast to partial and bribe-taking judges, God commanded those judges to be guided by the rules of justice. This would help guarantee that Israel prospered in the **land** God gave to them.
>
> > i. "'Show partiality' renders the Hebrew figure 'recognize faces' (Exod 23:3; Lev 19:15; 2 Chronicles 19:7; Ps 82:2; Prov 18:5; Mal 2:9)." (Kalland)

4. (21-22) Prohibition of idol trees and pillars.

"You shall not plant for yourself any tree, as a wooden image, near the altar which you build for yourself to the LORD your God. You shall not set up a sacred pillar, which the LORD your God hates.

a. **You shall not plant for yourself any tree, as a wooden image**: Such sacred totems were common among the Canaanites. In sympathy or sensitivity to the Canaanite culture, Israel may have been tempted to add such items to their worship of the God of Israel.

b. **Near the altar which you build**: Canaanite forms of worship (a **wooden image** or a **sacred pillar**) were prohibited anywhere in Israel. They were especially wrong at God's **altar**. It was even more important to guard the holiness and integrity of the house of the LORD.

i. "*Groves* were planted about idol temples for the purposes of the obscene worship performed in them. (See on chap. 12:3.) On this account God would have no groves or thickets about his altar, that there might be no room for suspicion that any thing contrary to the strictest purity was transacted there." (Clarke)

ii. "The worship of the Lord must not be with the paraphernalia of the gods of Canaan in an eclecticism that would allow Asherah poles and sacred stones alongside the altar of the Lord who hates those items of worship." (Kalland)

Deuteronomy 17 – Laws Pertaining to the Rulers of Israel

A. Laws regarding justice and courts.

1. (1-5) Religious offenses.

"You shall not sacrifice to the LORD your God a bull or sheep which has any blemish *or* defect, for that *is* an abomination to the LORD your God.

"If there is found among you, within any of your gates which the LORD your God gives you, a man or a woman who has been wicked in the sight of the LORD your God, in transgressing His covenant, who has gone and served other gods and worshiped them, either the sun or moon or any of the host of heaven, which I have not commanded, and it is told you, and you hear *of it,* then you shall inquire diligently. And if *it is* indeed true *and* certain that such an abomination has been committed in Israel, then you shall bring out to your gates that man or woman who has committed that wicked thing, and shall stone to death that man or woman with stones.

> a. **You shall not**: This section, much like Exodus 21-23, was meant to give instructions to the judges of Israel in how to administer justice for the nation. It was *case law,* upon which legal precedents for future cases could be understood.
>
> > i. This section of the second sermon of Moses in Deuteronomy (4:44-26:19) began at 16:18 with general instructions to judges. Then, matters of worship and sacrifice were addressed, starting at 16:21. Chapter 17 continues the instructions of judges regarding sacrifice and worship.
>
> b. **Which has any blemish or defect, for that is an abomination to the LORD your God**: God refused any sacrifice which had **any blemish or defect**, even calling it an **abomination** to Him. God did not recognize the

giving of cast-off, worthless items, as a true sacrifice to Him. It is human nature to give God second best – if not third or fourth best. But God will not receive such sacrifices.

> i. Israel did not always live up to this standard: *And when you offer the blind as a sacrifice, is it not evil? And when you offer the lame and sick, is it not evil? Offer it then to your governor! Would he be pleased with you? Would he accept you favorably?" Says the LORD of hosts* (Malachi 1:8).
>
> ii. King David powerfully illustrated the idea behind this commandment when he refused to accept the threshing floor of Araunah as a gift, which David was going to give to the LORD as the place to build the temple. David said, *nor will I offer burnt offerings to the LORD my God with that which costs me nothing* (2 Samuel 24:24). David understood that if it didn't *cost* something, it wasn't a true *sacrifice*.

c. Who has gone and served other gods and worshiped them: Judges are also commanded to make sure that any who had gone after idolatry were to be investigated (**inquire diligently**), and if found to be guilty, they were to be executed.

2. (6-7) The standard of evidence in capital crimes.

Whoever is deserving of death shall be put to death on the testimony of two or three witnesses; he shall not be put to death on the testimony of one witness. The hands of the witnesses shall be the first against him to put him to death, and afterward the hands of all the people. So you shall put away the evil from among you.

> a. **Whoever is deserving of death shall be put to death on the testimony of two or three witnesses**: The judges of Israel were to uphold the standard that a death-sentence for any crime had to be based on evidence from at least two independent, unimpeachable sources. The Law of Moses specifically noted that one witness was not enough for conviction (Numbers 35:29-30).
>
> > i. The **two or three witnesses** required need not necessarily be two or three individuals. A piece of strong, tangible evidence (such as the ancient equivalent of a fingerprint on a murder weapon) also served as a witness.
> >
> > ii. The requirement of **two or three witnesses** inherently demands that the witness is present publicly, guarding against secret accusations. This requirement also inherently demands that the witness is available for questioning (cross-examination) by the accused or the representatives of the accused, confirming that they are indeed **witnesses** and to judge the reliability of their testimony.

iii. Though God commanded Israel to carry out the death penalty for certain crimes, there was also great concern for the rights of the accused. When the standard of **two or three witnesses** was observed, the innocent or falsely accused would not be sentenced to death.

iv. This high standard of evidence also meant that there would be some murderers who would not be prosecuted and brought to justice because there were not adequate witnesses to convict. In such cases, final justice would wait for God's court beyond this life. This assurance of final justice would give small solace to the survivors of those murdered under such circumstances.

v. This standard of evidence for the accused is also stated in the New Testament, in reference to the murder of reputation. God commands that one should *not receive an accusation against an elder except from two or three witnesses* (1 Timothy 5:19) – the same standard as for proving murder.

b. **The hands of the witnesses shall be the first against him to put him to death**: Additionally, the witnesses had to be so certain of what they saw, that they were willing to initiate the actual execution. This made certain that no one would be executed for a crime they did not commit.

i. "The hands of the witnesses were to be the first to administer punishment." (Kalland)

ii. This puts the words of Jesus regarding the woman taken in adultery in John 8 in perspective: *He who is without sin among you, let him throw a stone at her first* (John 8:7). Jesus asked for the official witness to step forward and identify themselves on record as having witnessed this act of adultery yet had been hypocritical enough to bring the woman and not the man.

c. **And afterward the hands of all the people**: The execution was a community event, in the sense that it was supported by the community. The whole village would know the justice of what was being done.

i. **So you shall put away the evil from among you**: "When Paul told the Corinthian church members that they should expel the wicked man from among them [1 Corinthians 5:13], he quoted this injunction, which appears, with slight variation, nine times in Deuteronomy." (Kalland)

3. (8-13) Provision made for higher courts.

"If a matter arises which is too hard for you to judge, between degrees of guilt for bloodshed, between one judgment or another, or between one punishment or another, matters of controversy within your gates,

then you shall arise and go up to the place which the LORD your God chooses. And you shall come to the priests, the Levites, and to the judge *there* in those days, and inquire *of them;* they shall pronounce upon you the sentence of judgment. You shall do according to the sentence which they pronounce upon you in that place which the LORD chooses. And you shall be careful to do according to all that they order you. According to the sentence of the law in which they instruct you, according to the judgment which they tell you, you shall do; you shall not turn aside *to* the right hand or *to* the left from the sentence which they pronounce upon you. Now the man who acts presumptuously and will not heed the priest who stands to minister there before the LORD your God, or the judge, that man shall die. So you shall put away the evil from Israel. And all the people shall hear and fear, and no longer act presumptuously.

a. **If a matter arises which is too hard for you to judge**: In ancient Israel, God provided for courts of appeal. These were higher courts where cases were taken beyond the local judges to the **priests, the Levites** – who were understood to be wiser judges because of their greater knowledge of God's word.

i. **Too hard for you to judge**: "The verb 'be difficult' or 'be baffling' is related in its root to the noun *pele*, which connotes something wonderful or miraculous, e.g. the mighty acts of God's deliverance in Egypt (Exod. 3:20; 15:11; 34:10). The case in question was, then, one that had some very unusual features." (Thompson)

b. **Degrees of guilt for bloodshed**: God's law recognized there are different **degrees of guilt** when a person is killed. This was the foundation for the cities of refuge (Numbers 35, Joshua 20). Not every killing is the same, and some are worthy of more severe judgment than others.

c. **Now the man who acts presumptuously and will not heed the priest…that man shall die**: The authority of the judges had to be respected. Therefore, to treat God's appointed court with contempt was a capital crime. God thought it was essential that the courts and judges were respected in Israel.

B. Laws pertaining to kings.

1. (14-15) God's indirect promise of a future king for Israel.

"When you come to the land which the LORD your God is giving you, and possess it and dwell in it, and say, "I will set a king over me like all the nations that *are* around me," you shall surely set a king over you whom the LORD your God chooses; *one* **from among your brethren you**

shall set as king over you; you may not set a foreigner over you, who *is* not your brother.

    a. **I will set a king over me like all the nations that are around me**: God looked forward – some 400 years forward – to Israel's future, to the time when they would demand a king. God warned them to look for and support a king **whom the LORD your God chooses**, and that person had to be an Israelite and not a foreigner.

        i. Although kingship was foreseen even in the days of the patriarchs (Genesis 17:6, 17:16, 35:11, 49:10), for more than 500 years of its history, Israel had no king. "Moses, in spite of his authoritative position, was not a king. Joshua, his successor, received an appointment charismatically, as did Moses. The judges that followed were not kings." (Kalland)

    b. **I will set a king over me**: When Israel eventually said this in 1 Samuel 8:6-9, it was not motivated by a desire to keep God's law here in Deuteronomy 17. It was motivated by a desire to be like the other nations, and by the desire to reject God's leadership over Israel.

        i. God eventually wanted Israel to have a king. These commands in Deuteronomy anticipate a king, and most of the time when Israel did not have a king was not a time of national glory (the time of the book of Judges).

        ii. God wanted Israel to have a king, but of *His* choosing, and at *His* timing. Saul was a perfect example of a king not from God's will, who was chosen by the nation and at their timing; David is an example of a king chosen by God and in His timing.

2. (16-17) Commands for the king.

But he shall not multiply horses for himself, nor cause the people to return to Egypt to multiply horses, for the LORD has said to you, "You shall not return that way again." Neither shall he multiply wives for himself, lest his heart turn away; nor shall he greatly multiply silver and gold for himself.

    a. **He shall not multiply horses for himself**: The future king of Israel must not put undue trust in military might, here represented by **horses** that were mighty weapons in a time when most soldiers fought on foot.

        i. "Lest the people might depend on a well-appointed *cavalry* as a means of security, and so cease from trusting in the strength and protection of God." (Clarke)

b. **Neither shall he multiply wives for himself**: The future king of Israel must not put undue emphasis on physical indulgence and personal status, here represented by having multiple wives.

> i. "A large harem of many wives also represented a likeness to the Oriental courts of other kingdoms, and having many wives envisaged the usual procedure of acquiring those wives from families of other kings and so sealing treaties by marriage. Such wives would bring the impact of foreign cultures into the palace, particularly the worship of other gods, and so lead the heart of the king astray." (Kalland)

c. **Nor shall he greatly multiply silver and gold for himself**: The future king of Israel must not put undue emphasis on personal wealth, here represented by the **silver and gold** he would accumulate.

d. **Lest his heart turn away**: Each of these were a matter of balance. The king had to have some military power, but not too much; one wife and certain comforts, but not too much; some personal wealth, but not too much. Such balances are often the hardest to keep.

> i. Solomon was a notorious breaker of these commands. He had *forty thousand stalls of horses for his chariots* (1 Kings 4:26), and *Solomon had horses imported from Egypt* (1 Kings 10:28). He had *seven hundred wives, princesses, and three hundred concubines; and his wives turned away his heart* (1 Kings 11:3). He *surpassed all the kings of the earth in riches* (1 Kings 10:23).
>
> ii. Yet, all along, we might see Solomon knowing the commands of Deuteronomy 17, yet deceiving himself by asking the self-justifying questions, "How much is 'multiply'? This isn't an exact number. I haven't gone too far." It might seem self-evident that 700 wives and 300 concubines is multiplying wives, but the human heart has an astounding ability to deceive itself.
>
> iii. "Military aggrandisement, a large harem, and the amassing of wealth were typical of Eastern potentates long before Moses' day." (Thompson)
>
> iv. "This is a remarkable portrait of God's ideal of kingship. It would be an interesting exercise to measure the kings of men throughout history by this ideal.... the measure by which they have violated these principles has been the measure of the disaster resulting from their rule." (Morgan)
>
> v. Each of these three areas reflects the places where many modern Christian leaders fall: power, pleasure, or money. God's commands for

leaders have not changed; and neither has the need to be on guard against the self-deception in these things which made Solomon fall.

3. (18-20) The king and the word of God.

"**Also it shall be, when he sits on the throne of his kingdom, that he shall write for himself a copy of this law in a book, from *the one* before the priests, the Levites. And it shall be with him, and he shall read it all the days of his life, that he may learn to fear the LORD his God and be careful to observe all the words of this law and these statutes, that his heart may not be lifted above his brethren, that he may not turn aside from the commandment *to* the right hand or *to* the left, and that he may prolong *his* days in his kingdom, he and his children in the midst of Israel.**

a. **He shall write for himself:** God commanded the king of Israel, when he was appointed king, to write a copy of the law for himself. It is striking to picture the king of Israel, laboring over parchment with a pen, making a personal copy of the law of Israel. This shows how greatly God wanted the word of God to be on the hearts of His rulers; God wanted every king to also be a scribe.

i. **From the one before the priests**: "It is likely this means, that the copy which the king was to write out was to be taken from the *autograph* kept in the tabernacle before the Lord, from which, as a standard, every copy was taken, and with which doubtless every copy was compared; and it is probable that the priests and Levites had the revising of every copy that was taken off, in order to prevent errors from creeping into the sacred text." (Clarke)

ii. "The king's copy was to be made from the 'official' version, that retained by the priests, presumably in or near the ark of the covenant (cf. Deut 31:9, 25–26). This is most likely the 'book of the law' found by Josiah's priests and scribes in the days of Judah's reformation (cf. 2 Kgs 22:8–13)." (Merrill)

iii. "Incidentally, the phrase *a copy of this law* (Deuteronomy 17:18) appears incorrectly in the LXX [Septuagint] as 'this second law', *to deuteronomion touto*. It was this misunderstanding that gave rise to the English name Deuteronomy." (Thompson)

b. **It shall be with him, and he shall read it all the days of his life:** The word of God was to be a constant companion of the king of Israel, and something he read every day.

i. "Only the study of this law could preserve him from the temptations which beset a king." (Thompson)

ii. "The corrective suggested here is meditation on the Word of God. The king was to write out a copy with his own hand, and meditate on it all the days of his life; this would keep him in the lowlands of humility. The Bible is so true in its analysis of the heart; like a mirror it reveals a man to himself. It gives such exalted views of the greatness and holiness of God, compared with which the greatest human state is like the royalties of an ant-heap." (Meyer)

iii. Everyone needs the word of God. But the greater our responsibilities, the greater our need to depend on the truth of God's word.

iv. John Trapp of the 17th century praised an English monarch for her love of God's word: "Queen Elizabeth, as she pass in triumphal state through the streets of London after her coronation, when the Bible was presented to her at the little conduit in Cheapside, received the same with both her hands, and kissing it, laid it to her breasts, saying that the same had ever been her chiefest delight, and should be the rule whereby she meant to frame her government."

c. **That he may learn to fear the LORD his God and be careful to observe all the words of this law**: Staying in the word of God was intended to build in the king a reverence for God and a holy life.

i. "As a result of failing to follow carefully the law, notice the mistake David made when he first attempted to bring the ark of the covenant to Jerusalem and the correction of that mistake at the second and successful attempt (1 Chronicles 13:1–10; 15:2, 13)." (Kalland)

ii. It is wonderful to consider that reading a book – the great book, the Bible – can keep a person from sin. We may not understand all the spiritual work behind the word of God, but staying in the word will keep one from sin. It has been well written in many Bibles: "This book will keep you from sin. Sin will keep you from this book."

d. **That his heart may not be lifted up**: Staying in the word of God would keep the king properly humble and help him to not think of himself as above those he ruled over.

i. "The Scriptures, diligently read and studied, are a powerful and probable means to keep him humble, because they show him that, though a king, he is subject to a higher Monarch, to whom he must give an account…sufficient to abate the pride of the haughtiest person in the world, if he duly consider it." (Poole)

ii. **He and his children**: Adam Clarke, a British Methodist of the 19th century, had a comment on this phrase appropriate to his time and place. "From this verse it has been inferred that the crown of Israel was designed to be *hereditary*, and this is very probable; for long experience has proved to almost all the nations of the world that *hereditary succession* in the regal government is, on the whole, the safest, and best calculated to secure the public tranquillity."

iii. "Those who forsook the Lord and disregarded the principles of godly rule would face personal disaster and lack of royal succession. The history of Israel would prove this to be all too true." (Merrill)

Deuteronomy 18 – Priests and Prophets

A. The provision for priests and Levites.

1. (1-2) The inheritance of the Levites.

"The priests, the Levites—all the tribe of Levi—shall have no part nor inheritance with Israel; they shall eat the offerings of the Lord made by fire, and His portion. Therefore they shall have no inheritance among their brethren; the Lord is their inheritance, as He said to them.

> a. **The priests, the Levites…shall have no part nor inheritance with Israel**: The Levites – those of the tribe of Levi, who were the paid ministers for the nation of Israel – were to **have no inheritance among their brethren**. In other words, they were not to have allotted portions of land for their own possession. Instead, they were distributed throughout the land of Israel (Joshua 21).
>
> b. **They shall eat the offerings of the Lord made by fire, and His portion**: The Levites were to be supported by the gifts and offerings of God's people. They were permitted to receive at least a portion of most animals sacrificed to the Lord, and by this were provided with meat for food (Numbers 18:8-9).
>
> c. **The Lord is their inheritance**: God calls some among His people to focus more on Him, His service, and the service of His people. These ones may have less in terms of tangible assets and material security, but they are still provided for because the **Lord is their inheritance**.

2. (3-5) The specific portions of the sacrificial animal set apart to the priests.

"And this shall be the priest's due from the people, from those who offer a sacrifice, whether *it is* bull or sheep: they shall give to the priest the shoulder, the cheeks, and the stomach. The firstfruits of your grain and your new wine and your oil, and the first of the fleece of your sheep, you shall give him. For the Lord your God has chosen him out of all your

tribes to stand to minister in the name of the LORD, him and his sons forever.

a. **The priest's due from the people, from those who offer a sacrifice**: From a typical sacrifice, the priests received the **shoulder, the cheeks, and the stomach**. The rest of the animal was either burnt before the LORD or returned to the one bringing the sacrifice, so he could enjoy his own fellowship meal with his family before the LORD.

b. **Your grain and your new wine and your oil and the first of the fleece of your sheep**: The priests also received these offerings of firstfruits from the people.

i. **The fleece of your sheep**: "The prescriptions of verse 4 are similar to those in other places in the Old Testament (cf. Num. 18:12; 2 Chr. 31:5). The *fleece*, however, is mentioned only here." (Thompson)

3. (6-8) All the Levites had equal rights to the offerings.

"So if a Levite comes from any of your gates, from where he dwells among all Israel, and comes with all the desire of his mind to the place which the LORD chooses, then he may serve in the name of the LORD his God as all his brethren the Levites *do*, who stand there before the LORD. They shall have equal portions to eat, besides what comes from the sale of his inheritance."

a. **From where he dwells among all Israel**: The Levites would not have their own province or state in Israel, as the other tribes did. At God's instruction, they would be distributed throughout the land of Israel (Joshua 21), to serve the people and to teach God's word.

b. **Comes with all the desire of his mind to the place which the LORD chooses**: If a Levite who lived in one of the appointed cities wanted to live and serve at the tabernacle (and later, the temple), he had the right to (**then he may serve**). Not every Levite would have a calling or passion to serve at the house of the LORD, but those who did were permitted to do so.

i. "Special provision was now made for any priest whose heart prompted him to special service." (Morgan)

ii. "It is a blessed thing to feel an impulse like this. It may prompt to home or foreign missions, to some enterprise of self-denying ministry to the helpless and sad, to service for God or man. It may come on you like a strong current, fresh from the ocean, sweeping up into some quiet river or harbour basin, and lifting the ponderous barges. But when it comes, be true to it, nurse it, reverence it, thank God for it, trust and follow it where it leads." (Meyer)

c. **They shall have equal portions to eat**: Ideally, the Levite who lived far away from the tabernacle or temple would receive the same amount from the tithes and offerings of God's people as those who lived closer to the tabernacle (**who stand there before the LORD**).

> i. **Besides what comes from the sale of his inheritance**: "So we find that, though the Levites might have no part of the land by lot, yet they were permitted to make purchases of houses, goods, and cattle, yea, of fields also. See the case of Abiathar, 1 Kings 2:26, and of Jeremiah, Jer. 32:7, 8." (Clarke)

B. Prescriptions for prophets.

1. (9-11) The command to reject all the occult practices of the Canaanites.

"When you come into the land which the LORD your God is giving you, you shall not learn to follow the abominations of those nations. There shall not be found among you *anyone* who makes his son or his daughter pass through the fire, *or one* who practices witchcraft, *or* a soothsayer, or one who interprets omens, or a sorcerer, or one who conjures spells, or a medium, or a spiritist, or one who calls up the dead.

> a. **You shall not learn**: God knows that many people have a natural curiosity regarding the occult, and that curiosity often leads them to seek spiritually dangerous experiences. God wisely commanded His people to avoid dark spiritual powers and experiences altogether, to not seek after them.

> b. **Anyone who makes his son or his daughter to pass through the fire**: This refers to the debased worship of the Canaanite god Molech, to whom children were sacrificed by burning. Following are eight offices or roles played by those given over to demonic and dark practices.

>> i. "Of the eight terms employed, the first three refer to different means of reading the future, the next two to different means of influencing events, and the last three to different ways of consulting the dead." (Maclaren)

> c. **Or one who practices witchcraft**: The word **witchcraft** here is a broad word, describing a variety of occult activities. Basically, anything that contacts the demonic or dark spiritual world.

>> i. Thompson on **practices witchcraft**: "A variety of devices were in use in various lands, but all were designed to discern the will of the gods. The same word in Ezekiel 21:21 refers to the practice of whirling arrows in a quiver and deciding the answer to the question by the first arrow thrown out."

ii. There is a modern revival of witchcraft, or Wicca, and many people claim that "white" witchcraft (as opposed to "black" witchcraft) is a use of spiritual powers for good, as well as being a more feminist, ecology-friendly understanding of god and spirituality. Whether a witch claims to be "white" or "black," they still use occultic powers. This should be completely rejected by the people of God.

d. **Or a soothsayer**: This has reference to astrological-type divination, predicting the future or seeking guidance through the stars, planets, clouds, or weather.

i. Kalland says that the **soothsayer**: "Is…predicting the future by means of physical signs (astrology)." Thompson points out "it seems to refer to divination by reading clouds, or from a root which occurs in Arabic meaning 'to make unusual noises', 'croon', 'hum', in which case it may refer to some kind of incantation."

ii. Even though astrology is unscientific – it is based on the supposition that the sun circles the earth, and the positions of the planets and stars have shifted, and are never consistently uniform; therefore, the houses of the Zodiac have shifted – despite all that, millions of people still believe in astrology to some degree.

iii. The Bible clearly forbids participation in astrology, which includes reading horoscopes, studying signs, and computing natal charts. Astrology is an occult art, meaning that it involves "knowledge of hidden things," seeking spiritual knowledge apart from God's revelation. It is a foundational art, which means it is the building block for all occultists. It is studied by witches and magicians alike. Every Christian should renounce any involvement that they have ever had with astrology.

e. **Or one who interprets omens**: The word for **omens** comes from the root "to hiss" or "to whisper" and refers to psychics and fortune-tellers who use "aids" other than naturally created things to gain knowledge, tell the future, and cast spells.

i. Today, those who interpret **omens** can be found among the tarot card readers, crystal ball seers, tea-leaf readers, palm readers, Ouija board users, and the like. A Christian has *no business* participating or approving of any of these practices, because either the practitioners are greedy frauds (at best!), or worse, they gain their knowledge from satanic, demonic, spiritual sources. Parents must prevent their children from any such involvement, even if it seems innocent or only to be play.

ii. It is worth noting that Satan or his demons cannot absolutely know the future, but they can reasonably predict the future. This may be based on their superior knowledge of people and circumstances. Alternatively, they may predict events that they have had a hand in shaping through their own demonic influence.

f. **Or a sorcerer**: This has reference to those who use drugs or potions to cast spells, gain spiritual knowledge, or enter altered states of consciousness. Modern drug abuse easily falls into this category, and the use of drugs has a definite *occult* connection that the drug taker may not desire, but is exposed to nonetheless.

i. Clarke says of **sorcerer**: "Those who by means of drugs, herbs, perfumes, and so forth, pretended to bring certain celestial influences to their aid." Thompson adds, "derived from the root…'to cut up', may denote one who cuts up herbs and brews them for magical purposes (*cf.* LXX [Septuagint] *pharmaka*, drug). The term is used in Micah 5:12 for some such material as drugs or herbs used superstitiously to produce magical effects."

g. **Or one who conjures up spells**: This is literally, "a charmer of charms" and refers to those who cast spells or charms for what is thought to be good or evil on others, using spiritual powers apart from God and not directed by His word.

i. It is a glorious thing to bless others in the name of the LORD; or even to pray to God against the evil of another person. But it is always and forever wrong to use demonic, dark, pagan, or occult powers to cast spells or charms.

h. **Or a medium**: The idea is of someone who "stands between" the physical world and the psychic world; they channel knowledge from the psychic world into the physical world. Such mediums and psychics must be rejected by Christians, and they do great harm with their connections to demonic spirits.

i. Thompson notes that the **medium**: "Spoke from within a person (Leviticus 20:27) with a twittering voice (Isaiah 29:4). Those who practiced this art called up the departed from the realm of the dead, or rather, professed to do so."

i. **Or a spiritist**: Literally, this word refers to the "knowing ones" – those who claim unique occult or psychic knowledge and powers – such as those on the many psychic hotlines that one can pay to call. Again, a Christian must have no participation with, or approval of, any of these practices, because the practitioners are greedy frauds (at best), or worse, they gain their knowledge from satanic, demonic, spiritual sources.

j. Or one who calls up the dead: This refers to the practice of necromancy, which is the conjuring up or the contacting of the dead.

i. This refers to "One who investigates, looks into, and seeks information from the dead" (Kalland). This is another practice that should be rejected and avoided by Christians.

2. (12-14) Why rejection of all these occultic actions is commanded.

For all who do these things *are* an abomination to the Lord, and because of these abominations the Lord your God drives them out from before you. You shall be blameless before the Lord your God. For these nations which you will dispossess listened to soothsayers and diviners; but as for you, the Lord your God has not appointed such for you.

a. **For all who do these things are an abomination to the Lord**: God did not take these occult actions lightly then, nor does God take them lightly now. The practices mentioned in verses 9-11 are participation with the powers of darkness and are always to be rejected by Christians. The people of God have reason to be concerned when these abominations are treated lightly by the wider culture and are accepted and promoted.

i. "The concern of the passage is that God's people must avoid any heathen means of achieving revelation and must, rather, avail themselves of those prophetic instruments whom he himself would raise up and through whom exclusively he would reveal himself." (Merrill)

ii. "It may be pertinent to comment that in our own day, when spiritualism, astrology, teacup reading and the like are widely practised, these injunctions given to ancient Israel have a particular relevance. Not only is it impossible to discover the future by such practices, but the practices themselves are forbidden by God to men who call themselves members of the covenant family." (Thompson)

b. **Because of these abominations the Lord your God drives them out from before you**: God's judgment was upon the Canaanites because of these occult practices, and if Israel took up the same occult practices, they could also expect to receive the judgment of God.

i. Yes, the Canaanites were sex-worshippers (in their service of the goddess Ashtaroth); and yes, they were money and success worshippers (in their service of the god Baal). Added to these, what made the Canaanites particularly ripe for judgment was their occult practices, practices the people of God were strictly forbidden to imitate.

c. **You shall be blameless**: This was more than a general call to a holy life. This was a solemn warning to keep from *any* involvement with these detestable practices of the occult. Such occult practices are things that the **LORD your God has not appointed** for His people.

i. Believers are to be *blameless* regarding such things, even as the Ephesian Christians, who destroyed all things that marked the occult in their lives (Acts 19:19-20). This is why it is dangerous for people to seek or approve of the occult, even if they don't really believe it and even if it is considered fun or acceptable in the wider culture.

3. (15-19) The promise of a true Prophet to come.

"The LORD your God will raise up for you a Prophet like me from your midst, from your brethren. Him you shall hear, according to all you desired of the LORD your God in Horeb in the day of the assembly, saying, 'Let me not hear again the voice of the LORD my God, nor let me see this great fire anymore, lest I die.'

"And the LORD said to me: 'What they have spoken is good. I will raise up for them a Prophet like you from among their brethren, and will put My words in His mouth, and He shall speak to them all that I command Him. And it shall be *that* whoever will not hear My words, which He speaks in My name, I will require *it* of him.

a. **The LORD your God will raise up for you a Prophet like me**: In contrast to the dark, false, and dangerous spiritual practices described in the previous verses, God promised a coming Prophet. By inspiration of the Holy Spirit, Moses promised a prophet to come; a prophet that would first be **like me** – that is, like Moses.

i. **Like me**: "It would be a very interesting task for the young people to work out all the points in which Moses is a personal type of the Lord Jesus. The points of resemblance are very many, for there is hardly a single incident in the life of the great Lawgiver, which is not symbolical of the promised Saviour." (Spurgeon)

ii. "The 'prophet like you from among their brothers' (v.18) was seen as a messianic prediction, a prophet par excellence. This interpretation was widespread in NT times, being mentioned in the NT and among the Essenes as well as among the Jews, Gnostics, and others (cf. John 1:21; 6:14; 7:40; Acts 3:22-23)." (Kalland)

b. **From your midst, from your brethren**: Like Moses, this Prophet would be from the midst of Israel. This not only meant that He would be an Israelite, but that He would be a "man of the people" – He would be one of them.

c. **Him you shall hear**: Like Moses, this Prophet would command the attention of the nation. This means both that Israel *should* listen to this Prophet, and that they *would* listen to this Prophet.

i. "Men and brethren, if our hearts were right, the moment it was announced that God would speak to us through Jesus Christ there would be a rush to hear him. If sin had not maddened men they would listen eagerly to every word of God through such a Mediator as Jesus is." (Spurgeon)

d. **According to all you desired of the LORD your God in Horeb**: At Mount Sinai (**Horeb**), Israel begged for a mediator (Exodus 20:19-21). Like Moses, this Prophet to come would be a mediator, representing God to the people, and representing the people before God.

e. **Will put My words in His mouth**: Like Moses, this Prophet would speak God's word.

f. **I will require it of him**: Like Moses, this Prophet's message would be rejected at a great penalty. God would hold accountable (**require**) all those who rejected the Prophet.

i. "The day will come when he will require it of you in a much more violent sense than he does to-day; when you shall have passed beyond the region of mercy he will say, 'I called you and you refused, why is this?'" (Spurgeon)

g. **I will raise up for them a Prophet**: People looked for this Prophet in the days of Jesus, and there are many references in the New Testament to this Prophet and these words of Moses.

- John the Baptist said that he was not this Prophet whom Moses promised (John 1:21, 25).
- Philip understood that Jesus was the One whom Moses wrote about (John 1:45).
- Many people in the days of Jesus recognized Him as this Prophet (John 6:14, 7:40).
- Jesus specifically said that Moses wrote about Him (John 5:46).
- Peter specifically said this promise was fulfilled in Jesus (Acts 3:22-23).
- Stephen specifically said this promise was fulfilled in Jesus (Acts 7:37).

i. "This prophet is the Lord Jesus, who was in the bosom of the Father, and who came to *declare him* to mankind. Every word spoken by him is a living infallible oracle from God himself; and must be received and obeyed as such, on pain of the eternal displeasure of the Almighty." (Clarke)

ii. In describing the office of prophet, Moses completed a section dealing with the office of a king (17:14-20), the office of a priest (18:1-8), and the office of a prophet (18:15-22). All these offices are perfectly fulfilled in Jesus Christ. "He was the true King; of His brethren, appointed by God, knowing, doing, and administering the law. He was the true Priest; of His brethren, without inheritance in His own land, abiding in the service of God, ministered to by the people of God. He was the true Prophet; of His brethren, uttering the Word of God in purity and fullness." (Morgan)

iii. Jesus is not only the **Prophet like** Moses, He is also greater than Moses (Hebrews 3:1-6).

4. (20) The penalty for a false prophet.

But the prophet who presumes to speak a word in My name, which I have not commanded him to speak, or who speaks in the name of other gods, that prophet shall die.'

a. **But the prophet who presumes to speak a word in My name**: There may be one who **presumes to speak a word** in God's name. That is, they claim that they speak for God, but they do not. For this reason, believers must always be cautious at any claim to speak for God and must guard against presumption if they themselves believe they speak for God.

i. "The difference was that, whereas the true prophet spoke for God, the false prophet spoke presumptuously, *i.e.* he blurted out personal opinions for which there was no backing from Yahweh." (Thompson)

ii. "Of the three major institutions of ancient Israelite social and religious life—royalty, the priesthood, and prophetism—only the last was charismatic and nonsuccessive. Prophets were men and women raised up individually by God and called and empowered by him to communicate his purposes to the theocratic community." (Merrill)

b. **Which I have not commanded him to speak**: It was possible for a prophet to hear from God, yet it was not a word that God **commanded him to speak**. God may speak to an instrument, yet not intend for that prophet to speak to others.

c. **Or speaks in the name of other gods**: Obviously, those who presumed to "prophesy" in the name of Baal or Ashtoreth, or any number of the other false gods of the Canaanites were false prophets. They must be rejected.

d. **That prophet shall die**: Simply stated, the penalty in ancient Israel for false prophets was death. Presumptuous speaking in the name of the LORD, disobedient speaking in the name of the LORD, and speaking in the name of false gods were never to be tolerated in Israel.

5. (21-22) The test of a false prophet.

And if you say in your heart, 'How shall we know the word which the LORD has not spoken?'—when a prophet speaks in the name of the LORD, if the thing does not happen or come to pass, that *is* the thing which the LORD has not spoken; the prophet has spoken it presumptuously; you shall not be afraid of him.

a. **How shall we know**: It was easy to tell if a prophet spoke in the name of Baal or Ashtoreth. But how could one know if a prophet spoke presumptuously or disobediently in the name of the LORD? One way to know was by their accuracy.

b. **If the thing does not happen or come to pass, that is the thing which the LORD has not spoken**: If a prophet said, "Thus says the LORD," claiming that something would happen, and it did not happen, then that prophet must be held accountable for the false prophecy. The prophet was also no longer to be regarded as a true or reliable prophet.

i. This principle does not exclude the principle of Deuteronomy 13:1-5. There, God commands that even if a supposed prophet was able to authenticate his message with some kind of sign and wonder, if that claimed messenger from God would lead people to follow and serve other gods, they must be rejected, and in ancient Israel, be put to death. Whether a predicted thing happened or not was one test of a prophet, but not the only test of a prophet. It was the first test, not the final test.

ii. "This answer is not comprehensive: it speaks of only one of the ways to determine the validity of a prophet and a prophecy. It does not cover all circumstances." (Kalland)

c. **The prophet has spoken presumptuously; you shall not be afraid of him**: Genuine prophets were to be treated with respect, as those who proclaimed God's authentic message. False prophets could be disregarded. At best, such false prophets spoke from themselves (**presumptuously**). At worst, they were instruments of demonic deception (as in verses 9-11).

i. There continues to be an emphasis on "prophets" in some Christian circles. Many of these supposed prophets claim things will happen, and the things do not come to pass. Such false prophecies are sometimes excused with the claim that the prophets were "learning" and "experimenting" and "under grace," therefore, they should not be regarded as false prophets.

ii. While it is true that experience is a help in the use of spiritual gifts, no one should claim that a message is from God unless they are assured that it is – and if they are wrong, then their own discernment and ability to hear from God are rightly called into question.

iii. Besides, if prophets were held to this standard under the old covenant, it isn't right to have a lesser standard under the new covenant. Under the new covenant, there is a greater outpouring of the Holy Spirit, not less. Under the new covenant, the *penalty* for false prophecy has changed; they should not be executed. Yet false prophets among Christians today should not be respected, and not be given the title or position of "prophet."

iv. Instead, the New Testament says all prophecy should be judged: *Let two or three prophets speak, and let the others judge* (1 Corinthians 14:29; also 1 John 4:1). While God may communicate today through the gift of prophecy, it is essential that those through whom God may communicate be humble in their perceived ability to hear from God, and that their supposed prophecies be appropriately judged.

v. Pastor Tom Stipe, in the foreword to *Counterfeit Revival*, spoke powerfully about the problem of false prophets in the church:

"After only a couple of years, the prophets seemed to be speaking to just about everyone on just about everything. Hundreds of…members received the 'gift' of prophecy and began plying their trade among both leaders and parishioners. People began carrying around little notebooks filled with predictions that had been delivered to them by the prophets and seers. They flocked to the prophecy conferences that had begun to spring up everywhere. The notebook crowd would rush forward in hopes of being selected to receive more prophecies to add to their prophetic diaries.

"Not long after 'prophecy du jour' became the primary source of direction, a trail of devastated believers began to line up outside our pastoral counseling offices. Young people promised teen success and stardom through prophecy were left picking up the pieces of their shattered hopes because God had apparently gone back on His promises. Leaders were deluged by angry church members who had received prophecies about the great ministries they would have but had been frustrated by local church leaders who failed to recognize and 'facilitate' their 'new anointing.'

"After a steady diet of the prophetic, some people were rapidly becoming biblically illiterate, choosing a 'dial-a-prophet' style of Christian living rather than studying God's Word. Many were left to continually live from one prophetic 'fix' to the next, their hope always in danger of failing because God's voice was so specific in pronouncement, yet so elusive in fulfillment. Possessing a prophet's phone number was like having a storehouse of treasured guidance. Little clutched notebooks replaced Bibles as the preferred reading material during church services."

vi. God's people must always guard against letting an emphasis on the supposedly prophetic overshadow a simple emphasis on God's word: *The prophet who has a dream, let him tell a dream; And he who has My word, let him speak My word faithfully. What is the chaff to the wheat?" says the* LORD. (Jeremiah 23:28)

Deuteronomy 19 – Concerning Criminal Law

A. Cities of refuge to be provided.

1. (1-3) Three special cities.

"When the LORD your God has cut off the nations whose land the LORD your God is giving you, and you dispossess them and dwell in their cities and in their houses, you shall separate three cities for yourself in the midst of your land which the LORD your God is giving you to possess. You shall prepare roads for yourself, and divide into three parts the territory of your land which the LORD your God is giving you to inherit, that any manslayer may flee there.

a. **When the LORD your God has cut off the nations**: The three sermons of Moses recorded in Deuteronomy were given a few weeks before Israel crossed the Jordan and began their conquest of Canaan. This section describes something they were to do when they were established in the land.

i. "Still with his mind on the fact that the people were coming into the land, Moses made further applications of the laws to the new conditions. His words now had to do with life and land and truth and justice." (Morgan)

b. **You shall separate three cities for yourself in the midst of the land**: God instructed Israel to establish three cities of refuge in the Promised Land and instructed them to spread the cities across Israel (**in the midst of the land**).

i. The cities of refuge were anticipated in Exodus 21:12-14. Numbers 35:9-28 gave the initial command to establish the cities of refuge, and Joshua 20:7-8 is the record of their establishment. Moses had already established Bezer, Ramoth, and Golan as the cities of refuge on the east side of the Jordan River (Deuteronomy 4:41-43).

ii. The three cities later established by Joshua were Kedesh, Shechem, and Hebron (Joshua 20:7-9). "Kedesh served the Galilee region, Shechem the central hill country, and Hebron the highlands of Judah." (Merrill)

c. **Prepare roads for yourself:** The people of Israel were to build good roads to each city of refuge, so the cities would be accessible to travelers.

i. "The Jews inform us that the roads to the cities of refuge were made very broad, thirty-two cubits; and even, so that there should be no impediments in the way; and were constantly kept in good repair." (Clarke)

2. (4-7) The purpose for the cities of refuge.

"And this *is* the case of the manslayer who flees there, that he may live: Whoever kills his neighbor unintentionally, not having hated him in time past—as when *a man* goes to the woods with his neighbor to cut timber, and his hand swings a stroke with the ax to cut down the tree, and the head slips from the handle and strikes his neighbor so that he dies—he shall flee to one of these cities and live; lest the avenger of blood, while his anger is hot, pursue the manslayer and overtake him, because the way is long, and kill him, though he *was* not deserving of death, since he had not hated the victim in time past. Therefore I command you, saying, 'You shall separate three cities for yourself.'

a. **The case of the manslayer who flees there, that he may live**: The cities of refuge were for the protection of the person who killed another accidentally or in self-defense. In ancient Israel, when one was killed, it was the responsibility of the **avenger of blood** to make certain the murder was punished.

i. This practice was based upon a correct understanding of Genesis 9:6: *Whoever sheds man's blood, by man his blood shall be shed; for in the image of God, He made man.*

ii. John Trapp considered the phrase **not having hated him in time past**, and the nature of such hatred when it does exist: "There is, *first*, a *passion* of hatred. This is a kind of averseness and rising of the heart against a man, when one sees him, so that he cannot away with him, nor speak to him, nor look courteously or peaceably upon him, and by his goodwill he would have nothing to do with him. *Secondly*, there is a *habit* of hatred, when the heart is so settled in this alienation and estrangement, that it grows to wish, and desire, and seek his hurt. Both these must be mortified." (Trapp)

b. **Lest the avenger of blood**: The **avenger of blood** was an appointed member of the family (the *goel*), designated to protect the honor and lives of the family. His interest would not be in gathering evidence, but in avenging the honor of the family – so, in the case of an accidental killing, the **manslayer** would need protection from the **avenger of blood**.

i. The case study given here in Deuteronomy 19 illustrates the point. Two men are working together, chopping down trees, when one man takes a swing of an ax and the ax head flies off, striking the other man in the head and instantly killing him. The surviving man had good reason to believe the avenger of blood from the dead man's family would track him down and kill him, believing the death was murder.

ii. Therefore, such a man could flee to a city of refuge – an appointed Levitical city, where he could stay, safe from the avenger of blood, until the issue was settled, and he could leave the city of refuge safely.

iii. "It was not that the next of kin was deprived of his right of blood revenge, but only that restraints were placed on the indiscriminate exercise of the right." (Thompson)

3. (8-10) Appointment of additional cities of refuge.

"Now if the LORD your God enlarges your territory, as He swore to your fathers, and gives you the land which He promised to give to your fathers, and if you keep all these commandments and do them, which I command you today, to love the LORD your God and to walk always in His ways, then you shall add three more cities for yourself besides these three, lest innocent blood be shed in the midst of your land which the LORD your God is giving you *as* an inheritance, and *thus* guilt of bloodshed be upon you.

a. **Now if the LORD your God enlarges your territory**: As Israel expanded, there were to be more cities of refuge. If a city of refuge was too far to be readily reached by the manslayer, it would do him no good. The avenger of blood would overtake him before he could reach the city of refuge.

i. "Even under David and Solomon, this did not occur; so the third set of cities of refuge was never appointed." (Kalland)

b. **Then you shall add three more cities for yourself**: Ultimately, there were to be six cities of refuge; with three on each side of the Jordan River. Each of the three cities on either side would be positioned as north, central, and south.

i. Joshua 20:7-8 tells of the actual cities chosen, and they fulfilled the plan of being evenly distributed across the territory of Israel.

4. (11-13) What to do with the guilty who seeks protection in the city of refuge: **your eye shall not pity him**.

"But if anyone hates his neighbor, lies in wait for him, rises against him and strikes him mortally, so that he dies, and he flees to one of these cities, then the elders of his city shall send and bring him from there, and deliver him over to the hand of the avenger of blood, that he may die. Your eye shall not pity him, but you shall put away *the guilt of* **innocent blood from Israel, that it may go well with you.**

a. **But if anyone hates his neighbor, lies in wait for him, rises against him and strikes him mortally**: The city of refuge was never intended to protect the person who was truly guilty of murder. It is easy to imagine that someone who was truly guilty of murder would seek protection in the city of refuge. Therefore, whenever a manslayer came to seek protection at a city of refuge, **the elders of the city** were to judge his case and determine if he was truly worthy of protection.

b. **Deliver him over to the hand of the avenger of blood**: If, after an investigation, it was determined at his trial that the man was truly guilty of murder, then he would be delivered **to the hand of the avenger of blood, that he may die**. There was no protection for the guilty within the walls of a city of refuge, only for the innocent.

i. "So heinous was murder its penalty was to be inflicted without pity or compassion of any kind. The reason is that humankind is the image of God (cf. Gen 1:27; 9:6) and therefore murder was deemed to be an assault on God himself, an ultimate act of insubordination and rebellion (Gen 9:5–6)." (Merrill)

c. **Put away the guilt of innocent blood from Israel, that it may go well with you**: God was just as concerned that the *guilty* be punished as He was that the *innocent* be protected (*lest innocent blood be shed in the midst of your land*, Deuteronomy 19:10).

5. The cities of refuge as a picture of Jesus.

a. The Bible applies this picture of the city of refuge to the believer finding refuge in God on more than one occasion:

i. Psalm 46:1: *God is our refuge and strength, A very present help in trouble.* More than 15 other times, the psalms speak of God as being our refuge.

ii. Hebrews 6:18 also explains, *that by two immutable things, in which it is impossible for God to lie, we might have strong consolation, who have fled for refuge to lay hold of the hope set before us.*

b. There are many points of similarity between the cities of refuge and the refuge that the believer finds in Jesus Christ.

- The cities of refuge were *within easy reach* of the needy person; they were of no use unless someone could get to the place of refuge. This is also true of the refuge the believer finds in Jesus Christ.
- The cities of refuge were *open to all*, not just the Israelite; no one needed to fear they would be turned away from their place of refuge in their time of need (Numbers 35:15). This is also true of the refuge the believer finds in Jesus Christ.
- The cities of refuge became a place where the one in need would *live*. Someone in need didn't come to a city of refuge to casually visit (Numbers 35:25). This is also true of the refuge the believer finds in Jesus Christ.
- The cities of refuge were the *only alternative* for the one in need; without this specific protection, they would be destroyed. This is also true of the refuge the believer finds in Jesus Christ.
- The cities of refuge provide protection *only within their boundaries*; to go outside meant death (Numbers 35:26-28). This is also true of the refuge the believer finds in Jesus Christ.
- With the cities of refuge, full freedom came with the *death of the High Priest* (Numbers 35:25). This is also true of the refuge the believer finds in Jesus Christ.

c. There is a crucial distinction between Israel's cities of refuge and the refuge the believer finds in Jesus Christ.

- The cities of refuge only helped the *innocent*, but the *guilty* can come to Jesus and find refuge.

B. Other legal principles.

1. (14) The principle of the landmark.

"You shall not remove your neighbor's landmark, which the men of old have set, in your inheritance which you will inherit in the land that the LORD your God is giving you to possess.

a. **You shall not remove your neighbor's landmark**: When Israel possessed the land of Canaan, they would divide the land by tribes, clans, and families. These individual plots of land would be distinguished by a **landmark**, normally a stone property boundary marker. To move your **neighbor's landmark** was to enlarge your own property, and to steal your neighbor's property. These boundary markers were to be respected and not moved.

> i. "Before the extensive use of fences, landed property was marked out by *stones* or *posts*, set up so as to ascertain the divisions of family estates. It was easy to remove one of these landmarks, and set it in a different place; and thus the dishonest man enlarged his own estate by contracting that of his neighbour." (Clarke)
>
> ii. "The right to hold property was a cornerstone of Israel's inheritance from the Lord. It is still a primary right of free people on the earth, and without it freedom is greatly limited." (Kalland)
>
> iii. "No man was to remove an ancient landmark. The far-reaching importance of this will be understood when it is remembered how absolutely man depends on the land for physical sustenance." (Morgan)
>
> iv. This command reinforced the eighth commandment, *you shall not steal* (Exodus 20:15). This both established and supported the basic right to private property. The land of Israel ultimately belonged to God, but He distributed it to Israel by tribe, clan, and family. Individual plots of land belonged to one family and did not belong to another family.
>
> v. This command supports an important foundation for human society: The right to personal property. God has clearly entrusted certain possessions to certain individuals, and other people or states are not permitted to take that property without due process of law.
>
> vi. This command is repeated in the wisdom of the Proverbs: *Do not remove the ancient landmark, which your fathers have set* (Proverbs 22:28).

b. **Which the men of old have set**: This law also reflects an important spiritual principle: It isn't wise to ignore what the **men of old have set** in life, and especially when doing the work of the LORD. Many a young man, or a new man, has greatly hindered his own work by being a revolutionary – and ignoring the "landmarks" which the **men of old have set**.

> i. A **landmark** – a custom, a tradition, or a value – should not be removed lightly. We should never assume that **men of old** set such landmarks for no reason or for a bad reason. We should not defend tradition for the sake of tradition, but neither should we destroy tradition just for the sake of destroying it.

2. (15-20) The requirements for testimony and witnesses.

"One witness shall not rise against a man concerning any iniquity or any sin that he commits; by the mouth of two or three witnesses the matter shall be established. If a false witness rises against any man to testify against him of wrongdoing, then both men in the controversy shall stand before the LORD, before the priests and the judges who serve in those days. And the judges shall make careful inquiry, and indeed, *if* the witness *is* a false witness, who has testified falsely against his brother, then you shall do to him as he thought to have done to his brother; so you shall put away the evil from among you. And those who remain shall hear and fear, and hereafter they shall not again commit such evil among you.

> a. **One witness shall not rise**: In the system of law God established for ancient Israel, one witness was never enough to convict an accused person. One needed **two or three witness** to confirm the guilt of the accused.
>
>> i. This wasn't only because it was possible for one witness to lie without having their story corroborated. It was also because one witness can be confused or mistaken in their testimony. This is a basic standard of evidence, lifting accusations above a standard of "my word against theirs."
>>
>> ii. In this context, a witness can also be an independent line of evidence. Clear physical evidence from a crime (such as the ancient equivalent of fingerprints on a murder weapon) can serve as a witness.
>>
>> iii. "Even Jezebel knew that she had to hire more than one witness to testify against Naboth if her case were to have any merit (1 Kgs 21:10, 13)." (Merrill)
>
> b. **If a false witness rises against any man to testify**: A **false witness** was to be discovered by careful examination (**the judges shall make careful inquiry**) and was to be punished by giving the false witness the same penalty which would have gone to the man he falsely accused (**you shall do to him as he thought to have done to his brother**).
>
>> i. **You shall do to him as he thought to have done to his brother**: "Nothing can be more equitable or proper than this, that if a man endeavour to do any injury to or take away the life of another, on detection he shall be caused to undergo the same evil which he intended for his innocent neighbour. Some of our excellent English laws have been made on this very ground." (Clarke)
>>
>> ii. At the trial of Jesus, many false witnesses testified against Him, and were demonstrated to be false witnesses by their confused and contradictory testimony (Matthew 26:59-60). Those false witnesses,

under Jewish law, should have been put to death, because that was the punishment they sought for Jesus.

c. **And those who remain shall hear and fear**: In the present day, it is often doubted that the just punishment of others is an effective deterrent to crime, but the Bible clearly says that it is. Weak, delayed, or inconsistent punishment does not deter crime, but effective punishment does.

i. "Others' woes should be our warnings, others' sufferings our sermons, yea, standing sermons (1 Corinthians 10:5-12). God's house of correction is the school of instruction." (Trapp)

3. (21) A basic legal principle: **eye for eye, tooth for tooth**.

Your eye shall not pity: life *shall be* for life, eye for eye, tooth for tooth, hand for hand, foot for foot.

a. **Your eye shall not pity**: This was an important principle for the biblical court of law, here connected to the punishment described for false witness. In this immediate context, it means that the penalty for false witness should be carried out.

i. It is a pity that this law were not still in force: it would certainly prevent many of those savage acts which now both disgrace and injure society." (Clarke)

b. **Life shall be for life, eye for eye**: However, justice was always limited by the **eye for eye** principle. An individual or a mob may want to inflict a greater judgment, but the law was not to be used to satisfy the desire for revenge.

i. It is common to want to do *more* against the offending party than what they had done against their victim. Under God's law, punishment was not to come from the motive of revenge, only from the motive of justice.

ii. "Far from encouraging vengeance it limits vengeance and stands as a guide for a judge as he fixes a penalty suited to the crime. The principle was thus not license or vengeance, but a guarantee of justice." (Thompson)

c. **Eye for eye, tooth for tooth**: In Matthew 5:38-39, Jesus quoted this passage in His teaching on the true interpretation of the law. Jesus did not say that the **eye for eye** principle was wrong; rather, He simply condemned the use of it to create an *obligation* to carry out revenge against someone who had *personally* offended an individual.

i. Many Rabbis in Jesus' day taught that the **eye for eye** law meant that people were obligated to avenge themselves of a personal insult or attack. Jesus rightly disallowed the application of this law in personal relationships. This was a law intended to guide the judges of Israel in the work of their law courts, not to guide personal relationships.

ii. "Jesus' criticism of this law (Mt. 5:38f.) arose from its use to regulate conduct between individuals. He did not reject it as a principle of justice which should operate in the courts of the land. For private relationships He proposed the ideal of brotherhood, a strong principle throughout the book of Deuteronomy. To extend the *lex talionis* [eye for an eye principle] to this interpersonal domain was to destroy the law of God." (Thompson)

Deuteronomy 20 – Instructions Concerning Warfare

A. The spiritual and practical preparation of the army.

1. (1) The command to trust in God.

"When you go out to battle against your enemies, and see horses and chariots *and* people more numerous than you, do not be afraid of them; for the LORD your God *is* with you, who brought you up from the land of Egypt.

> a. **When you go out to battle against your enemies**: Israel, a relatively small nation surrounded by great empires, rarely had a superior military compared to their rivals. In battle, they usually fought against **horses and chariots** and **people more numerous** than Israel.
>
> b. **Do not be afraid of them**: Despite the disadvantages Israel normally faced, they also had a clear command from God to not fear. Israel was commanded to not fear what any smart military man *would* normally fear: superior numbers, superior technology, and superior equipment.
>
> c. **For the LORD your God is with you**: God gave Israel a *reason* to not be afraid. God did not deny that the enemies of Israel would usually have more horses, chariots, and people than Israel. But God asked them to recognize a greater fact: That **the LORD…God** was **with** Israel.
>
>> i. In spiritual application, Paul explained this principle in Romans 8:31: *If God is for us, who can be against us?* One with God makes an unbeatable majority.
>>
>> ii. This implies that Israel fought in wars at God's direction. "Divine assistance could not be expected in wars which were not undertaken by the Divine command." (Clarke)
>
> d. **Who brought you up from the land of Egypt**: Israel was also given *evidence* for their faith. God didn't ask Israel to have a blind, uninformed trust in Him. They could trust Him as they went into battle because He had

proven Himself mighty and faithful before. The LORD had demonstrated that He could be trusted.

> i. God delivered Israel when Pharaoh came against them with **horses and chariots** at the Red Sea (Exodus 14:26-28). Israel did not need to fear enemies equipped with horses and chariots.

2. (2-4) The command to encourage people before battle.

So it shall be, when you are on the verge of battle, that the priest shall approach and speak to the people. And he shall say to them, 'Hear, O Israel: Today you are on the verge of battle with your enemies. Do not let your heart faint, do not be afraid, and do not tremble or be terrified because of them; for the LORD your God *is* He who goes with you, to fight for you against your enemies, to save you.'

> a. **When you are on the verge of battle**: At the critical time before the battle, it was the duty of the **priest** to encourage the soldiers to trust in God. Priests were not normally to go into battle themselves, in that they were not numbered among the fighting men of Israel (Numbers 1:47-53). Yet the priests still had an important job when Israel went to war – to teach and encourage the soldiers.
>
>> i. The believer is not called to the same kind of warfare Israel faced in their conquest of Canaan. For the Christian, their warfare is not against flesh and blood, but against spiritual powers (Ephesians 6:12-13). Yet even as ancient Israel was encouraged by the **priest** before battle, so should the believer today be encouraged by Jesus Christ, their High Priest (Hebrews 4:14-16) and the captain of their salvation (Hebrews 2:10). In spiritual warfare, the believer should look first to Jesus Christ.
>
> b. **The LORD your God is He who goes with you, to fight for you against your enemies, to save you**: This was the reason for courage. When Israel was obedient and trusting in God, they would not be defeated in battle. But when they were disobedient or not trusting, they could not win in battle, even if they had superior forces.
>
>> i. **To fight for you**: "Though God promised them such protection, yet they were to expect it in the diligent use of their own prudence and industry. The priests, the officers, and the people, had their respective parts to act in this business; if they did their duty respectively, God would take care that they should be successful. Those who will not help themselves with the strength which God has already given them, shall not have any farther assistance from him. In all such cases, the parable of the *talents* affords an accurate rule." (Clarke)

3. (5-9) How to shrink an army and make it more effective.

"Then the officers shall speak to the people, saying: 'What man *is there* who has built a new house and has not dedicated it? Let him go and return to his house, lest he die in the battle and another man dedicate it. Also what man *is there* who has planted a vineyard and has not eaten of it? Let him go and return to his house, lest he die in the battle and another man eat of it. And what man *is there* who is betrothed to a woman and has not married her? Let him go and return to his house, lest he die in the battle and another man marry her.'

"The officers shall speak further to the people, and say, 'What man *is there who is* fearful and fainthearted? Let him go and return to his house, lest the heart of his brethren faint like his heart.' And so it shall be, when the officers have finished speaking to the people, that they shall make captains of the armies to lead the people.

a. **What man is there who has built a new house and has not dedicated it?** God first told the **officers** of the Israelite army to send home all the soldiers who had unfinished business at home. This could include a home the soldier had not used, a vineyard he had not harvested, or an engaged woman he had not married. Those soldiers were told to go home.

i. "In each of these instances death in war resulted in the dispossession of blessing and its appropriation by someone else who otherwise had no just claim to it." (Merrill)

ii. "This privilege might encourage men to build and plant, which is good and profitable for the commonwealth, as the apostle speaketh in a like case (Titus 3:8)." (Trapp)

iii. **Dedicated it**: The phrasing here implies something sacred about a family home. According to Merrill, this verb was also used for Solomon's dedication of the temple (1 Kings 8:63, 2 Chronicles 7:5), the consecration of the altar (2 Chronicles 7:9), and the walls of Jerusalem (Nehemiah 12:27). "In all cases there are strong religious overtones, suggesting that what was being done was a sacred ceremony before the Lord." (Merrill)

b. **What man is there who is fearful and fainthearted?** Next, the officers of Israel were to send home all the soldiers who were **fearful and fainthearted**. Their fear and lack of courage might have a bad influence on the other soldiers. In His service, God only wants willing and courageous soldiers.

c. **When the officers have finished speaking to the people**: Though the exceptions made Israel's army smaller, this was God's command. All the exemptions – remarkable among any army – were a powerful testimony that Israel trusted in Yahweh for military victory, not in their own ability to raise a mighty, large army.

>i. To God, the *size* of the army was not more important than the *heart* of the army. Yahweh didn't want soldiers who might be distracted by worries about the cares of everyday life (their home, their vineyard, their fiancée); nor did Yahweh want people who did not really trust Him. God could do more through a *smaller* army that was truly committed to Him than through a *bigger* army that was full of compromise.

>ii. The story of Gideon (Judges 7) is a powerful illustration of this principle. Gideon started with an army of 32,000, but it was too big – so he sent home those who were afraid, and 22,000 departed. But the army was still too big, so God had Gideon send home 7,700 more, so he only had an army of 300 to fight against a Midianite army of 135,000. Despite their small numbers, God gave Gideon and Israel victory in battle.

d. **Make captains of the armies to lead the people**: God commanded that His army have leadership. Their trust in God and His promise of blessing did not eliminate their need for good leadership.

B. Instructions for battle.

1. (10-11) The offer of peace.

"When you go near a city to fight against it, then proclaim an offer of peace to it. And it shall be that if they accept your offer of peace, and open to you, then all the people *who are* found in it shall be placed under tribute to you, and serve you.

a. **When you go near a city to fight against it**: The following verses describe the normal battle procedures for Israel. There were many times when God gave specific instructions which would supersede these normal instructions, such as with the battle of Jericho or the conquest of Canaan in general.

>i. This begins a section where Yahweh told Israel how to conduct war. There are, in God's way of doing things, rules for war. It cannot be conducted in any way conceivable or in any way that might bring victory. These principles were later reflected in the ancient Christian teachings regarding just war.

b. **Proclaim an offer of peace**: It was important that Israel did not fight unnecessarily. If the city they fought against would agree to terms of peace, then they should come to an agreement.

c. **It shall be placed under tribute to you**: The conquered city would be made a tribute city to Israel, subservient to the people of God.

2. (12-15) Conquering a city through siege and battle.

Now if *the city* will not make peace with you, but makes war against you, then you shall besiege it. And when the LORD your God delivers it into your hands, you shall strike every male in it with the edge of the sword. But the women, the little ones, the livestock, and all that is in the city, all its spoil, you shall plunder for yourself; and you shall eat the enemies' plunder which the LORD your God gives you. Thus you shall do to all the cities *which are* very far from you, which *are* not of the cities of these nations.

    a. **You shall besiege it**: Typically, a walled city was conquered by use of the *siege*. Enemy armies surrounded a city and cut off all their supplies and contact with the outside world. When the city was sufficiently weakened through hunger or thirst, they either surrendered or were conquered. Sometimes a siege would last for years.

        i. There are a few terrible sieges described in the Scriptures, such as a siege of Samaria in 2 Kings 6:24-33.

    b. **You shall strike every male**: Cities that were **very far** from Israel and refused Israel's terms of surrender established themselves as chronic enemies of Israel and Yahweh, the God of Israel. Having rejected their chance at a peaceful resolution, every soldier or potential soldier would be put to death.

        i. "The death of the men was not only to induce other cities to a more ready submission to Israel but to prevent future uprising in the city that had just been taken." (Merrill)

        ii. This kind of warfare was rare. Israel did not often send their army **very far** and lay siege against other cities.

    c. **You shall plunder for yourself**: Plunder provided the wages for the army in ancient warfare and underwrote the expenses for the battle. There were times when the army of Israel was specifically prohibited from taking plunder in battle (as in Joshua 6:17-19), but normally **plunder** was allowed.

3. (16-18) The command to destroy the Canaanites.

"But of the cities of these peoples which the LORD your God gives you *as* an inheritance, you shall let nothing that breathes remain alive, but you shall utterly destroy them: the Hittite and the Amorite and the Canaanite and the Perizzite and the Hivite and the Jebusite, just as the LORD your God has commanded you, lest they teach you to do according

to all their abominations which they have done for their gods, and you sin against the LORD your God.

> a. **You shall let nothing that breathes remain**: The previous commands regarding warfare did not apply to the upcoming conquest of Canaan. There, not only was Israel not to offer peace to the cities, but they were also to destroy everything, not only the adult males. This was a unique war of judgment, more than a war of conquest or defense.
>
>> i. "All the inhabitants that remained in the conquered cities of Canaan were to be completely destroyed so that Israel would not be enticed into the supreme sin of defecting from the Lord and turning to the worship of other gods." (Kalland)
>>
>> ii. Adam Clarke suggested that **you shall utterly destroy them** be translated, "*thou shalt utterly subdue them*—slaying them if they resist, and thus leaving nothing alive that breathed; or *totally expel them from the land*, or reduce them to a state of slavery in it, that they might no longer exist as a *people*." Using the examples of the Gibeonites (Joshua 9) and Rahab (Joshua 2), Clarke suggests "it does not appear that the Israelites believed that they were bound to put every Canaanite *to death*." Clarke believed this command was for the destruction of the Canaanites as organized nations occupying the land.
>>
>> iii. John Trapp made an interesting speculation regarding the Canaanite tribes listed here: "The Girgashites are not reckoned among the rest, as neither are they in Joshua 9:1, haply because they accepted of conditions of peace."
>
> b. **Lest they teach you to do according to their abominations which they have done for their gods**: This explains why such a complete destruction was commanded. The culture of the Canaanites was so corrupt – socially, morally, and spiritually – that God considered it irredeemable, and ripe for judgment. In this unique war, the armies of Israel were to bring God's judgment upon the Canaanites.

4. (19-20) The command to save trees for food during a siege.

"When you besiege a city for a long time, while making war against it to take it, you shall not destroy its trees by wielding an ax against them; if you can eat of them, do not cut them down to use in the siege, for the tree of the field *is* man's *food*. Only the trees which you know *are* not trees for food you may destroy and cut down, to build siegeworks against the city that makes war with you, until it is subdued.

> a. **When you besiege a city for a long time**: When an army surrounded a city during a siege, the army would forage around the countryside for

supplies. Needing wood for building and fuel, it would be common for the besieging army to cut down trees in the area around the city.

b. **Only the trees which you know are not trees for food you may destroy and cut down**: However, God commanded Israel against cutting down **trees for food** when they besieged a city. They had to take a long-term view (one good for the ecology) and see that their immediate need for wood was less important than the long-term good of the area. This is another example of how God did not allow Israel to conduct total war or win a battle at any cost.

i. "It was a merciful provision to spare all fruit-bearing trees, because they yielded the fruit which supported man's life; and it was sound policy also, for even the conquerors must perish if the means of life were cut off." (Clarke)

ii. "Had this law been observed by invaders throughout the centuries, Palestine today would not be so denuded of trees." (Thompson)

Deuteronomy 21 – Various Laws

A. The law of unsolved murders.

1. (1) The presence of an unsolved murder.

"If *anyone* is found slain, lying in the field in the land which the LORD your God is giving you to possess, *and* it is not known who killed him,

> a. **If anyone is found slain**: Presumably, this deals with a case where death from natural causes had been ruled out and it was evident that the deceased had been murdered. Yet, it was **not known who killed him**.
>
> b. **It is not known who killed him**: An unsolved murder was important for Israel to deal with because of a principle stated in Numbers 35:33-34. That passage shows that the blood of unsolved, unavenged murder defiled and polluted the land. Therefore, if there is a murder unavenged, some kind of cleansing was necessary, so the land would not be defiled.

2. (2-6) The procedure for atoning for murder-polluted land.

Then your elders and your judges shall go out and measure *the distance* from the slain man to the surrounding cities. And it shall be *that* the elders of the city nearest to the slain man will take a heifer which has not been worked *and* which has not pulled with a yoke. The elders of that city shall bring the heifer down to a valley with flowing water, which is neither plowed nor sown, and they shall break the heifer's neck there in the valley. Then the priests, the sons of Levi, shall come near, for the LORD your God has chosen them to minister to Him and to bless in the name of the LORD; by their word every controversy and every assault shall be *settled*. And all the elders of that city nearest to the slain *man* shall wash their hands over the heifer whose neck was broken in the valley.

> a. **The elders of the city nearest to the slain man**: First, the matter of jurisdiction had to be settled. Measurements would be made, and the

elders of the city closest to the scene of the crime were responsible to sacrifice a heifer to atone for and cleanse the land polluted by murder.

b. **A heifer which has not been worked**: Then, appropriate sacrifice had to be made. This **heifer** was sacrificed by the **priests** in the presence of the city elders, who washed their hands over the sacrificed animal.

> i. "The heifer, the valley and the water were undefiled, because they had never been contaminated by common use." (Thompson)

> ii. This washing of the hands, done in the presence of the **priests**, who **by their word every controversy and every assault shall be settled**, was a powerful proclamation by the elders: "We have done all we could to settle this case, but cannot. We are clean from all guilt in the matter of this slain man."

> iii. "The act of washing hands as a sign of exculpation is known elsewhere in the Old Testament (cf. Pss 26:6; 73:13)." (Merrill)

> iv. Of course, this *ceremony* of washing the hands over the sacrificed animal meant nothing if the elders had in fact *not* done what they could to avenge the murder. Apart from that, this washing of the hands was just as much an empty gesture as Pilate's washing of his hands at the trial of Jesus (Matthew 27:24).

3. (7-9) The prayer said by the elders as they washed their hands.

Then they shall answer and say, 'Our hands have not shed this blood, nor have our eyes seen *it*. Provide atonement, O LORD, for Your people Israel, whom You have redeemed, and do not lay innocent blood to the charge of Your people Israel.' And atonement shall be provided on their behalf for the blood. So you shall put away the *guilt of* innocent blood from among you when you do *what is* right in the sight of the LORD.

a. **Provide atonement, O LORD**: Again, Numbers 35:33-34 makes the principle clear, that unavenged murders defile and pollute the land and atonement must be made for the land itself.

> i. "Though the word *kapar* ('atone') appears twice in v.8, the atonement mentioned is not an atonement within the sacrificial system; for the blood of the heifer was not offered. It is rather an atonement for justice; the heifer suffered death in place of the unknown criminal, in order to clear the land of guilt." (Kalland)

> ii. "Possibly the meaning of the ritual was that, since the murderer could not be found, an animal was put to death in place of the murderer (cf. Exod. 13:13), i.e. a kind of ceremonial judicial execution took place

in which the heifer served as a substitute for the unknown murderer." (Thompson)

b. **So you shall put away the guilt of innocent blood**: When Israel followed God's instructions for atonement, He honored His word by taking away their guilt. But the removal of guilt was always based on blood sacrifice, on a substitutionary atonement – looking forward to the work of Jesus on the cross for the entire world.

B. Laws relevant to family and home situations.

1. (10-14) Laws regarding the taking of a wife from conquered peoples.

"When you go out to war against your enemies, and the LORD your God delivers them into your hand, and you take them captive, and you see among the captives a beautiful woman, and desire her and would take her for your wife, then you shall bring her home to your house, and she shall shave her head and trim her nails. She shall put off the clothes of her captivity, remain in your house, and mourn her father and her mother a full month; after that you may go in to her and be her husband, and she shall be your wife. And it shall be, if you have no delight in her, then you shall set her free, but you certainly shall not sell her for money; you shall not treat her brutally, because you have humbled her.

a. **And you see among the captives a beautiful woman, and desire her**: In the ancient world, it was not uncommon for a man to take a wife from **among the captives**, especially if she was **a beautiful woman**. Yet obviously, this custom could be used to terribly abuse the captive women. For this reason, God gave specific commands to govern this practice in Israel.

i. "Women taken prisoner as a result of conquest could be taken as wives by Israelites, another indication that they were not from among the Canaanite nations (v. 11; cf. Exod 34:16; Deut 7:3)." (Merrill)

ii. "No forcible possession was allowed even in this case, when the woman was taken in war, and was, by the general consent of ancient nations, adjudged as a part of the spoils." (Clarke)

b. **Shave her head and trim her nails**: First, the captive woman had to be *purified and humbled*. This denoted a complete break with her past, and the willingness to start anew, humbly as a child.

i. **Shave her head**: "This was in token of her renouncing her religion, and becoming a proselyte to that of the Jews. This is still a custom in the East; when a Christian turns Mohammedan his head is shaven." (Clarke)

c. **Put off the clothes of her captivity, remain in your house**: Second, the captive woman had to show a *change of allegiance*. This showed that the captive woman no longer regarded her former nation and her former family; now she was a citizen of Israel.

i. "Certainly the change of garments suggests a change of status." (Thompson)

d. **Mourn her father and mother a full month**: Third, the captive woman had to *mourn her past associations*. This would be time when she could resolve issues in her heart regarding her family, and when her husband-to-be could live with her a month without intimate relations. In this time, he could see if he really wanted to take this woman as a wife, and to make sure he was not deciding based only on her attractiveness.

i. Taken together, all these requirements imply the willingness of the woman. "This presupposes a degree of willingness on the part of the maiden to forsake the past and to embrace a new and different way of life, for one can hardly conceive of all this taking place coercively." (Merrill)

e. **You certainly shall not sell her for money; you shall not treat her brutally**: After the month of mourning, the potential husband was free to marry the captive woman – yet, he did not have to. But if he decided not to, he had to set her free with dignity. All this together provided remarkable protection of the rights of a captive woman.

i. "The relationship rested on a legal basis. If it were dissolved, the woman's social status was not to be impaired. She was not a slave to be sold, but was free to go where she wished." (Thompson)

2. (15-17) The protection of inheritance rights.

"If a man has two wives, one loved and the other unloved, and they have borne him children, *both* the loved and the unloved, and *if* the firstborn son is of her who is unloved, then it shall be, on the day he bequeaths his possessions to his sons, *that* he must not bestow firstborn status on the son of the loved wife in preference to the son of the unloved, the *true* firstborn. But he shall acknowledge the son of the unloved wife *as* the firstborn by giving him a double portion of all that he has, for he *is* the beginning of his strength; the right of the firstborn *is* his."

a. **If a man has two wives**: Obviously, there were going to be problems in a home like this, especially if one wife was **loved** and the other was **unloved**.

Yet, God commanded that the inheritance rights of the firstborn son be respected, even if he were the son of the **unloved** wife.

b. **A double portion of all that he has**: This was the **right of the firstborn** in ancient Israel. The firstborn son was to receive twice as much inheritance as any other son. For example, if there were three sons, the inheritance would be divided into four parts, with the firstborn receiving two parts, and the other two sons each receiving one part.

i. "This rule was not followed in the case of Solomon." (Kalland)

ii. A **double portion**: "According to this phrase, Elisha (2 Kings 2:9) doth not desire a greater measure of the spirit than rested upon his master; but only to excel the other children of the prophets by a right of primogeniture." (Trapp)

3. (18-21) The penalty for a rebellious son.

"If a man has a stubborn and rebellious son who will not obey the voice of his father or the voice of his mother, and *who*, when they have chastened him, will not heed them, then his father and his mother shall take hold of him and bring him out to the elders of his city, to the gate of his city. And they shall say to the elders of his city, 'This son of ours is stubborn and rebellious; he will not obey our voice; he is a glutton and a drunkard.' Then all the men of his city shall stone him to death with stones; so you shall put away the evil from among you, and all Israel shall hear and fear.

a. **A stubborn and rebellious son**: This does not mean a small child, or even a young teen – but a son past the age of accountability, who set himself in determined rebellion against his father and mother.

i. **Stubborn** and **rebellious**: These words "occur paired together in Jer 5:23 where Israelite wickedness, which was bringing on the destruction of the nation, is described. In Ps 78:8 the forefathers who were not loyal to God are called 'a stubborn and rebellious generation.'" (Kalland)

ii. **Glutton** and a **drunkard**: "The two vices occur together elsewhere (cf. Prov 23:20–21) and apparently serve as a cliché for self-indulgence and lack of constructive activity." (Merrill)

b. **Who, when they have chastened him, will not heed them**: To call a rebellious son to account as described in this passage, the parents must have done a good job raising the son, calling him to obedience, and disciplining him as appropriate before the LORD.

c. **Bring him out to the elders of his city**: Such a **stubborn and rebellious son** was to be put on trial before the elders of the city. If they determined him to be chronically rebellious, then the son was to be stoned to death.

i. It is important to note that the parents could not, by themselves, carry out this penalty. They had to bring the son on trial before impartial judges. This contrasts with ancient Greek and Roman law, which gave fathers the absolute right of life or death over their children. This was a *control* of parental authority more than it was an *exercise* of it.

ii. "If the elders found the man guilty, the sentence was death by stoning. The parents were not required to participate, perhaps out of a sense of delicacy, although more likely in order to stress the point that the power of life and death over their children was not theirs." (Thompson)

iii. The parents had to take the boy to the elders of the community; not only because the decision of life or death should be taken out of their direct hands, but because the sin of the **stubborn and rebellious son** was not only against his parents, but against the whole community. His rebellion against his parents sowed the seeds for cultural ruin in Israel.

d. **And all Israel shall hear and fear**: This law was clearly intended to protect the social order of ancient Israel. No society can endure when the young are allowed to make war against the old.

i. Perhaps just the presence of this law was deterrent enough; we never have a Scriptural example of a son being stoned to death because of these commands in the Law of Moses.

ii. "Yet the Jews say this law was never put into practice, and therefore it might be made for terror and prevention, and to render the authority of parents more sacred and powerful." (Poole)

iii. "Stoning was the punishment appointed for blasphemers and idolaters; which if it seem severe, it is to be considered that parents are in God's stead, and entrusted in good measure with his authority over their children; and that families are the matter and foundation of the church and commonwealth, and they who are naughty members and rebellious children in them, do commonly prove the bane and plague of these, and therefore no wonder if they are nipped in the bud." (Poole)

iv. "If such a law were in force now, and duly executed, how many deaths of disobedient and profligate children would there be in all corners of the land!" (Clarke)

4. (22-23) The curse upon one who hangs on a tree.

"If a man has committed a sin deserving of death, and he is put to death, and you hang him on a tree, his body shall not remain overnight on the tree, but you shall surely bury him that day, so that you do not defile the land which the LORD your God is giving you *as* an inheritance; for he who is hanged *is* accursed of God.

a. **And you hang him on a tree**: In the thinking of ancient Israel there was something worse than being put to death. The worse fate was to die and have your corpse left exposed to shame, humiliation, and to scavenging animals and birds.

i. **Hang him on a tree** does not have the idea of being executed by strangulation but of having the corpse mounted on a tree or other prominent place. This would expose the executed one to disgrace and the elements.

b. **His body shall not remain overnight on the tree, but you shall surely bury him that day**: Therefore, if anyone was executed and deemed worthy of such disgrace (being hanged **on a tree**), the humiliation to his memory and his family must not be excessive. This was a way of tempering even the most severe judgment with mercy.

i. "The presence of the corpse hanging up to the public gaze, with crime, as it were, clinging to it and God's curse resting on it, might result in untold calamities. Hence as soon as the necessary amount of publicity had been achieved and other likely offenders had been warned, the corpse was buried, and that before sunset." (Thompson)

ii. "Its exposure for the space of *one day* was judged sufficient.... It is worthy of remark that in the infliction of punishment prescribed by the Mosaic law, we ever find that *Mercy* walks hand in hand with *Judgment*." (Clarke)

c. **For he who is hanged is accursed of God**: The punishment of being hanged on a tree, and left to open exposure, was thought to be so severe, that it was reserved only for those for which it was to be declared, "this one is **accursed of God**."

i. "The man was accursed of God because he was hanged on a tree. He was hanged on the tree because he was accursed of God. The hanging was the outward sign of the curse upon him." (Morgan)

ii. Paul expounded on Deuteronomy 21:23 in Galatians 3:13-14: *Christ has redeemed us from the curse of the law, having become a curse for us (for it is written, "Cursed is everyone who hangs on a tree"), that the blessing of Abraham might come upon the Gentiles in Christ Jesus, that we might receive the promise of the Spirit through faith.*

iii. Jesus not only died in the place of His people; but He also took their place as the **accursed of God**, being hanged on a "tree" in open shame and degradation. He received this curse, which believers deserved, and He did not, so that His people could receive the *blessing of Abraham*, which He deserved, and believers did not.

iv. "But He became sin for us; cursed, that we might be blessed; cast out, that we might be for ever welcomed; naked, that we might be clothed; hungry, that we might feed on his flesh; poor, that we might be enriched; dying, that we might live beyond the range of the curse for evermore." (Meyer)

v. God's people are *redeemed from the curse of the law* by the work of Jesus on the cross in their place. Believers no longer need to fear that God will curse them. God wants to *bless* His people, not because of who they are, or what they have done, but because of what Jesus Christ has done on behalf of believers.

Deuteronomy 22 – Various Laws

A. Laws to demonstrate kindness and purity.

1. (1-4) Kindness to your brother regarding his animals and lost property.

"You shall not see your brother's ox or his sheep going astray, and hide yourself from them; you shall certainly bring them back to your brother. And if your brother *is* not near you, or if you do not know him, then you shall bring it to your own house, and it shall remain with you until your brother seeks it; then you shall restore it to him. You shall do the same with his donkey, and so shall you do with his garment; with any lost thing of your brother's, which he has lost and you have found, you shall do likewise; you must not hide yourself.

"You shall not see your brother's donkey or his ox fall down along the road, and hide yourself from them; you shall surely help him lift *them* up again.

> a. **You shall not see…and hide yourself**: God here condemned the sin of doing *nothing*. To see your brother in need, and to do nothing, is to do evil. When people can do good, then they **must not hide**.
>
> > i. "In these words we discover an element of responsibility which outruns all ordinary standards of righteousness. According to it, we are not only responsible that we do no harm to our fellow-men; we are also responsible to prevent harm from being done to them when it is in our power to do so." (Morgan)
> >
> > ii. "The priest and the Levite, when they saw the wounded man, passed by on the other side of the way, Luke 10:31, 32. This was a notorious breach of the merciful law mentioned." (Clarke)
>
> b. **Until your brother seeks it; then you shall restore it to him**: When something is lost (here the examples are of a **donkey** and a **garment**), a finder cannot claim it as their possession without taking proper effort to

restore it to the owner. If the owner seeks the missing object, it must be restored to him.

> i. Exodus 23:4-5 also commands Israel to help recover stray animals but extends the obligation to the stray animals of an *enemy*, not only a brother.
>
> ii. "The implication is that animals left to roam would eventually become prey to harm or death by the elements or at the hand of unscrupulous thieves." (Merrill)

c. **You shall surely help him lift them up again**: Moses gave another command with an example of how God wanted His people to treat each other. If someone's donkey fell, and another had the ability to help them, then they must. To pass by a brother in need and to **hide yourself from them** was to sin against the brother and against God.

> i. "While the succinct statement of Leviticus 19:18b, 'You shall love your neighbour as yourself', does not occur in Deuteronomy, it is implied here and in many parts of the book. The covenant law was comprehensive in its demand for love, love for God and love for one's fellows." (Thompson)

2. (5) A command to keep distinction between the sexes in clothing.

"A woman shall not wear anything that pertains to a man, nor shall a man put on a woman's garment, for all who do so *are* an abomination to the LORD your God.

a. **Anything that pertains to a man**: In Old Testament times, men and women wore clothing that was superficially similar – long robes and wrapping garments were worn by both sexes. Yet, the specific types of garments and the way in which they were worn made a clear distinction between the sexes, and this command instructs God's people to respect those distinctions.

> i. This command reflects a principle that is of great issue in the early 21st century: the importance of maintaining gender distinctions, and the outward signs of gender distinctions. A man should not dress like a woman, and a woman should not dress like a man. What clothing or other adornment says "man" or "woman" may differ slightly across cultures and generations, but these slight differences do not make this principle invalid. There are ways for men to deliberately dress like women, and for women to dress like men. When this is done, it goes against God's principles as revealed in His commandments and is disruptive to natural order.

ii. This is not a command against women wearing a garment that in some ways might be common between men and women. A woman can wear trousers without looking like a man. It is a command against dressing in a manner which deliberately crosses or blurs the distinction between the sexes.

iii. "As elsewhere, Scripture considers the natural differences between male and female to be the Lord's creation and so should not be disregarded or camouflaged." (Kalland)

b. **Nor shall a man put on a woman's garment**: This does not prohibit a man from wearing a kilt; yet it clearly prohibits a man from dressing like a woman. The phenomenon of men dressing like women is a clear breaking of the principle behind this command.

i. The dramatic rise in cross-dressing, transvestitism, androgynous behavior, and transgender behavior in our culture is a shocking trampling of this command and will continue to reap a bitter harvest in more perversion and more gender confusion in our culture.

ii. "The close-shaved gentleman may at any time appear like a woman in the female dress, and the woman appear as a man in the male's attire. Were this to be tolerated in society, it would produce the greatest confusion." (Clarke)

c. **All who do so are an abomination to the LORD your God**: The principle behind this command to observe the distinction between the sexes is so important, those who fail to observe it are called **an abomination to the LORD**. This was not only because cross-dressing was a feature of pagan, idolatrous worship in the ancient world, but also because of the terrible cultural price that is paid when it is pretended that there is no difference between men and women.

i. "Because it is against both natural and civil honesty." (Trapp)

3. (6-7) A command to show kindness to animals.

"If a bird's nest happens to be before you along the way, in any tree or on the ground, with young ones or eggs, with the mother sitting on the young or on the eggs, you shall not take the mother with the young; you shall surely let the mother go, and take the young for yourself, that it may be well with you and *that* you may prolong *your* days.

a. **If a bird's nest happens to be before you along the way**: God simply and plainly commanded His people to show kindness to animals. Even **a bird's nest** was to be given special consideration and care.

i. **You shall surely let the mother go**: Puritan commentator Matthew Poole wrote on this, "Partly for the bird's sake, which suffered enough by the loss of its young; for God would not have cruelty exercised towards the brute creatures; and partly for men's sake, to restrain their greediness and covetousness, that they should not monopolize all to themselves, but might leave the hopes of a future seed for others."

ii. "Perhaps reverence for motherhood in general gave rise to the law." (Thompson)

iii. Some Jewish commentators claim this was the smallest, or the least of all the commandments. Yet even with this command, there is a promise of blessing for the obedient: **That it may be well with you and that you may prolong your days**.

b. **That it may be well with you and that you may prolong your days**: If Israel obeyed this commandment, they would find blessing and long life, both as individuals and as a nation. There is a definite connection between showing kindness to God's creatures and national survival.

i. First, because obedience to the smallest of God's commands brings blessing. It puts us into a properly submitted relationship to Him, and this always brings blessing.

ii. Second, because kindness and gentleness in the small things often (but not always) speaks to the ability to be kind and gentle in weightier matters. If someone is cruel to animals, not only is that sin, but those who show such cruelty are also much more likely to be cruel to people. If Israel allowed such cruelty to flourish, it would harm the nation.

4. (8) Liability and building codes.

"When you build a new house, then you shall make a parapet for your roof, that you may not bring guilt of bloodshed on your household if anyone falls from it.

a. **You shall make a parapet for your roof**: God commanded that a railing be made for the rooftop, so someone was protected against falling.

i. "The roofs of houses were often used for various purposes. Consequently, without some kind of restraining wall, one could easily fall off and be hurt. In 1 Samuel 9:25–26, Samuel conversed with Saul on the roof and spent the night there. David was walking on the roof of the palace when he saw Bathsheba (2 Sam 11:2)." (Kalland)

ii. One may imagine a homeowner thinking, "I don't need a rail around my roof. I won't fall." But the homeowner had to think of more than himself. As Philippians 2:4 says, *Let each of you look out not only for his own interests, but also for the interests of others.*

iii. "This careful command clearly shows us that God holds life to be very valuable, and that, as he would not permit us to kill by malice, so he would not allow us to kill by negligence." (Spurgeon)

b. **That you may not bring guilt of bloodshed on your house**: Failure to build with consideration of the safety of others would **bring guilt** (liability) on the owner or builder of the home. The owner of the home was responsible for the safety of those who would use the home.

i. In his sermon on Deuteronomy 22:8 titled *Battlements*, Charles Spurgeon applied the principle of the command for a railing for the protection of people on the roofs of Israel's homes to the idea of spiritual railings for protection. Many people, regarding sin, get too close to the edge and fall off. Then it's too late. There are some wise "railings" that provide protection from falling over the edge, spiritually speaking. Such railings protect the individual and those they may influence.

ii. "The fact is that, if professors do not stop till they are certainly in the wrong, they will stop nowhere. It is of little use to go on till you are over the edge of the roof, and then cry, 'Halt.'" (Spurgeon)

5. (9-12) Four laws of separation.

"You shall not sow your vineyard with different kinds of seed, lest the yield of the seed which you have sown and the fruit of your vineyard be defiled.

"You shall not plow with an ox and a donkey together.

"You shall not wear a garment of different sorts, *such as* **wool and linen mixed together.**

"You shall make tassels on the four corners of the clothing with which you cover *yourself.*

a. **You shall not sow your vineyard with different kinds of seed**: Each of these laws was meant to separate Israel from her pagan neighbors. Canaanites would commonly combine different things to achieve what was thought to be a magical combination.

i. "It is generally supposed that mixtures of different sorts in seed, breed, &c., were employed for superstitious purposes, and therefore prohibited in this law." (Clarke)

ii. "While this might be possible in the world of actual agriculture, it was not to be undertaken in Israel because it symbolized an admixture of spiritual elements that is abhorrent to the Lord." (Merrill)

b. **You shall not plow with an ox and a donkey together**: According to the principle that there was spiritual or "magical" power in combining different things, Canaanites commonly combined contrasting things.

- They might combine **different kinds of seed** in a **vineyard**.
- They might **plow** a field **with an ox and a donkey together**.
- They might wear a garment of **wool and linen mixed together**.

When God commanded Israel to *not* do these things, it wasn't so much for the sake of the combinations themselves, but so Israel would not imitate the pagan, occult customs of their neighbors.

i. There is a spiritual application of this principle. The commands forbidding unholy combinations, "though in themselves small and trivial, are given…to forbid all mixture of their inventions with God's institutions, in doctrine or worship." (Poole)

ii. The apostle Paul later expressed the principle of this command like this: *Do not be unequally yoked together with unbelievers. For what fellowship has righteousness with lawlessness? And what communion has light with darkness?* (2 Corinthians 6:14)

iii. In a curious explanation, one commentator believed that these laws were also given (in part) to protect other animals from the poisonous breath of donkeys: "Besides, the ass, from feeding on coarse and poisonous weed, has a fetid breath, which its yoke-fellow seeks to avoid, not only as poisonous and offensive, but producing leanness, or, if long continued, death." (Jamieson-Fausset-Brown)

c. **You shall make tassels on the four corners of the clothing**: This command was also given to distinguish Israel from their pagan neighbors. When this command was obeyed, an Israelite man was immediately known by the clothes he wore.

i. "A symbolic meaning is given to these tassels in Numbers 15:37-41, namely that they are a reminder to Israel to keep God's law." (Thompson)

ii. Like most good commands of God, men have the capability to twist and corrupt these commands. In Jesus' day, He had to condemn the Pharisees, saying they *enlarge the borders of their garments* (Matthew 23:5) In other words, they made the tasseled portion of their garments larger and more prominent to show how spiritual they were.

B. Laws of sexual morality.

1. (13-21) Resolving an accusation of marital deception.

"If any man takes a wife, and goes in to her, and detests her, and charges her with shameful conduct, and brings a bad name on her, and says, 'I took this woman, and when I came to her I found she *was* **not a virgin,' then the father and mother of the young woman shall take and bring out** *the evidence of* **the young woman's virginity to the elders of the city at the gate. And the young woman's father shall say to the elders, 'I gave my daughter to this man as wife, and he detests her. Now he has charged her with shameful conduct, saying, "I found your daughter** *was* **not a virgin," and yet these** *are the evidences of* **my daughter's virginity.' And they shall spread the cloth before the elders of the city. Then the elders of that city shall take that man and punish him; and they shall fine him one hundred** *shekels* **of silver and give** *them* **to the father of the young woman, because he has brought a bad name on a virgin of Israel. And she shall be his wife; he cannot divorce her all his days.**

"But if the thing is true, *and evidences of* **virginity are not found for the young woman, then they shall bring out the young woman to the door of her father's house, and the men of her city shall stone her to death with stones, because she has done a disgraceful thing in Israel, to play the harlot in her father's house. So you shall put away the evil from among you.**

> a. **Charges her with shameful conduct**: The idea is that the man accused his wife of not being a virgin when they were married. Apparently, this was discovered on their wedding night, when they first had intimate relations **(when I came to her I found she was not a virgin)**.
>
> > i. In ancient Israel virginity was valued. It was seen as a great *loss* to give up one's virginity before marriage, and if a woman was known to have lost her virginity, it reduced her chances of getting married.
> >
> > ii. According to this same principle, if a husband believed that his wife had lied about her virginity, he felt cheated. What follows is an attempt to resolve the issue.
>
> b. **Then the father and mother...bring out the evidence of the young woman's virginity.... they shall spread the cloth before the elders of the city**: According to custom, a Jewish woman would first be intimate with her husband upon a special cloth, which would be marked by the drops of blood which were accepted as **evidence of the young woman's virginity**. This bloodstained cloth would then become the property of

the married woman's parents, who kept it as the **evidence of the young woman's virginity**.

i. Many people argue that this custom of proving a woman's virginity is absurd because it doesn't always work. Some people have answered by saying it does "work" when ladies are given in marriage at twelve or thirteen years of age, as was the custom in Old Testament times.

ii. Nonetheless, for whatever reasons, the custom was practiced long after biblical times, and is still practiced in some parts of the world. "The proofs of virginity, the blood-spotted bedclothes or garments, which, though not infallible, were widely accepted in the ancient Near East as indications of prior virginity, are still accepted among some peoples today" (Kalland). Clarke also adds: "A custom similar to that above is observed among the Mohamedans to the present day."

c. **The elders of the city shall take that man and punish him**: If the parents could produce the evidence, then the man was found to have made a false accusation against his wife and it was commanded that a fine be paid to the father of his wife.

i. The sin was great; he had **brought a bad name** upon his wife. "Which is a kind of murder (Ezekiel 22:9). God shall clear the innocency of his slandered servants (Psalm 37:6; Isaiah 54:17)." (Trapp)

ii. Additionally, the man had forfeited his future right to divorce his wife: **he cannot divorce her all his days**. "The law protected the innocent bride from the caprice of her husband and discouraged premarital infidelity among young women." (Kalland)

iii. The strong penalty against a man who made a false accusation (**one hundred shekels of silver**), and the loss of any future right to divorce his wife was an effective deterrent against wild, false accusations by a husband against his wife.

iv. "The amount of the fine was considerable relative to that economy. David, for example, later bought Araunah's threshing floor and oxen for only fifty silver shekels (2 Sam 24:24). Such an enormous penalty would clearly deter young husbands from such frivolous and fallacious allegations." (Merrill)

d. **But if the thing is true, and evidences of virginity are not found for the young woman**: If this were the case, the woman was to be executed by stoning. This was not only for her sexual promiscuity (**to play the harlot**) but also for the deception of her husband.

i. This law must be seen in connection with the command in Exodus 22:16-17, which commands that a man who *entices a virgin* must *surely pay the bride-price for her to be his wife.* This law in Deuteronomy is directed against the truly wanton woman, who had given up her virginity, yet not claimed her rights under Exodus 22:16-17. She did not value her virginity at the time she gave it up, yet she wanted to later claim the benefit of it by deceiving her husband.

ii. All this simply reinforces the principle that virginity was valued, highly valued, in Israel. Modern culture would benefit enormously by a re-capturing of this value.

2. (22) The penalty for adultery.

"If a man is found lying with a woman married to a husband, then both of them shall die—the man that lay with the woman, and the woman; so you shall put away the evil from Israel.

a. **If a man is found lying with a woman married to a husband**: This was a clear case of adultery. It isn't stated if the offending man was married or not, but the woman in this case was.

b. **Both of them shall die**: God commanded the death penalty for adultery. The breaking of the marriage bond by adultery does significant harm not only to the individuals involved, but also to the wider community as marriages are endangered and families broken apart. Therefore, God commanded the ultimate penalty against adultery.

i. God also specifically instructed that **both the man that lay with the woman** and **the woman** were under this penalty. Adultery was not to be condemned with a double standard; if it was wrong for the woman, it was wrong for the man, and vice-versa.

c. **Then both of them shall die**: As a practical matter, this death penalty was rarely carried out for adultery. This was the case for most crimes in Israel where the death penalty was commanded. This was because any capital crime required two or three witnesses, and the witnesses had to be so certain of what they saw that they were willing to "cast the first stone" – that is, initiate the execution (Deuteronomy 17:6-7).

i. Particularly in a case of adultery (or other sexual sins) there would rarely be two eyewitnesses willing to initiate the execution. Without such witnesses, the death penalty would not be carried out.

ii. This also helps us to understand the actions of Jesus when He confronted the leaders who brought the woman taken in adultery. By their presence and words, they claimed to have caught the woman in the act. Yet, they did not also bring the guilty man. This explains, in part, why no one was willing to cast the first stone – that is, to initiate the execution (John 8:1-12).

d. **So you shall put away the evil from Israel**: Though the death penalty for adultery was rarely carried out, it still had value. It clearly communicated an *ideal* that Israel was to live up to, and it made people regard their sin much more seriously. Today, society often ignores this ideal, and people don't care much about adultery. As a result, modern society suffers greatly.

> i. "While in the modern world we would not follow all the penalties for breach of the laws, we need to recognize that purity and fidelity are essential to the well-being of society.... Great nations in centuries past lost their nationhood in considerable measure because of their unrestrained licence in sexual matters." (Thompson)

3. (23-29) Laws concerning rape.

"If a young woman *who is* a virgin is betrothed to a husband, and a man finds her in the city and lies with her, then you shall bring them both out to the gate of that city, and you shall stone them to death with stones, the young woman because she did not cry out in the city, and the man because he humbled his neighbor's wife; so you shall put away the evil from among you.

"But if a man finds a betrothed young woman in the countryside, and the man forces her and lies with her, then only the man who lay with her shall die. But you shall do nothing to the young woman; *there is* in the young woman no sin *deserving* of death, for just as when a man rises against his neighbor and kills him, even so *is* this matter. For he found her in the countryside, *and* the betrothed young woman cried out, but *there was* no one to save her.

"If a man finds a young woman *who is* a virgin, who is not betrothed, and he seizes her and lies with her, and they are found out, then the man who lay with her shall give to the young woman's father fifty *shekels* of silver, and she shall be his wife because he has humbled her; he shall not be permitted to divorce her all his days.

a. **If a young woman who is a virgin is betrothed to a husband**: This law used the example of a man who had sexual relations with a virgin who was engaged to be married (**betrothed to a husband**). If the crime happened **in the city**, and no one immediately hears the woman **cry out** to stop the man, then both the man and the woman were to be executed.

> i. The woman was to be executed because her lack of resistance – offering not even a **cry** of resistance – gave no proof that she was not a willing participant. It's important to understand that these laws were given to Israel and her judges as case law, and the principles revealed in the law could be adapted to various situations. Based on the *principle*

of this law, if there was a non-verbal way the woman expressed her resistance, she could be found innocent, and the man found guilty of rape.

ii. The man was to be executed **because he humbled his neighbor's wife**. Interestingly, the woman was considered the **wife** of another man, even though she was only **betrothed**, and was still a **virgin**, having not yet consummated the marriage.

b. **But if a man finds a betrothed young woman in the countryside**: This law next considered the case of a man who had sexual relations with a virgin who was **betrothed**, yet it happened **in the countryside**. In a remote place, no one could hear the woman's resistance, and she would also have less incentive to offer even verbal resistance.

i. In such a case, only the man was to be executed, because the woman was presumed to be the victim of rape. Significantly, the woman was not blamed for the rape, and it was *presumed* that she was innocent in this circumstance. This is clear in the phrasing used in verse 25: **the man forces her**, phrasing not used in verse 23.

ii. "A *rape* also, by these ancient institutions, was punished with death, because a woman's honour was considered equally as precious as her life; therefore the same punishment was inflicted on the ravisher as upon the murderer." (Clarke)

c. **If a man finds a young woman who is a virgin, who is not betrothed**: If a man had intimate relations with a virgin who was **not betrothed**, then he had to pay a fine and was obligated to marry the woman (presumably, if she would have him). He also forfeited his right to divorce her in the future.

i. It is likely that the **fifty shekels of silver** were to be paid to the father *in addition to* the dowry.

4. (30) A law concerning incest.

"A man shall not take his father's wife, nor uncover his father's bed.

a. **A man shall not take his father's wife**: This probably described the case of a son marrying his stepmother after his father had died. This was considered incest, even though they were not blood relations, because the son was considered to have uncovered **his father's bed**.

i. "A man in his old age may have married a young wife, and on his dying, his son by a former wife may desire to espouse her: this the law prohibits." (Clarke)

ii. This emphasized the community's interest in guarding the institution of marriage, and in de-sexualizing family relationships.

b. **Nor uncover his father's bed**: Significantly, this was the same kind of immoral relationship that the Corinthian Christians – to their shame – accepted. The apostle Paul had to rebuke them regarding this, *that a man has his father's wife* (1 Corinthians 5:1-2).

i. "This was regarded as an incestuous union and a particularly dangerous one, since it struck deeply at the maintenance of family life (cf. 27:20; Lev. 18:8; 20:10). The expression *uncover her who is his father's* is a euphemism…. 'To uncover' means to encroach on his father's marital rights." (Thompson)

Deuteronomy 23 – Instructions to the Assembly, Various Laws

A. Those excluded from leadership in Israel.

1. (1) Eunuchs are excluded from leadership in the congregation of Israel.

"He who is emasculated by crushing or mutilation shall not enter the assembly of the LORD.

a. **By crushing or mutilation**: This refers to those **emasculated** by a birth defect, accident, or by deliberate emasculation.

b. **Shall not enter the assembly of the LORD**: The idea of the **assembly of the LORD** often refers to the nation gathered before the LORD in worship, such as when Israel gathered at Mount Sinai (Deuteronomy 5:22, 9:10, 10:4, and 18:16). But it doesn't always have this sense.

i. There are several suggestions for what comprised the **assembly of the LORD**. (1) The general community of Israel. (2) "Citizens" of Israel, distinct from "residents." (3) Those permitted and welcome to gather for public worship and celebration of the feasts. (4) The broad group of civil leaders and officials in Israel. There are reasons to regard the last sense here.

ii. Deuteronomy 31:30 refers to *all the congregation of Israel*, while Deuteronomy 31:28 makes it clear that "all the congregation" was represented by *all the elders of your tribes, and your officers*. So, in some contexts, *the congregation* can refer to *elders* and *officers*. It may very well be that these exclusions from the **assembly of the LORD** are exclusions not from the religious life of Israel, but from the political life of the nation.

iii. Poole suggests that the idea of **the assembly of the LORD** is the leadership or the rulers of Israel. These people were barred not from the religious life of Israel, but from the political life of the nation. Trapp agrees, saying on **shall not enter the assembly of the Lord**: "Shall not go in and out before the people as a public officer." Clarke adds, "If by entering into the congregation be meant the bearing a *civil* office among the people, such as magistrate, judge, &c., then the reason of the law is very plain."

    c. **Shall not enter the assembly of the Lord**: To whatever extent eunuchs were excluded, it was because God's covenant with Israel was vitally connected with the idea of the *seed*, and emasculation is a "crime" against the seed of man. Additionally, most eunuchs were made to be so in pagan ceremonies where they, in their emasculated condition, were dedicated to pagan gods.

        i. Isaiah 56:3-5 shows that even eunuchs and foreigners could be accepted before the Lord if they would obey Him, and they would be received before those who were complete in their body but disobeyed God. Acts 8:27-38 is the record of a eunuch coming to faith in Jesus.

2. (2) Those of unknown parentage are excluded from the assembly of Israel (civil leadership in Israel).

"One of illegitimate birth shall not enter the assembly of the Lord; even to the tenth generation none of his *descendants* shall enter the assembly of the Lord.

    a. **One of illegitimate birth**: It is difficult to define exactly what is meant by the term **of illegitimate birth**. Some later Jewish writers defined this as someone who was born of an incestuous relationship between Jews; others said it refers to those born of mixed marriages between the people of Israel and their pagan neighbors (as in Nehemiah 13:23).

        i. **To the tenth generation**: "The temporal reference in vv.2–3 "to the tenth generation," as v.6 indicates, means as long as the nation exists. The generations are not to be counted but should be understood rather as in the Lord Jesus' statement that one's brother should be forgiven seventy-seven times (i.e., always; cf. Matt 18:22)." (Kalland)

    b. **The assembly of the Lord**: This exclusion of those of **illegitimate birth**, as with the case of those emasculated in verse 1, probably applied to the civil leadership of Israel, not to membership in the community of Israel as a whole.

3. (3-6) Ammonites and Moabites are excluded from the congregation of Israel (civil leadership in Israel).

"An Ammonite or Moabite shall not enter the assembly of the Lord; even to the tenth generation none of his *descendants* shall enter the

assembly of the LORD forever, because they did not meet you with bread and water on the road when you came out of Egypt, and because they hired against you Balaam the son of Beor from Pethor of Mesopotamia, to curse you. Nevertheless the LORD your God would not listen to Balaam, but the LORD your God turned the curse into a blessing for you, because the LORD your God loves you. You shall not seek their peace nor their prosperity all your days forever.

    a. **An Ammonite or Moabite shall not enter the assembly of the LORD**: The Moabites and the Ammonites not only treated Israel cruelly on their way to the Promised Land, but they also were a people with a disgraceful beginning. Moab and Ammon were the two sons born to the daughters of Lot through their incest with their father (Genesis 19:30-38).

        i. The story of the strange prophet **Balaam** and Balak, the Moabite king who hired him to curse Israel, is found in Numbers 22-24.

    b. **The assembly of the LORD**: This had the same application as the previous laws in this section, concerning the civil leadership of Israel. It did not apply to membership in the community of Israel as a whole.

        i. "Disbarment from the assembly was not synonymous with exclusion from the covenant community itself as the one example of Ruth the Moabite makes clear.... There can be no doubt that Ruth was welcomed among the people of the Lord as one of their own." (Merrill)

4. (7-8) The descendants of Edomites and Egyptians are permitted to be among the congregation of Israel (civil leadership in Israel).

"You shall not abhor an Edomite, for he *is* your brother. You shall not abhor an Egyptian, because you were an alien in his land. The children of the third generation born to them may enter the assembly of the LORD.

    a. **You shall not abhor an Edomite**: The Edomites were ethnically related to Israel, because Jacob's brother Esau was the father of the Edomite peoples. Therefore, Israel was commanded to **not abhor an Edomite**. Starting with the third generation, the descendants of an Edomite or an Egyptian could be part of the leadership of Israel.

        i. "The verb *abhor* (*tieb*) is from the same root as the noun 'abomination' (*toeba*) and is generally used of ritual uncleanness. The verb form here means 'to treat as ritually unclean' (cf. Deuteronomy 7:26)." (Thompson)

        ii. Interestingly, one of the most famous Edomites in history was hated by Israel – Herod the Great. Many of his spectacular building projects in Judea were intended to not only glorify his own name, but to win the favor of the Jews who despised him as an Edomite.

b. **You shall not abhor an Egyptian**: The Egyptians were also to receive more favor than the Moabites or Ammonites, because Israel was a "guest" in Egypt for almost 400 years. Though the years Israel spent in Egypt were hard, God had a great purpose for them. Egypt was like a mother's womb for Israel; they went in as a large family and came out as a distinct nation.

i. "There were the most cogent reasons why Israel should make no political affinity with Egypt, but she was not to harbour abhorrence in her heart against the Egyptian people." (Morgan)

B. Miscellaneous laws.

1. (9-14) Cleanliness in the camp.

"When the army goes out against your enemies, then keep yourself from every wicked thing. If there is any man among you who becomes unclean by some occurrence in the night, then he shall go outside the camp; he shall not come inside the camp. But it shall be, when evening comes, that he shall wash with water; and when the sun sets, he may come into the camp.

"Also you shall have a place outside the camp, where you may go out; and you shall have an implement among your equipment, and when you sit down outside, you shall dig with it and turn and cover your refuse. For the LORD your God walks in the midst of your camp, to deliver you and give your enemies over to you; therefore your camp shall be holy, that He may see no unclean thing among you, and turn away from you.

a. **When the army goes out against your enemies, then keep yourself from every wicked thing**: God commanded *ceremonial* cleanliness among the army of Israel. **Some occurrence in the night** probably refers to nocturnal emissions, and the cleansing ceremony for this was described in Leviticus 15:16-18. After observing the ceremonial washing, that soldier **may come into the camp again**.

i. "Though the passage in no way suggests that bodily emissions (whether or not of a quasi-sexual kind) are in themselves inherently evil or even cultically impure, it does underscore the importance of a proper time and place for such things." (Merrill)

b. **And you shall have an implement among your equipment**: God commanded *sanitary* cleanliness among the army of Israel. In addition to his weapons, each soldier was to carry some type of shovel, used to cover **refuse**.

i. Spurgeon completely passed over verse 13, and said this of verse 14: "I will scarcely allude to the context, which you ought to notice at home, but I must say as much as this: the Lord cared for the cleanliness of his people while they were in the wilderness, literally so; and this text is connected with a sanitary regulation of the wisest possible kind." (Spurgeon)

c. **For the LORD your God walks in the midst of your camp**: Israel had the tabernacle and the ark of the covenant, which in some sense symbolized or pointed to the presence of Yahweh among them. At the same time, they also understood that God's presence was not *restricted* to the tabernacle or the ark of the covenant. Yahweh was present everywhere, as if He walked through the camp of Israel.

i. "No part of the camp was exempt from God's walking in it. Not merely in the holy place was God, or in the Holy of holies between the cherubim, but he was everywhere in the streets of the canvas city, and in the outskirts thereof." (Spurgeon)

ii. "God went up and down the long avenues of the tents, He would see nothing to offend his gaze and make Him turn away. How deep a lesson! God is ever patrolling the avenues of our life. The most secret processes of our daily existence, our innermost relationships, the thoughts and intents of our heart, are all manifest to Him." (Meyer)

iii. **And turn away from you**: "Note well the fearful warning which is added. If there be in the camp an unclean thing tolerated and delighted in, and he see it – if it becomes conspicuous and grievous to him, then the worst consequences will follow – 'Lest he turn away from thee.'" (Spurgeon)

2. (15-16) Israel to provide asylum for the foreign escaped slave.

"You shall not give back to his master the slave who has escaped from his master to you. He may dwell with you in your midst, in the place which he chooses within one of your gates, where it seems best to him; you shall not oppress him.

a. **You shall not give back to his master the slave who has escaped from his master to you**: This probably dealt with a slave from a foreign land, enslaved by kidnapping (prohibited in Exodus 21:16). At times, there were escaped slaves roaming the land in Israel (1 Samuel 25:10).

i. "Israel was to be a refuge for the oppressed slaves of other people." (Morgan)

ii. "The refugee slave referred to had evidently come from a foreign land. Otherwise there would have been legal complications, since slaves were a valued possession." (Thompson)

b. **He may dwell with you in your midst**: An Israelite was not to take an escaped slave and enslave them again. The escaped slave was free and entitled to live in whatever **place** that **he chooses**.

3. (17-18) Sacred prostitution banned.

"There shall be no *ritual* harlot of the daughters of Israel, or a perverted one of the sons of Israel. You shall not bring the wages of a harlot or the price of a dog to the house of the Lord your God for any vowed offering, for both of these *are* an abomination to the Lord your God.

a. **Ritual harlot**: This refers to a female prostitute. The term **perverted one** refers to a male prostitute, both of which were common among the pagan religions of the Canaanites and others in the ancient world.

i. Later, in the reigns of Asa (1 Kings 15:12) and Josiah (2 Kings 23:7) we are told that the *perverted persons* (male prostitutes) were expelled from Israel. This means that for some period before they were expelled, they were allowed to practice their "sacred prostitution," which was clearly an **abomination to the Lord your God**.

b. **You shall not bring the wages of a harlot or the price of a dog to the house of the Lord your God**: The pay of a female prostitute (**the hire of a harlot**) and the pay of a male prostitute (**the price of a dog**) were never to be offered to the Lord. This was a common practice among the sacred prostitution cults that abounded in the ancient world.

i. "The female prostitute is described in verse 18 as a *harlot* (*zona*) and the male a *dog*. This usage of the term *dog* is known outside the Old Testament." (Thompson) Goliath's question to young David, "Am I a dog?" (1 Samuel 17:43) should probably be understood in this context. This is also true in 2 Kings 8:13, and perhaps behind Paul's warning in Philippians 3:2.

ii. The work of the Lord does not need money from immoral or ill-gotten gains. "Whole guilds of male and female temple personnel participated in grossly sexual rituals designed to induce the various gods and goddesses to release their procreative powers on the earth. Nowhere was this more commonly practiced than among the peoples of Syria and Canaan, hence the special need to warn Israel against it." (Merrill)

4. (19-20) Against stealing from a fellow Israelite through unfair interest on a loan.

"You shall not charge interest to your brother—interest on money *or* food *or* anything that is lent out at interest. To a foreigner you may charge interest, but to your brother you shall not charge interest, that the LORD your God may bless you in all to which you set your hand in the land which you are entering to possess.

a. **You shall not charge interest to your brother—interest on money or food**: The mention of **food**, and the similar command in Exodus 22:25, leads most people to understand that interest was prohibited on loans made to the poor for their basic needs, and did not prohibit the taking of interest on loans that were not for relief of the poor.

i. Verse 19 could be translated, "You shall not lend at biting interest," referring to excessive interest or usury. "Heb., Upon biting usury." (Trapp)

ii. "To exact penalties of a brother is to put the 'bite' (so Heb. *nesek*, 'interest,' or *nasak*, 'pay interest') on him." (Merrill)

iii. "The rate of interest in the ancient Near East was exorbitant, e.g. some contracts in Northern Assyria at Nuzi in the fifteenth century BC show that the interest was fifty per cent." (Thompson)

b. **To a foreigner you may charge interest**: Such loans to foreigners were made for business and commercial purposes, not to sustain or help the poor.

i. "But since merchants from other nations might come for business reasons to Israel, or make loans on interest to Israelites, foreigners could be charged interest." (Kalland)

5. (21-23) Against stealing from the LORD by failing to pay a vow.

"When you make a vow to the LORD your God, you shall not delay to pay it; for the LORD your God will surely require it of you, and it would be sin to you. But if you abstain from vowing, it shall not be sin to you. That which has gone from your lips you shall keep and perform, for you voluntarily vowed to the LORD your God what you have promised with your mouth.

a. **You shall not delay to pay it**: A vow before God is no small thing. God expressly commanded that Israel should be careful to keep its vows and to fulfill every oath made, **for the LORD your God will surely require it of you, and it would be sin to you**.

i. In many circles today, the breaking of an oath is just standard business practice. Before God, it is simply sin.

ii. "Payment of vows is often mentioned by psalmist and prophet (Pss 22:25; 50:14; et al.; Isa 19:21; Jonah 2:9; Nah 1:15). Jeremiah and Malachi speak of improper vows (Jer 44:25; Mal 1:14)." (Kalland)

b. **If you abstain from vowing**: Some ask if vows or oaths are permitted for a Christian today, based on what Jesus said in Matthew 5:34-37: *But I say to you, do not swear at all: neither by heaven, for it is God's throne; nor by the earth, for it is His footstool; nor by Jerusalem, for it is the city of the great King. Nor shall you swear by your head, because you cannot make one hair white or black. But let your 'Yes' be 'Yes,' and your 'No,' 'No.' For whatever is more than these is from the evil one.* James 5:12 expresses a similar thought.

i. In the context of the rest of Scripture, we see that Jesus was not forbidding oaths, rather telling His people that the integrity of their words should make an oath unnecessary. Jesus answered under oath in a court (Matthew 26:63-64), and God Himself swears oaths (Luke 1:73, Acts 2:30, Hebrews 3:18, 6:13, 17).

c. **But if you abstain from vowing, it shall not be sin to you**: God never *requires* vows; many times, it is better not to make a vow.

d. **That which has gone from your lips you shall keep and perform**: This shows how important it is to keep a vow once made. As it says in Ecclesiastes 5:4-5, *When you make a vow to God, do not delay to pay it; for He has no pleasure in fools. Pay what you have vowed—better not to vow than to vow and not pay.*

i. Many vows are just plain foolish – "I'll never do that again" is usually a foolish vow, and it is foolish and unwise to demand such a vow from someone else.

ii. Of course, there is a vow we all can and should make – a vow to praise God: *Vows made to You are binding upon me, O God; I will render praises to You* (Psalm 56:12). *So I will sing praise to Your name forever, that I may daily perform my vows* (Psalm 61:8).

6. (24-25) Against stealing from a traveler by refusing the right to glean a grainfield.

"When you come into your neighbor's vineyard, you may eat your fill of grapes at your pleasure, but you shall not put *any* in your container. When you come into your neighbor's standing grain, you may pluck the heads with your hand, but you shall not use a sickle on your neighbor's standing grain.

a. **When you come into your neighbor's vineyard**: The idea was that, as you traveled, you had the right to pick off a few grapes or heads of grain to eat along the way. It wasn't the right to harvest from your neighbor's fields, but to provide for your own immediate needs.

b. **You may pluck the heads with your hand**: This is the law Jesus and His disciples were operating under when they *plucked the heads of grain and ate them, rubbing them in their hands* (Luke 6:1-5). They were accused by the Pharisees of breaking the Sabbath, but not of stealing grain, because the Pharisees knew this law in the book of Deuteronomy.

> i. "On the other hand, this advantage was not to be abused by putting grapes in a basket or putting a sickle to the neighbor's grain for one's future use." (Kalland)

Deuteronomy 24 – The Law of Divorce and Other Various Laws

A. Divorce, remarriage, and marriage.

1. (1) The law of divorce in ancient Israel.

"When a man takes a wife and marries her, and it happens that she finds no favor in his eyes because he has found some uncleanness in her, and he writes her a certificate of divorce, puts *it* in her hand, and sends her out of his house,

> a. **A certificate of divorce**: According to these laws, divorce was allowed in Israel, but carefully regulated. Under God's law, the marriage agreement could not be simply dissolved as soon as one partner wanted it to end. There had to be a cause for **a certificate of divorce**.
>
> i. "The legislation here neither commands nor condones divorce in general but only regulates its practice for ancient Israel." (Merrill)
>
> ii. Even with cause, divorce was never to be seen as a preferred or easy option. The Hebrew word translated **divorce** has as its root the idea of "a hewing off, a cutting apart" – it is the amputation of that which is intended to be one.
>
> iii. "[Christians] all regard divorce as something like cutting up a living body, as a kind of surgical operation. Some think that the operation is so violent that it cannot be done at all; others admit that it is a desperate remedy in extreme cases. They are all agreed that it is more like having your legs cut off than it is like dissolving a business partnership or even deserting a regiment." (C.S. Lewis, *Christian Behaviour*)
>
> b. **He writes her a certificate of divorce**: God commanded through Moses that any divorce be sealed with **a certificate of divorce**. In other words, it was not enough for a man to just declare, "we're divorced" to his wife.

The divorce had to be recognized legally just as the marriage had been, so **a certificate of divorce** – a legal document – must be issued, and properly served (**puts it in her hand**).

c. **She finds no favor in his eyes because he has found some uncleanness in her**: This describes the *grounds* of divorce and indicates that a **certificate of divorce** could not be written for just any reason. It had to be founded on these two important clauses.

i. There must be **some uncleanness** in the spouse. Some later Rabbis defined **uncleanness** as anything in the wife which might displease the husband. At the time of Jesus, some Rabbis taught that if a wife burned her husband's breakfast, of if he found a more attractive woman to marry, he could then divorce her.

ii. But Matthew 19:3-10 is the record of Jesus carefully and properly defining what **uncleanness** meant in Deuteronomy 24:1. He said, *whoever divorces his wife, except for sexual immorality, and marries another, commits adultery* (Matthew 19:9). Jesus explained that **uncleanness** referred to *sexual immorality*, using a broad term referring to sexual sin, which includes, but is not restricted to, sexual intercourse with a person not your spouse. The Hebrew word translated **uncleanness** implies the meaning of sexual immorality; it is literally, "nakedness of a thing."

iii. So, if a husband found **some uncleanness** in his spouse, he had the right to give his wife **a certificate of divorce**. But he was not *obligated* to do so. It also had to be true that the loss of favor was **because** of the discovery of **some uncleanness** in the spouse. In other words, it must be that the husband was so troubled at his wife's sexual immorality that he simply could not look on her with **favor in his eyes** anymore. The lack of **favor in his eyes** had to be prompted by her **uncleanness**.

iv. This helps us understand what Jesus explained in Matthew 19:8: *Moses, because of the hardness of your hearts, permitted you to divorce your wives, but from the beginning it was not so.*

- If a woman did not have a hard heart, she would never commit sexual immorality against her husband, and there would be no need for divorce.

- If a husband did not have any hardness in his heart, he could forgive and still look upon his repentant wife with **favor in his eyes**, even though she was guilty of sexual immorality.

Yet because God knows there is hardness in our hearts – both in the offending and offended parties – He grants *permission* for divorce.

v. In the days of Jesus, some Rabbis taught that it was the *duty* of a godly man to divorce his wife if she displeased him. Both Moses and Jesus clearly said that God *permits* divorce in certain circumstances, but never *commands* it.

vi. Yet, if someone has biblical grounds of divorce (which, according to 1 Corinthians 7:15, also includes abandonment by an unbelieving spouse), they certainly do have *permission* to divorce, and God does not charge them with wrong. An exception to this would be if the testimony of the Holy Spirit to the individual believer would be to remain in the marriage, and that believer was disobedient to the specific guidance of the Spirit.

d. **He writes her a certificate of divorce**: Because this passage only speaks of husbands divorcing their wives, some people think that wives had no right to divorce their husbands on the grounds of sexual immorality (**uncleanness**). However, Deuteronomy and the Law of Moses in general deal with case law, giving principles with specific examples, with the understanding that Israel's judges would apply the same principle to similar situations. The same principle applies for the wife regarding the husband.

i. In addition, when Jesus referred to this passage in Mark 10:12, He explained that the principle applies in the case when *a woman divorces her husband and marries another*. This statement of Jesus applied the principle to the wife regarding the husband.

2. (2-4) The law of remarriage in ancient Israel.

When she has departed from his house, and goes and becomes another man's *wife, if* the latter husband detests her and writes her a certificate of divorce, puts *it* in her hand, and sends her out of his house, or if the latter husband dies who took her as his wife, *then* her former husband who divorced her must not take her back to be his wife after she has been defiled; for that *is* an abomination before the Lord, and you shall not bring sin on the land which the Lord your God is giving you *as* an inheritance.

a. **Her former husband who divorced her must not take her back**: This is a strong law, saying that if a divorced woman marries again, she could not return to her first husband, should her second marriage end through divorce or death. To break this law was **an abomination before the Lord**.

i. "The story of Hosea (1–3) is the story of a man who refused to divorce his wife, despite her unfaithfulness. He was thus in a position to take her back when he had found her. So God was faithful to Israel despite her unfaithfulness and did not put her away irrevocably (cf. Jer. 3:1–8)." (Thompson)

b. **An abomination before the Lord**: It seems that it might be a good thing for the first husband and wife to get back together. But this command was made because God wanted both marriage and divorce to be seen as serious, lasting things. One couldn't be married or divorced casually; it had to be carefully thought out because it was intended to last.

i. "The present law would have had the effect of making divorce a more serious affair.... it would discourage the easy transfer of a woman from one man to another which resulted in the defilement of the woman. The net result would be the elevation of the status of women." (Thompson)

ii. This law would also strengthen the second marriage. In this example, it would discourage a spouse from thinking that they might as well just leave their second marriage and go back to their first partner. Usually, the preferred option was to remain in the marriage and work things out.

iii. **Bring sin on the land**: "The idea that unchastity defiled the land is found in several other passages in the Old Testament (e.g. Lev. 18:25, 28; 19:29; Num. 5:3; Jer. 3:2, 9; Hos. 4:3)." (Thompson)

3. (5) The law honoring marriage.

"When a man has taken a new wife, he shall not go out to war or be charged with any business; he shall be free at home one year, and bring happiness to his wife whom he has taken.

a. **He shall be free at home one year**: A similar principle was previously stated in Deuteronomy 20:7. This was one way that God honored and blessed the marriage covenant. The law of Israel allowed men who were newly married to be exempt from military or other state service for **one year**. This was not only to enjoy the bond of marriage, but also to begin a family and establish descendants.

b. **Bring happiness to his wife**: This is an important job for every husband. The disciples of Jesus Christ find their lives by losing them (Matthew 10:39), so a husband will find happiness if he purposes to **bring happiness to his wife**.

i. This doesn't mean that the husband should focus on pleasing the wife's opinion or preference on every occasion. That can be a profound abandonment of the husband's leadership, allowing the wife's every whim to guide the direction of the home. It means for the husband to take leadership in the home that constantly takes account of what is best for the entire family, giving the home the stability and security that brings happiness.

ii. As the role of the husband in Ephesians 5 is described, God emphasizes the essential oneness between husband and wife. On this principle, the husband cannot make his wife happy without also bringing happiness into his own life. Conversely, he cannot bring misery into the life of his spouse without also bringing misery into his own life.

iii. A wife made happy through the godly leadership of the husband is one part of the foundation for a happy home. A bitter or contentious wife makes for a miserable home (Proverbs 27:15, 21:9, 21:19).

B. Other various laws.

1. (6) Do not take someone's livelihood as a pledge.

"No man shall take the lower or the upper millstone in pledge, for he takes *one's* living in pledge.

a. **No man shall take the lower or the upper millstone in pledge**: A **millstone** was something essential to a family's livelihood, their ability to provide regular food for the family. Therefore, it was forbidden to take a **millstone** as a guarantee for a loan.

i. This warns God's people against taking advantage of each other in times of great need. Believers must take care that they never unfairly profit from the poverty or difficulty of others.

b. **For he takes one's living in pledge**: Non-essential items could be taken as a **pledge**, to guarantee the repayment of a loan. Although interest could not be charged on a loan to an Israelite in need, a **pledge** could be taken – collateral to guarantee the repayment of the loan. This command forbids the taking of collateral that would take away a man's ability to provide for his family and get himself out of debt.

2. (7) The punishment for kidnapping.

"If a man is found kidnapping any of his brethren of the children of Israel, and mistreats him or sells him, then that kidnapper shall die; and you shall put away the evil from among you.

a. **If a man is found kidnapping any of his brethren of the children of Israel**: **Kidnapping** was usually done in the ancient world not so much for return and ransom, but so that one could sell the one abducted to slavery, just as was done to Joseph by his brothers (Genesis 37:28).

b. **That kidnapper shall die**: This crime was serious enough before God to command the death penalty. The same principle is stated in Exodus 21:16. As Israel carried out this command, it would help to **put away the evil** among Israel.

> i. "The offence must have been common in the ancient Near East, to judge from other law codes which legislate against the practice…. whether the kidnapper possessed his fellow or sold him abroad, he was to be put to death." (Thompson)

3. (8-9) The command to act swiftly when leprosy breaks out.

"Take heed in an outbreak of leprosy, that you carefully observe and do according to all that the priests, the Levites, shall teach you; just as I commanded them, *so* you shall be careful to do. Remember what the LORD your God did to Miriam on the way when you came out of Egypt!

> a. **Take heed in an outbreak of leprosy**: Leviticus 13 and 14 describe in detail how God wanted lepers examined and quarantined. Because leprosy was such a dreaded disease, God commanded that they **take heed in an outbreak of leprosy**, so it would not become a plague among the people.
>
>> i. "The term for *leprosy* (*sara'at*) is a wide one and covers a variety of skin diseases. Indeed, the term is also applied to clothes and houses (Lev. 14:55)." (Thompson)
>
> b. **Remember what the LORD your God did to Miriam**: In Numbers 12, Miriam led her brother Aaron in a rebellion against Moses, and for it, God struck her with leprosy. Though Moses prayed for her to be healed, God let her be a leper for seven days before healing her, and she was *shut out of the camp seven days* (Numbers 12:14). If someone as prominent as Miriam was quarantined as a leper, it showed that every other leper in Israel should also be quarantined according to God's instructions in Leviticus 13-14.

4. (10-13) Handling a pledge for a loan rightly.

"When you lend your brother anything, you shall not go into his house to get his pledge. You shall stand outside, and the man to whom you lend shall bring the pledge out to you. And if the man *is* poor, you shall not keep his pledge overnight. You shall in any case return the pledge to him again when the sun goes down, that he may sleep in his own garment and bless you; and it shall be righteousness to you before the LORD your God.

> a. **You shall not go into his house to get his pledge**: When a **pledge** was taken for a loan, it had to be received in a way that guarded the poor man's dignity. The lender couldn't burst into the home of the borrower and seize the pledge. The borrower delivered it to the lender.

i. "What courtesy and respect for the feelings of another prompted this injunction!.... If the poor man asked a loan, he must choose his own pledge, and fetch it from his house with his own hand; it must be his act." (Meyer)

ii. God did not condemn the *principle* of taking a pledge, only commanding that it be received humanely. The idea of taking collateral for a loan is valid because it encourages personal responsibility in the one receiving the loan.

b. **You shall not keep his pledge overnight**: Assuming the pledge was something to keep the man warm (such as a garment or a blanket, which would often be the only pledge a poor man could make), the pledge had to be returned so the man could use it to keep warm overnight.

i. "Instructions were given concerning loans and pledges which were full of mercy to the poor, and provided that nothing really necessary for the well-being of anyone should be withheld from him after sundown. Those who were in need were not to be oppressed." (Morgan)

ii. **It shall be righteousness to you before the LORD**: "God will reckon it for a good work, and graciously reward it, he will turn paymaster to thee; thy righteousness, and thy riches too, shall endure for ever (Psalm 112:3)." (Trapp)

iii. "The Jews in several cases did act contrary to this rule, and we find them cuttingly reproved for it by the Prophet Amos, Amos 2:8." (Clarke)

5. (14-15) The command to pay your workers.

"You shall not oppress a hired servant *who is* poor and needy, *whether* one of your brethren or one of the aliens who *is* in your land within your gates. Each day you shall give *him* his wages, and not let the sun go down on it, for he *is* poor and has set his heart on it; lest he cry out against you to the LORD, and it be sin to you.

a. **You shall not oppress a hired servant**: A servant might be oppressed by not being paid, by brutal or unsafe working conditions, or in other ways. God commanded employers to treat their workers fairly and kindly.

b. **Lest he cry out against you to the LORD**: The LORD hears the cry of the oppressed, and this should be a warning to the one who would oppress others (James 5:4).

i. "The fact that he was 'only a hireling' (Heb. *sakir*), a person of a lower socioeconomic status, was no excuse to deny him his rights. In fact, he enjoyed such status with God that he could and might cry out to the Lord against the stingy, dishonest employer and thus invoke God's verdict of guilt." (Merrill)

6. (16) Each shall bear his own sin.

"Fathers shall not be put to death for *their* children, nor shall children be put to death for *their* fathers; a person shall be put to death for his own sin.

   a. **A person shall be put to death for his own sin**: God commanded that everyone be responsible for his or her own sin. A father cannot be blamed and responsible for the sin of their (grown) children, and the children cannot be blamed and responsible for the sin of their parents.

      i. By this same principle, it is often wrong for a parent to automatically blame themselves for their wayward children; though they may have a part in the problem, it isn't always the case.

      ii. "Though shame and other consequences of crime fall naturally on one's family and descendants according to the governance of God, the punishment to be exacted for a crime falls on the perpetrator alone." (Kalland)

   b. **For his own sin**: There are instances when God commands that a whole family be punished for sin, such as with the family of Achan in Joshua 7:16-26. When God deals with a whole family, it usually shows that there must have been some conspiracy between family members, for each is responsible **for his own sin**.

      i. "This law is explained and illustrated in sufficient detail, Ezekiel 18." (Clarke)

7. (17-18) A command to be compassionate and fair.

"You shall not pervert justice due the stranger or the fatherless, nor take a widow's garment as a pledge. But you shall remember that you were a slave in Egypt, and the Lord your God redeemed you from there; therefore I command you to do this thing.

   a. **You shall not pervert justice due the stranger or the fatherlessness**: The foreigner (**stranger**) or the orphan (**fatherless**) where among those who were often denied justice in the ancient world, because they normally had no one to advocate for them or support their cause.

      i. **Nor take a widow's garment**: "The widow's cloak must not be taken in pledge (though taking a cloak in pledge, temporarily, was allowed for others, vv.12–13)." (Kalland)

   b. **You shall remember**: As Israel remember how much God had done for them, it should make them more compassionate to the disadvantaged. It is good for God's people to deal with others remembering how much God has blessed and forgiven them.

8. (19-22) Leave behind some of the harvest for the poor.

"When you reap your harvest in your field, and forget a sheaf in the field, you shall not go back to get it; it shall be for the stranger, the fatherless, and the widow, that the LORD your God may bless you in all the work of your hands. When you beat your olive trees, you shall not go over the boughs again; it shall be for the stranger, the fatherless, and the widow. When you gather the grapes of your vineyard, you shall not glean *it* afterward; it shall be for the stranger, the fatherless, and the widow. And you shall remember that you were a slave in the land of Egypt; therefore I command you to do this thing.

> a. **It shall be for the stranger, the fatherless, and the widow**: This was one of God's support programs for the poor in Israel, giving them the right of the gleaner. Farmers were instructed to not completely harvest their fields, so that some would be left behind for the hard-working poor to gather for themselves. Dropped or forgotten bundles of grain were to be left behind in the field. This was what Boaz did for Ruth (Ruth 2:2-3, 2:16).
>
>> i. This was not the only care given to the poor in Israel. Deuteronomy 14:28-29 and 26:12-15 also command that every three years the poor were to be supported by Israel's tithe.
>
> b. **Therefore I command you to do this thing**: This was a wonderful way of helping the poor. It commanded farmers to have generous hearts, and it encouraged the poor to be active and work for their food. It made a way for Israel's poor to provide for their own needs with dignity.
>
>> i. "This permitted the recipient to salvage his own honor while at the same time delivering the landowner from any sense of arrogant control over the lives of those dependent on him." (Merrill)

Deuteronomy 25 – More Laws on Various Subjects

A. Two laws to protect criminals and animals.

1. (1-3) A limit on corporal punishment.

"If there is a dispute between men, and they come to court, that *the judges* may judge them, and they justify the righteous and condemn the wicked, then it shall be, if the wicked man deserves to be beaten, that the judge will cause him to lie down and be beaten in his presence, according to his guilt, with a certain number of blows. Forty blows he may give him *and* no more, lest he should exceed this and beat him with many blows above these, and your brother be humiliated in your sight.

a. **If there is a dispute between men, and they come to court**: By the direction of God, Israel's legal system made the distinction between criminal cases (where rulers punished crime through judges) and civil cases (where the people brought disputes before judges). This was a way to resolve disputes apart from violence.

b. **They justify the righteous and condemn the guilty**: Regarding both criminal and civil cases, the duty of Israel's **judges** was simple. They were to approve and encourage the **righteous** and condemn those who were guilty. When the righteous are penalized and the guilty are rewarded, courts of justice are not fulfilling their God-given responsibility (Romans 13:4).

c. **If the wicked man deserves to be beaten**: The context is of a civil case, a dispute between men. Those who were found to be **wicked** in their treatment of others, even in disputes between men, received physical punishment (or presumably, the equivalent). This would discourage those who were in the wrong from bringing the case before judges, and encourage disputes to be settled without bringing the matter before judges.

i. The law did not require 40 lashes; the punishment of the guilty man would be **according to his guilt**, and not more. However, the total number of strokes could not exceed 40.

ii. "Among the Mohammedans there are very few law-suits, and the reason is given…because they that sue others without just cause are to be whipped publicly." (Trapp)

d. **Forty blows may he give him and no more**: Though sometimes a beating was the appropriate punishment, God's law also recognized that punishment could be excessive, and therefore gave limits to penalties. The penalty was to be given in the **presence** of the judge, so he could make sure the punishment was not excessive.

i. In 2 Corinthians 11:24, Paul listed this among his apostolic credentials: *From the Jews five times I received forty stripes minus one.* The *forty stripes minus one* means Paul was beaten by the Jewish authorities with thirty-nine blows on five different occasions. One was subtracted both out of caution of a miscount, and as a small expression of mercy.

e. **Lest…your brother be humiliated in your sight**: God commanded that the dignity of even the guilty man be respected. To flog a man more than his wrong deserved would be to treat him more like an animal than a man.

i. "His sinful conduct against a brother was not sufficient cause to rob him of his full dignity." (Merrill)

ii. "It is interesting to notice what excessive punishment is to the mind of God. It is anything which makes our brother appear vile in our sight." (Morgan)

2. (4) The command to not muzzle the ox.

"You shall not muzzle an ox while it treads out *the grain*.

a. **You shall not muzzle an ox**: This law commanded the humane treatment of a working animal. In those days, grain could be broken away from its husk by having an ox walk on it repeatedly (usually around a circle). It would be cruel to force the ox to walk on all the grain, yet to **muzzle** him so he couldn't eat of it.

i. "The care for dumb creatures is part of our religious duty…. Oh, when will the travail of creation cease! Man's sin has indeed worked woe for the lower orders of creation." (Meyer)

ii. "The prohibition here (Deut 25:4) about muzzling the working ox reflects the spirit of mercy that pervades all of God's dealings with his creation, human or otherwise. The purpose clearly was not only to provide for the ox itself but to make the point by *a fortiori* argument that if a mere animal was worthy of humane treatment, how much more so was a human being created as the image of God." (Merrill)

b. **You shall not muzzle an ox**: In 1 Corinthians 9:9 and 1 Timothy 5:18 the apostle Paul applied this principle to the minister's right to be supported by the people he serves. Under normal circumstances, it is not right to expect a minister to serve a congregation and to receive no support from the congregation.

i. 1 Corinthians 9:9-10 suggests the application to God's ministers was the real point of this command, because in that passage Paul asked, *is it oxen God is concerned about? Or does He say it altogether for our sakes?*

B. Two laws dealing with family matters.

1. (5-10) The marriage obligation of surviving brothers.

"If brothers dwell together, and one of them dies and has no son, the widow of the dead man shall not be *married* to a stranger outside *the family;* her husband's brother shall go in to her, take her as his wife, and perform the duty of a husband's brother to her. And it shall be *that* the firstborn son which she bears will succeed to the name of his dead brother, that his name may not be blotted out of Israel. But if the man does not want to take his brother's wife, then let his brother's wife go up to the gate to the elders, and say, 'My husband's brother refuses to raise up a name to his brother in Israel; he will not perform the duty of my husband's brother.' Then the elders of his city shall call him and speak to him. But *if* he stands firm and says, 'I do not want to take her,' then his brother's wife shall come to him in the presence of the elders, remove his sandal from his foot, spit in his face, and answer and say, 'So shall it be done to the man who will not build up his brother's house.' And his name shall be called in Israel, 'The house of him who had his sandal removed.'

a. **One of them dies and has no son**: In ancient Israel it was seen as a great tragedy for a man to die without leaving descendants to carry on his name, with no one to give his family inheritance to. Therefore, if a man **dies and has no son**, it was the responsibility of one of his brothers to take the deceased brother's widow as a wife and **perform the duty of a husband's brother to her**. This custom is sometimes called *levirate marriage*.

i. "The practice of levirate marriage (Lat. *levir*, brother-in-law or husband's brother) was not peculiar to Israel, for it was practised among the Hittites and Assyrians as well as in countries such as India, Africa and South America.... The purpose of the custom was to ensure that a man who died before he had produced a male heir might nevertheless have an heir." (Thompson)

ii. "Was the law of levirate marriage an approval of polygamy? Hardly! It was rather an alternate arrangement under specific bounds to make possible the retention of landed property throughout the families of Israel." (Kalland)

b. **The firstborn son which she bears will succeed to the name of his dead brother, that his name may not be blotted out of Israel**: When a son was born to this union, he would not be counted as the son of the surviving brother, but as the son to the deceased brother.

i. **Son** here may simply mean *child*. "In the history of the interpretation of this Deuteronomic law, difference of opinion existed among Jewish expositors whether *ben* in v.5 meant 'son' or 'child.' The LXX [Septuagint] and Josephus render it 'child.' Moses had already established that when no male heir existed, daughters would be heirs of their father's property (Num 27:1-8)." (Kalland)

c. **He will not perform the duty of my husband's brother**: If the brothers of the deceased man refused to take this responsibility, they were to be called to open shame by the widow. The shame was compounded as they would **remove his sandal** and the widow would **spit in his face**.

i. "The legislation makes possible the release of the brother-in-law from his duty, while definitely discouraging such failure by the shame involved in being brought to court, spit upon, and labeled as 'The Family of the Unsandaled.'" (Kalland)

ii. This explains the circumstances of Ruth 4, where one relative of Ruth's deceased husband refused to take this responsibility, and the removal of the sandal demonstrated the refusal (Ruth 4:6-8). There is no reference to spitting in the face in the record of Ruth 4.

iii. **Him who had his sandal removed**: "It is difficult to find the reason of these ceremonies of degradation. Perhaps the *shoe* was the emblem of *power;* and by *stripping it off, deprivation* of that power and authority was represented. *Spitting* in the face was a mark of the utmost ignominy; but the Jews, who are legitimate judges in this case, say that the spitting was not *in* his face, but *before* his face *on the ground.*" (Clarke)

2. (11-12) Wives forbidden to interfere in their husband's fights.

"If *two* men fight together, and the wife of one draws near to rescue her husband from the hand of the one attacking him, and puts out her hand

and seizes him by the genitals, then you shall cut off her hand; your eye shall not pity *her*.

    a. **The wife of one draws near to rescue her husband**: This unusual law condemned a woman who interfered in her husband's **fight**, battling for her husband in a dishonorable way (**seizes him by the genitals**).

    b. **Then you shall cut off her hand**: This extreme punishment was meant to give an example in similar cases, commanding strong punishment against those who would fight in a way that would be unlikely to murder a man, but could "murder" his potential descendants. It also reinforced the basic principle that there are some fights or battles that women should not involve themselves in.

        i. The woman faced a penalty broadly based on the "eye for an eye" principle. She had mutilated a man, ruining his ability to father children. Her body would also be mutilated by the amputation of her hand, the part of her body that committed the offence.

        ii. "Possibly it was representative of similar offences and provided a standard for judgment in all such cases. Perhaps also, the law arose from the desire to protect the reproductive organs and thus obviate anything that might prevent a man leaving descendants." (Thompson)

C. Two laws commanding justice.

1. (13-16) God commands weights and measures be just.

"You shall not have in your bag differing weights, a heavy and a light. You shall not have in your house differing measures, a large and a small. You shall have a perfect and just weight, a perfect and just measure, that your days may be lengthened in the land which the LORD your God is giving you. For all who do such things, all who behave unrighteously, *are* an abomination to the LORD your God.

    a. **You shall not have in your bag different weights**: God commanded that His people do business honestly. The use of **different weights** was to cheat either the buyer or the seller. The surrounding culture may believe that it doesn't matter if money is made ethically or not, but God commands a **perfect and just weight** to be used in trade. This idea is repeated in passages such as Proverbs 11:1, 16:11, and 20:23.

        i. "There obviously was no sin in possessing these things per se, but their very possession would inevitably lead to their use in unscrupulous transactions." (Merrill)

    b. **All who do such things…are an abomination to the LORD**: This is a stronger stating of a command introduced in Leviticus 19:35-36. Stealing from others under the cover of doing business is a serious crime before God.

2. (17-19) God commands Israel to justly destroy Amalek.

"Remember what Amalek did to you on the way as you were coming out of Egypt, how he met you on the way and attacked your rear ranks, all the stragglers at your rear, when you *were* tired and weary; and he did not fear God. Therefore it shall be, when the LORD your God has given you rest from your enemies all around, in the land which the LORD your God is giving you to possess *as* an inheritance, *that* you will blot out the remembrance of Amalek from under heaven. You shall not forget.

a. **Remember what Amalek did**: The Amalekites descended from Esau (Genesis 36:15-16, 1 Chronicles 1:36) and were a nomadic tribe that roamed the broader area of southern Canaan and its bordering lands. Amalek's attack on Israel is recorded in Exodus 17. In response, Joshua led the armies of Israel in victory over the Amalekites as Moses prayed for Israel, assisted by the continual prayer of Aaron and Hur.

i. "Amalek's failure to show mercy to the weak merited divine judgment, for God judged nations for crimes against natural law." (Thompson)

b. **Blot out the remembrance of Amalek from under heaven**: The nature of the Amalekite attack against Israel – focused on the **stragglers** and those who were **tired and weary** – made Amalek the permanent enemy of Israel, and Israel was to treat the Amalekites as they would the Canaanites, both being under the judgment of God.

i. Because of God's strong command to battle against Amalek, many see Israel's struggle with Amalek as a picture of the believer's struggle with the flesh, which constantly battles against the spirit and must be struggled against until completely conquered (Galatians 5:17).

ii. "It is supposed that this command had its final accomplishment in the death of Haman and his ten sons, Esth. 3, 7, 9, as from this time the memory and name of Amalek was blotted out from under heaven, for through every period of their history it might be truly said, *They feared not God.*" (Clarke)

c. **When the LORD your God has given you rest**: Israel was to carry out this war against the Amalekites later, when they were at rest in the land. Some 400 years later, God directed Saul to make war against the Amalekites, and his failure to destroy them was the primary act of disobedience which cost Saul the throne (1 Samuel 15:2-9; 28:18).

Deuteronomy 26 – Presenting Firstfruits and Tithes

A. Instruction for bringing the firstfruits and tithes.

1. (1-4) Bringing the firstfruits to the priest.

"And it shall be, when you come into the land which the LORD your God is giving you *as* an inheritance, and you possess it and dwell in it, that you shall take some of the first of all the produce of the ground, which you shall bring from your land that the LORD your God is giving you, and put *it* in a basket and go to the place where the LORD your God chooses to make His name abide. And you shall go to the one who is priest in those days, and say to him, 'I declare today to the LORD your God that I have come to the country which the LORD swore to our fathers to give us.'

"Then the priest shall take the basket out of your hand and set it down before the altar of the LORD your God.

>a. **When you come into the land**: The sermons of Deuteronomy were presented by Moses to Israel as they camped on the plains of Moab (Deuteronomy 1:1, 1:5), near where they would cross the Jordan River. Though there were formidable obstacles (such as a flood-swollen Jordan and the mighty armies of Canaanites), God still assured them that they would **come into the land**. These were commands for Israel as they would **possess** and **dwell** in Canaan.

>b. **Some of the first of all the produce of the ground**: Numbers 18:12 instructed Israel to regularly bring the first of their harvest as a sacrifice to the priests. Yet the firstfruits described here seem to be a special offering of firstfruits, from the first of the harvest that they would gain in the Promised Land.

c. **Set it down before the altar of the** LORD **your God**: The giving of firstfruits honored the LORD, because it gave priority to honoring God with the harvest He had graciously provided.

> i. "The point is made that it was Yahweh who had given the increase to his people. By inference, therefore, it was not Baal." (Thompson)

2. (5-10) The words of thanks and praise at the giving of firstfruits.

And you shall answer and say before the LORD **your God: 'My father** *was* **a Syrian, about to perish, and he went down to Egypt and dwelt there, few in number; and there he became a nation, great, mighty, and populous. But the Egyptians mistreated us, afflicted us, and laid hard bondage on us. Then we cried out to the** LORD **God of our fathers, and the** LORD **heard our voice and looked on our affliction and our labor and our oppression. So the** LORD **brought us out of Egypt with a mighty hand and with an outstretched arm, with great terror and with signs and wonders. He has brought us to this place and has given us this land, "a land flowing with milk and honey"; and now, behold, I have brought the firstfruits of the land which you, O** LORD**, have given me.'**

Then you shall set it before the LORD **your God, and worship before the** LORD **your God.**

a. **And you shall answer and say before the** LORD **your God**: This wonderful confession of thanks marked the history of Israel from the time of Jacob and his family in the land of Canaan, to the family's going down into Egypt, continuing to the eventual deliverance from Egypt, wilderness journey, and entrance to the Promised Land.

> i. "They were commanded to remember and publicly acknowledge their former degradation and wretchedness, that they might be ever kept humble and dependent; and they must bring their offering as a public acknowledgment to God that it was by his mercy their state was changed, and by his bounty their comforts were continued." (Clarke)

> ii. **My father was a Syrian**: "It is pretty evident, from the text, that by a *Syrian* we are to understand *Jacob*, so called from his long residence in Syria with his father-in-law Laban. And his *being ready to perish* may signify the hard usage and severe labour he had in Laban's service, by which, as his health was much impaired, so his life might have often been in imminent danger." (Clarke)

b. **He went down to Egypt and dwelt there**: The King James Version translates this phrase as *he went down into Egypt, and sojourned there*. The thought was that Israel's 400 years in Egypt are described as only a sojourn or a brief visit. In the course of God's eternal plan, the time was nothing more than a *sojourn*.

> i. It is possible for a believer to focus so much on their time of trial or misery that they come to think that it defines their whole life. In contrast, God saw Israel's experience in Egypt as a *sojourn*.

c. **Few in number; and there he became a nation, great, mighty, and populous**: This was the major reason that God sent Jacob and his family to Egypt. When they lived in Canaan, they risked assimilation with the wicked, pagan peoples around them. To prevent this, and to allow the nation to grow, God sent them down to Egypt. At that time Egypt was a racist, separated society, and there would not be much intermarriage with Israel. Therefore, though they went to Egypt **few in number**, over time they **became a nation, great, mighty, and populous** without assimilation with Egypt.

d. **And now, behold, I have brought the firstfruits of the land**: This initial giving of firstfruits when Israel came into the Promised Land was an appropriate way to give thanks to Yahweh. This giving, and all giving done with the right heart, is a proper way to **worship before the LORD your God**.

> i. "The peace and stability that would permit the inauguration of regular agricultural patterns would be irrefutable evidence that the Lord had indeed accomplished his word to the fathers. In recognition of this and in tribute to the Lord's electing and saving grace, the farmer would come to proffer the firstfruits of his fields." (Merrill)
>
> ii. "The case of the *ten lepers* that were cleansed, of whom only *one* returned to give God thanks, is an awful lesson. How many are continually living on the bounty of God, who feel no gratitude for his mercies! Reader, is this thy state? If so, then expect the just God to curse thy blessings." (Clarke)

3. (11) **So you shall rejoice**.

So you shall rejoice in every good *thing* which the LORD your God has given to you and your house, you and the Levite and the stranger who *is* among you.

> a. **Rejoice in every good thing which the LORD your God has given to you**: When God's people receive from the LORD, and they give back to Him, it should make them rejoice. This is the proper response of a creature to their Creator, who supplies all good things.
>
> b. **You and the Levite and the stranger**: Israel's joyful gratitude should also lead them to generosity with others. These would include those who

served them spiritually (the **Levite**) and the foreigners among them (the **stranger**).

> i. "They were to take care to share God's bounties among all those who were dependent on them. The *Levite* has no inheritance, let him rejoice with thee. The *stranger* has no home, let him feel thee to be his friend and his father." (Clarke)

4. (12-15) The prayer for the giving of the tithe.

"When you have finished laying aside all the tithe of your increase in the third year—the year of tithing—and have given *it* **to the Levite, the stranger, the fatherless, and the widow, so that they may eat within your gates and be filled, then you shall say before the L**ORD **your God: 'I have removed the holy** *tithe* **from** *my* **house, and also have given them to the Levite, the stranger, the fatherless, and the widow, according to all Your commandments which You have commanded me; I have not transgressed Your commandments, nor have I forgotten** *them.* **I have not eaten any of it when in mourning, nor have I removed** *any* **of it for an unclean** *use,* **nor given** *any* **of it for the dead. I have obeyed the voice of the L**ORD **my God, and have done according to all that You have commanded me. Look down from Your holy habitation, from heaven, and bless Your people Israel and the land which You have given us, just as You swore to our fathers, "a land flowing with milk and honey."'**

a. **When you have finished laying aside all the tithe**: The **tithe** was required of Israel every year, but every **third year** the tithe was given not only to the Levites for their support (Numbers 18:21-24, Deuteronomy 14:28-29) but was also to be shared by the needy. These would normally include the **stranger**, the **fatherless**, and the **widow**. This tithe was not brought to the tabernacle or temple (God's house); it was given to local Levites for its administration to the needy.

b. **Then you shall say**: The prayer described here shows the kind of heart God wanted Israel to have as they gave their tithe. God not only wants His people to give, but to give with the right heart.

> i. Right giving is done according to God's word: **According to all Your commandments which you have commanded me**.

> ii. Right giving is done within the context of a whole life of obedience: **I have not transgressed Your commandments, nor have I forgotten them**. "This is spoken, not by way of Pharisaical boasting or opinion of merit, but public testification of entire obedience." (Trapp)

iii. **I have not eaten any of it…nor have I removed any of it**: Right giving genuinely sets aside what is to be given to the LORD. It does not keep what should be surrendered to the LORD's service.

iv. **Nor given any of it for the dead**: Right giving is not done superstitiously. "Putting food in a grave with a dead body was a common Egyptian and Canaanite practice, which is most likely what the Israelites were not to emulate." (Kalland)

v. **Look down from Your holy habitation, from heaven, and bless Your people**: Right giving is done with the expectation that God will bless in response.

B. Moses' exhortation to Israel.

1. (16) A call to complete obedience.

"This day the LORD your God commands you to observe these statutes and judgments; therefore you shall be careful to observe them with all your heart and with all your soul.

a. **This day the LORD your God commands you to observe these statutes and judgments**: Deuteronomy 4:1 began this long section with the words *Now, O Israel, listen to the statutes and the judgments which I teach you to observe*. From Deuteronomy chapter 4 through chapter 26, Moses has reminded Israel of God's commands. Now, in concluding the second of the three sermons recorded in Deuteronomy, Moses exhorted Israel to *keep* the commands.

b. **Therefore you shall be careful to observe them**: Sometimes we need to be *instructed* regarding the law of God; sometimes we need to be *reminded* regarding the law of God. But most often, we need to be *exhorted* regarding the law of God. We know what to do, but we need to be encouraged to actually *do it*.

2. (17) Israel's proclamation.

Today you have proclaimed the LORD to be your God, and that you will walk in His ways and keep His statutes, His commandments, and His judgments, and that you will obey His voice.

a. **Today you have proclaimed the LORD to be your God**: This was the first of two things Israel was to proclaim. They were to proclaim their allegiance to Yahweh (**the LORD**), the covenant God of Israel. They should not recognize any of the pagan deities as true gods, especially the so-called gods of the Canaanites.

b. **You will walk in His ways and keep His statutes**: Israel was also to proclaim their allegiance to Yahweh by their obedience to Him. Honoring the LORD wasn't just a matter of religious or ceremonial observance; it should be seen in daily life.

3. (18-19) God's proclamation.

Also today the LORD has proclaimed you to be His special people, just as He promised you, that *you* should keep all His commandments, and that He will set you high above all nations which He has made, in praise, in name, and in honor, and that you may be a holy people to the LORD your God, just as He has spoken."

a. **The LORD has proclaimed you to be His special people**: The descendants of Abraham, Isaac, and Jacob were truly a **special people** to God. They were not special in the sense that they were all declared righteous and in right relationship with God, settling their standing with God in this life and life to come. That could come only through their faith in God as individuals, as was true for Abraham (Genesis 15:6, Romans 4:20-25). Israel was a **special people** in that they had, and continue to have, an important role in God's unfolding plan of the ages.

i. "It is true that Israel's selection as a 'kingdom of priests' and a 'holy nation' carried with it a heavy responsibility. Their faithful discharge of that responsibility would, however, result in the greatest privilege and honor." (Merrill)

b. **He will set you high above all nations**: Israel's obedience to the LORD would be more than rewarded. God promised that He would exalt an obedient Israel and set them superior to other peoples **in praise**, **name**, and **honor**. Yet this would be true only for Israel as they were obedient to their covenant with God.

i. "While Israel regarded God's word and kept his testimonies, they were the greatest and most respectable of all nations; but when they forsook God and his law, they became the most contemptible. O Britain! even more highly favoured than ancient Israel, learn wisdom by what they have suffered." (Clarke)

Deuteronomy 27 – Stones of Witness

A. The special altar on Mount Ebal.

1. (1-8) The command to set up a special altar.

Now Moses, with the elders of Israel, commanded the people, saying: "Keep all the commandments which I command you today. And it shall be, on the day when you cross over the Jordan to the land which the LORD your God is giving you, that you shall set up for yourselves large stones, and whitewash them with lime. You shall write on them all the words of this law, when you have crossed over, that you may enter the land which the LORD your God is giving you, 'a land flowing with milk and honey,' just as the LORD God of your fathers promised you. Therefore it shall be, when you have crossed over the Jordan, *that* **on Mount Ebal you shall set up these stones, which I command you today, and you shall whitewash them with lime. And there you shall build an altar to the LORD your God, an altar of stones; you shall not use an iron** *tool* **on them. You shall build with whole stones the altar of the LORD your God, and offer burnt offerings on it to the LORD your God. You shall offer peace offerings, and shall eat there, and rejoice before the LORD your God. And you shall write very plainly on the stones all the words of this law."**

    a. **Keep all the commandments which I command you today**: This begins the third sermon Moses gave to Israel recorded in Deuteronomy. These were preached shortly before Israel would cross the Jordan and enter Canaan under Joshua's leadership.

- The first sermon (1:1-4:43) emphasized *history* – what God had done for Israel in bringing them out of Egypt to the threshold of Canaan.
- The second sermon (4:44-26:19) emphasized *law* – God's commands to Israel for life in the Promised Land.

- The third sermon (27:1-33:29) emphasized *covenant* – God's covenant with Israel, established at Mount Sinai (Exodus 24) and here renewed on the plains of Moab.

    i. **With the elders of Israel**: "Not Moses alone, but Moses and the elders of Israel commanded the people. Nowhere else in Deuteronomy are the elders associated with Moses as spokesmen to the people." (Kalland)

b. **There you shall build an altar**: When Israel came into the Promised Land, they were to build a special altar on Mount Ebal. It was to be made of natural stone, with no **iron tool** used to carve the stones. With these **whole stones** making up the altar, they were also to **write very plainly on the stones all the words of this law**.

　i. "Such stipulations were intended to set Israelite altars apart from Canaanite ones that ordinarily were built of dressed stone." (Merrill)

　ii. This was a special altar. It was clearly to be used for sacrifice (**You shall offer peace offerings**), but it was also to be a memorial of the Law of Moses and his great sermon to Israel in the book of Deuteronomy.

　iii. This command was obeyed by Joshua in Joshua 8:30-32; there, at **Mount Ebal**, in Canaan, Joshua *in the presence of the children of Israel... wrote on the stones a copy of the law of Moses, which he had written.*

　iv. Probably, what was written was the summation of the law contained in the Ten Commandments.

c. **An altar of stones; you shall not use an iron tool on them**: God did not want the glory of the stone carver to be the center of attention at His altar. God, at His altar, refused to share His glory with man. The beauty and attractiveness would be found only in what God provided through sacrifice (in the **burnt offerings** and **peace offerings**), and in God's plainly revealed word, and not in the skill or talent of man.

　i. "The law insisted on the necessity for obedience, while the altar spoke of the only method of approach to God consequent on disobedience." (Morgan)

　ii. "Thus the moral law drove the Jews to the ceremonial, which was their gospel, as it doth now drive us to Christ, who is indeed 'the end of the law for righteousness to everyone that believeth' (Romans 10:4)." (Trapp)

d. **You shall whitewash them with lime**: This would make the engraved words easy to see. Anything done to make God's word more accessible to others is a good thing, if the integrity of God's word is preserved.

i. "Writing laws on stones…was common in the ancient Near East. Whitewashing stones before writing on them was a practice in Egypt. Large writing stones, some eight feet high, from before Moses' time have been found at Byblos." (Kalland)

ii. Any time God's word is presented, it must be presented **very plainly**. Every preacher and teacher must endeavor to make the word of God plain; clear in the understanding of those who receive it.

2. (9-10) Becoming the covenant people of Yahweh, the Lord God.

Then Moses and the priests, the Levites, spoke to all Israel, saying, "Take heed and listen, O Israel: This day you have become the people of the Lord your God. Therefore you shall obey the voice of the Lord your God, and observe His commandments and His statutes which I command you today."

a. **Then Moses and the priests, the Levites, spoke to all Israel**: Much of the book of Deuteronomy is written after the same pattern as ancient agreements between kings and their subjects. Here, the idea was clear: Yahweh was Israel's King, and the people of Israel were His subjects. He told them what He expected of them, and what they might expect from Him.

i. **All Israel**: "The point here is that there were no privileged persons who stand above or outside the covenant mandates. The fact that the tribe of Levi had to stand on Mount Gerizim with the other tribes makes this most clear." (Merrill)

b. **This day you have become the people of the Lord your God**: As the covenant was being formally confirmed with the second generation on the plains of Moab, it could again be said to Israel, **you have become the people of the Lord your God**. The covenant was agreed to, and Israel willingly submitted itself to the Lord God, recognizing Him as their King.

c. **You shall obey the voice of the Lord your God, and observe His commandments and His statutes**: If Yahweh is the King of His people, it is fitting that they obey Him this way. Considering their covenant with God, this was an obvious part of their obligation to the Lord.

B. The command to announce the curses from Mount Ebal.

1. (11-13) The division of the tribes between the two mountains.

And Moses commanded the people on the same day, saying, "These shall stand on Mount Gerizim to bless the people, when you have crossed over the Jordan: Simeon, Levi, Judah, Issachar, Joseph, and

Benjamin; and these shall stand on Mount Ebal to curse: Reuben, Gad, Asher, Zebulun, Dan, and Naphtali.

> a. **These shall stand on Mount Gerizim...and these shall stand on Mount Ebal**: When Israel came into Canaan, they were to separate the tribes according to these two groups. One group would gather on **Mount Gerizim**, and they would **bless the people**. The other group would stand on **Mount Ebal** and they would **curse** those who disobeyed the law of God.
>
>> i. "Though the instructions here do not say so, the Joshua narrative indicates that the ark of the covenant, with its Levitical bearers, remained in the valley between the mountains as representative of the presence of the Lord and as the receptacle containing the Ten Commandments (Josh 8:33)." (Merrill)
>
> b. **To bless the people...to curse**: This dramatic scene was fulfilled in Joshua 8:32-35. In Joshua's day, it happened after a bitter defeat, then a dramatic repentance and recovery at Ai (Joshua 7:1-8:29). After the victory at Ai, Joshua wanted to continue Israel's obedience to God, so he led the nation in the ceremony commanded in Deuteronomy 27 (Joshua 8:30-35).
>
>> i. By this, Joshua showed himself to be a man of the Book, and Israel a people of the Book. They would order their lives after God's word. This was done even at some cost or inconvenience. The distance from Ai to Ebal and Gerizim was not a small distance to move all the tribes of Israel (from 20 to 25 miles, or 32 to 40 km).
>>
>> ii. The rest of the chapter declares the curses; but does not announce a declaration of blessing. At Ebal and Gerazim, both the blessings and curses were read (Joshua 8:34).
>>
>> iii. "The absence of a list of blessings may simply mean that they were omitted, since they would have corresponded with the curses except that they negatived everyone in turn. Those who were blessed did not offend in the areas in which those who were cursed did." (Thompson)
>>
>> iv. "The blessings are not mentioned by Moses; that we might learn to look for them by the Messiah only." (Trapp)
>
> c. **These shall stand on Mount Gerizim...and these shall stand on Mount Ebal**: God commanded this open-air and audience-participation sermon to happen at **Mount Gerizim** and **Mount Ebal** for several important reasons.
>
>> i. This would be a beautiful place to do this. The whole nation could hear this reading of the law because the area has a natural amphitheater

effect given of the contour of the hills.

ii. Because Gerizim and Ebal were in the geographic middle of the Promised Land, Israel had to control the middle of Canaan and the highlands to have the luxury of such an assembly at these mountains.

iii. Finally, the mountains themselves were pictures of blessing and cursing: "On all hands it is allowed that *Gerizim* abounds with springs, gardens, and orchards, and that it is covered with a beautiful verdure, while *Ebal* is as *naked* and barren as a rock." (Clarke)

2. (14-26) The declaration of the curses.

"And the Levites shall speak with a loud voice and say to all the men of Israel: 'Cursed *is* the one who makes a carved or molded image, an abomination to the Lord, the work of the hands of the craftsman, and sets *it* up in secret.'

"And all the people shall answer and say, 'Amen!'

'Cursed *is* the one who treats his father or his mother with contempt.'

"And all the people shall say, 'Amen!'

'Cursed *is* the one who moves his neighbor's landmark.'

"And all the people shall say, 'Amen!'

'Cursed *is* the one who makes the blind to wander off the road.'

"And all the people shall say, 'Amen!'

'Cursed *is* the one who perverts the justice due the stranger, the fatherless, and widow.'

"And all the people shall say, 'Amen!'

'Cursed *is* the one who lies with his father's wife, because he has uncovered his father's bed.'

"And all the people shall say, 'Amen!'

'Cursed *is* the one who lies with any kind of animal.'

"And all the people shall say, 'Amen!'

'Cursed *is* the one who lies with his sister, the daughter of his father or the daughter of his mother.'

"And all the people shall say, 'Amen!'

'Cursed *is* the one who lies with his mother-in-law.'

"And all the people shall say, 'Amen!'

'Cursed *is* the one who attacks his neighbor secretly.'

"And all the people shall say, 'Amen!'

'Cursed *is* the one who takes a bribe to slay an innocent person.'

"And all the people shall say, 'Amen!'

'Cursed *is* the one who does not confirm *all* the words of this law by observing them.'

"And all the people shall say, 'Amen!'"

    a. **The Levites shall speak with a loud voice**: The loud reading of the blessings and curses would make a memorable impression on everyone present. The curses on covenant-breaking Israel would be declared by the Levites and the people were to answer **Amen!** to every declaration.

        i. It is good to remind ourselves that the word **amen** means something. It means "so be it." Every **amen** was a conscious agreement with the declaration of a curse.

    b. **Say to all the men of Israel**: Strictly speaking, these are not curses. Instead, they are a listing of sins that are proclaimed to be under God's curse. The particular way the curse will happen is not explained.

        i. Many of the sins that follow are sins that might not be discovered by others and brought to justice under the Law of Moses. The repeated theme of the following curse statements is that even if these sins are not discovered by man, they will be cursed by God.

    c. **Cursed is the one who**: The Levites were to declare, and the people were to agree to, curses on a covenant-breaking Israel.

        i. Curses on idolaters (**the one who makes any carved or molded image**).

        ii. Curses on those who dishonor their parents (**the one who treats his father or his mother with contempt**).

        iii. Curses on those who steal (**the one who moves his neighbor's landmark**).

        iv. Curses on those who are simply cruel (**the one who makes the blind to wander off the road**).

        v. Curses on **the one who perverts the justice due the stranger, the fatherless, and widow**.

        vi. Curses on those who disobey God's sexual standards (regarding incest and bestiality).

        vii. Curses on the violent (**the one who attacks his neighbor secretly**).

viii. Curses on those who cheat the courts (**the one who takes a bribe to slay an innocent person**).

d. Cursed is the one who does not confirm all the words of this law: Finally – if one believed they had escaped these curses – there was a curse pronounced on the **one who does not confirm all the words of this law**. Even if somehow, we have escaped all the previous curses, no one can **confirm all the words of this law** by obeying them all. In a sense, everyone is under the curse of the law.

i. When all are found guilty before the law, and they cannot **confirm all the words of this law**, there is still hope. A clue to this hope is found in the beginning of the chapter, where God declared that an altar be built – not upon Mount Gerizim, the mountain of blessing, but upon Mount Ebal, the mountain of curses. People need the covering and atoning sacrifice exactly at the point where their sin and failures are revealed, and God's curse is pronounced on sin.

ii. It is important to recognize that believers, in Jesus Christ, do not have an old covenant relationship with God. Believers expect to be blessed, not because of their obedience, but because of their position in Jesus. The curse God's people deserved was laid on Him (Galatians 3:10-14). Though there may be an inherent curse of consequences in disobedience, or even the correcting hand of God, under the new covenant, He does not punish His people or curse them – because all that they deserved, past, present, and future, was poured out on Jesus.

iii. **All the words of this law**: "The word *col*, all, is not found in any *printed* copy of the *Hebrew* text; but the *Samaritan* preserves it.... The *Septuagint* also, and *St. Paul* in his quotation of this place, Gal. 3:10. St. Jerome says that the Jews suppressed, the word, that it might not appear that they were bound to fulfill all the precepts in the law of Moses." (Clarke)

Deuteronomy 28 – Blessing and Cursing

A. Blessings on obedience.

1. (1-2) Overtaken by blessing.

"Now it shall come to pass, if you diligently obey the voice of the Lord your God, to observe carefully all His commandments which I command you today, that the Lord your God will set you high above all nations of the earth. And all these blessings shall come upon you and overtake you, because you obey the voice of the Lord your God:

> a. **If you diligently obey the voice of the Lord**: The word **if** has great importance here. In this chapter, Moses exhorted Israel to make a *choice*. The covenant God made with Israel contained three major features: The law, the sacrifice, and the choice.
>
>> i. The idea behind the choice was that God was determined to reveal Himself to the world through Israel. Yahweh would do this either by making them so blessed that the world would know only God could have blessed them so; or by making them so cursed that only God could have cursed them and cause them to still survive. The choice of blessing or cursing was up to Israel, based on their faithfulness to their covenant with God.
>>
>> ii. As a literary form, this chapter is like ancient treaties between a king and his people; this is Yahweh the King, making a covenant with His people, Israel.
>>
>> iii. "In the ancient Near East it was customary for legal treaties to conclude with passages containing blessings upon those who observed the enactments, and curses upon those who did not." (Harrison, commentary on Leviticus)
>
> b. **That the Lord your God will set you high above all nations of the earth**: Therefore, if Israel would obey the Lord, He would **set** them

high above other nations. The blessings would be so powerful that they would **come upon** and **overtake** Israel. They wouldn't be able to *escape* the blessings.

> i. "The list of blessings in these verses [28:3-14] provides a striking piece of Hebrew rhythmic prose with its succession of phrases without co-ordinates between them. The sense of rhythm is supported by the repetition of *Blessed*." (Thompson)

2. (3-14) God's promise to bless Israel as they obeyed the covenant.

"Blessed *shall* you *be* in the city, and blessed *shall* you *be* in the country.

"Blessed *shall be* the fruit of your body, the produce of your ground and the increase of your herds, the increase of your cattle and the offspring of your flocks.

"Blessed *shall be* your basket and your kneading bowl.

"Blessed *shall* you *be* when you come in, and blessed *shall* you *be* when you go out.

"The LORD will cause your enemies who rise against you to be defeated before your face; they shall come out against you one way and flee before you seven ways.

"The LORD will command the blessing on you in your storehouses and in all to which you set your hand, and He will bless you in the land which the LORD your God is giving you.

"The LORD will establish you as a holy people to Himself, just as He has sworn to you, if you keep the commandments of the LORD your God and walk in His ways. Then all peoples of the earth shall see that you are called by the name of the LORD, and they shall be afraid of you. And the LORD will grant you plenty of goods, in the fruit of your body, in the increase of your livestock, and in the produce of your ground, in the land of which the LORD swore to your fathers to give you. The LORD will open to you His good treasure, the heavens, to give the rain to your land in its season, and to bless all the work of your hand. You shall lend to many nations, but you shall not borrow. And the LORD will make you the head and not the tail; you shall be above only, and not be beneath, if you heed the commandments of the LORD your God, which I command you today, and are careful to observe *them*. So you shall not turn aside from any of the words which I command you this day, *to* the right or the left, to go after other gods to serve them.

> a. **Blessed shall you be**: An obedient Israel would be blessed everywhere. In the **city** and in the **country**, when they **come in** and when they **go**

out. An obedient Israel would be blessed in their farms (**produce, herds**), homes (the **fruit of your body**), and kitchens (**basket, kneading bowl**). Their **storehouses** would be blessed and full of food.

> i. "The expression *come in ... go out* is often used in the Old Testament to denote a man's ability to come and go in the affairs of life (31:2; Josh. 14:11; 1 Kgs 3:7; Ps. 121:8; Isa. 37:28). The blessings of Yahweh touch the whole range of a man's life and depict a comprehensive fullness of divine favour." (Thompson)

b. **They shall come out against you one way and flee before you seven ways**: An obedient Israel would be blessed in warfare. Under God's blessing, enemies would be **defeated** before the **face** of Israel.

c. **The LORD will establish you as a holy people to Himself**: Perhaps the best blessing had to do with Israel's own relationship with God. Yahweh would separate an obedient Israel to Himself, having a special relationship with Him. Without this blessing of God's presence, all the material blessings described previously would be empty.

> i. "This is the sum of all blessings, to be made *holy*, and be preserved in *holiness*." (Clarke)

d. **All the peoples of the earth shall see that you are called by the name of the LORD.... the LORD will make you the head and not the tail; you shall be above only, and not be beneath**: God's purpose in blessing Israel was greater than just enriching the nation for its own sake. He intended to glorify Himself through blessing Israel. The world would see and speak of God's hand of blessing on Israel.

> i. **To give the rain to your land in its season**: "The Israelites were facing a land where belief in the fertility gods of Baalism was common. The various Baals were thought to be in control of rain. The Canaanites believed that Baal had a house in the heavens with an opening in the roof from which the rains were sent.... Moses did insist that it was the Lord who would either bless Israel with abundant rain or withhold rain because of her disobedience." (Kalland)

> ii. When Israel walked after the LORD, these blessings were real. One example of this is when the queen of Sheba came to Solomon and saw a nation so blessed, she knew it had to be of God (1 Kings 10:1-13).

B. Curses on disobedience.

1. (15) Introduction to the curses.

"But it shall come to pass, if you do not obey the voice of the LORD your God, to observe carefully all His commandments and His statutes

which I command you today, that all these curses will come upon you and overtake you:

a. **If you do not obey the voice of the L**ORD **your God**: The covenant's aspect of the *choice* was a sword with two edges. Obedience would result in great blessing, but disobedience would result in terrible curses.

b. **All these curses will come upon you and overtake you**: Like the blessings for an obedient Israel, the curses for a disobedient Israel would be inevitable. It is helpful to remember that these curses were part of a covenant that Israel agreed to, both at Sinai (Exodus 24:1-8) and here in Deuteronomy.

i. Significantly, the description of the curses is much longer and more detailed than the description of the blessings. According to Thompson, this was common in treaties of that general time and place, and Trapp states: "Far more curses are mentioned than blessings. Such is the baseness of our natures, that we are sooner terrified with menaces than moved with mercies."

c. **All these curses**: The rest of the chapter is almost overwhelming. The repetition of the curse, in all its many aspects, was intended to make a deep impression on Israel. If they were not motivated by the blessings described in the previous verse, they should be motivated by these terrible curses.

i. "Actually, a logical analysis of the chapter is almost impossible, since the final aim was not to be logical but to build up a vivid impression by presenting picture after picture until the hearer could see and feel the import of the preacher's words." (Thompson)

2. (16-68) The curses upon Israel's disobedience.

"Cursed *shall* you *be* in the city, and cursed *shall* you *be* in the country.

"Cursed *shall be* your basket and your kneading bowl.

"Cursed *shall be* the fruit of your body and the produce of your land, the increase of your cattle and the offspring of your flocks.

"Cursed *shall* you *be* when you come in, and cursed *shall* you *be* when you go out.

"The LORD **will send on you cursing, confusion, and rebuke in all that you set your hand to do, until you are destroyed and until you perish quickly, because of the wickedness of your doings in which you have forsaken Me. The L**ORD **will make the plague cling to you until He has consumed you from the land which you are going to possess. The L**ORD **will strike you with consumption, with fever, with inflammation, with severe burning fever, with the sword, with scorching, and with mildew;**

they shall pursue you until you perish. And your heavens which *are* over your head shall be bronze, and the earth which is under you *shall be* iron. The LORD will change the rain of your land to powder and dust; from the heaven it shall come down on you until you are destroyed.

"The LORD will cause you to be defeated before your enemies; you shall go out one way against them and flee seven ways before them; and you shall become troublesome to all the kingdoms of the earth. Your carcasses shall be food for all the birds of the air and the beasts of the earth, and no one shall frighten *them* away. The LORD will strike you with the boils of Egypt, with tumors, with the scab, and with the itch, from which you cannot be healed. The LORD will strike you with madness and blindness and confusion of heart. And you shall grope at noonday, as a blind man gropes in darkness; you shall not prosper in your ways; you shall be only oppressed and plundered continually, and no one shall save *you*.

"You shall betroth a wife, but another man shall lie with her; you shall build a house, but you shall not dwell in it; you shall plant a vineyard, but shall not gather its grapes. Your ox *shall be* slaughtered before your eyes, but you shall not eat of it; your donkey *shall be* violently taken away from before you, and shall not be restored to you; your sheep *shall be* given to your enemies, and you shall have no one to rescue *them*. Your sons and your daughters *shall be* given to another people, and your eyes shall look and fail *with longing* for them all day long; and *there shall be* no strength in your hand. A nation whom you have not known shall eat the fruit of your land and the produce of your labor, and you shall be only oppressed and crushed continually. So you shall be driven mad because of the sight which your eyes see. The LORD will strike you in the knees and on the legs with severe boils which cannot be healed, and from the sole of your foot to the top of your head.

"The LORD will bring you and the king whom you set over you to a nation which neither you nor your fathers have known, and there you shall serve other gods—wood and stone. And you shall become an astonishment, a proverb, and a byword among all nations where the LORD will drive you.

"You shall carry much seed out to the field but gather little in, for the locust shall consume it. You shall plant vineyards and tend *them*, but you shall neither drink *of* the wine nor gather the *grapes;* for the worms shall eat them. You shall have olive trees throughout all your territory, but you shall not anoint *yourself* with the oil; for your olives shall drop off. You shall beget sons and daughters, but they shall not be yours; for they shall go into captivity. Locusts shall consume all your trees and the produce of your land.

"The alien who *is* among you shall rise higher and higher above you, and you shall come down lower and lower. He shall lend to you, but you shall not lend to him; he shall be the head, and you shall be the tail.

"Moreover all these curses shall come upon you and pursue and overtake you, until you are destroyed, because you did not obey the voice of the LORD your God, to keep His commandments and His statutes which He commanded you. And they shall be upon you for a sign and a wonder, and on your descendants forever.

"Because you did not serve the LORD your God with joy and gladness of heart, for the abundance of everything, therefore you shall serve your enemies, whom the LORD will send against you, in hunger, in thirst, in nakedness, and in need of everything; and He will put a yoke of iron on your neck until He has destroyed you. The LORD will bring a nation against you from afar, from the end of the earth, *as swift* as the eagle flies, a nation whose language you will not understand, a nation of fierce countenance, which does not respect the elderly nor show favor to the young. And they shall eat the increase of your livestock and the produce of your land, until you are destroyed; they shall not leave you grain or new wine or oil, *or* the increase of your cattle or the offspring of your flocks, until they have destroyed you.

"They shall besiege you at all your gates until your high and fortified walls, in which you trust, come down throughout all your land; and they shall besiege you at all your gates throughout all your land which the LORD your God has given you. You shall eat the fruit of your own body, the flesh of your sons and your daughters whom the LORD your God has given you, in the siege and desperate straits in which your enemy shall distress you. The sensitive and very refined man among you will be hostile toward his brother, toward the wife of his bosom, and toward the rest of his children whom he leaves behind, so that he will not give any of them the flesh of his children whom he will eat, because he has nothing left in the siege and desperate straits in which your enemy shall distress you at all your gates. The tender and delicate woman among you, who would not venture to set the sole of her foot on the ground because of her delicateness and sensitivity, will refuse to the husband of her bosom, and to her son and her daughter, her placenta which comes out from between her feet and her children whom she bears; for she will eat them secretly for lack of everything in the siege and desperate straits in which your enemy shall distress you at all your gates.

"If you do not carefully observe all the words of this law that are written in this book, that you may fear this glorious and awesome name, THE LORD YOUR GOD, then the LORD will bring upon you and your descendants extraordinary plagues—great and prolonged plagues—and serious and prolonged sicknesses. Moreover He will bring back on you all the diseases of Egypt, of which you were afraid, and they shall cling to you. Also every sickness and every plague, which *is* not written in this Book of the Law, will the LORD bring upon you until you are destroyed. You shall be left few in number, whereas you were as the stars of heaven in multitude, because you would not obey the voice of the LORD your God. And it shall be, *that* just as the LORD rejoiced over you to do you good and multiply you, so the LORD will rejoice over you to destroy you and bring you to nothing; and you shall be plucked from off the land which you go to possess.

"Then the LORD will scatter you among all peoples, from one end of the earth to the other, and there you shall serve other gods, which neither you nor your fathers have known—wood and stone. And among those nations you shall find no rest, nor shall the sole of your foot have a resting place; but there the LORD will give you a trembling heart, failing eyes, and anguish of soul. Your life shall hang in doubt before you; you shall fear day and night, and have no assurance of life. In the morning you shall say, 'Oh, that it were evening!' And at evening you shall say, 'Oh, that it were morning!' because of the fear which terrifies your heart, and because of the sight which your eyes see.

"And the LORD will take you back to Egypt in ships, by the way of which I said to you, 'You shall never see it again.' And there you shall be offered for sale to your enemies as male and female slaves, but no one will buy *you*."

    a. **In the city…in the country…. when you come in…when you go out**: A covenant-disobedient Israel would be cursed everywhere. There would be no place that they could go to escape the consequences of their covenant unfaithfulness.

    b. **The fruit of your body…the produce of your land and the increase of your cattle**: A covenant-disobedient Israel would be cursed in their homes, their farms, and in their kitchens (the **basket** and the **kneading bowl**).

    c. **Plague…. consumption…fever…. the boils of Egypt…the scab…the itch…. madness and blindness and confusion of heart**: A covenant-disobedient Israel would be cursed in their health.

        i. **Tumors**: "The 'tumors' that were to come on disobedient Israel were like those the Philistines later contracted when the ark of the covenant was held by them (1 Sam 5–6). The Hebrew word *opel* means 'a swelling' and is usually thought to be hemorrhoids, tumors, bubonic plague, or leprosy." (Kalland)

d. **Your heavens…shall be bronze…. the LORD will change the rain of your land to powder and dust**: A covenant-disobedient Israel would be cursed by the weather. The sky would not bring the rain essential to their agriculture. This would bring famine and starvation.

e. **To be defeated before your enemies**: A covenant-disobedient Israel would be cursed in warfare. God would not fight for them, and the bodies of their dead would be eaten by the **birds of the air** and the **beasts of the earth**.

f. **You shall betroth a wife, but another man shall lie with her…. Your ox shall be slaughtered before your eyes, but you shall not eat of it**: A covenant-disobedient Israel would be cursed by repeated and terrible injustices and tragedies. All these tragedies would bring a dreadful result: Israel would **be driven mad because of the sight which your eyes see**.

i. "Perhaps no people under the sun have been more oppressed and spoiled than the rebellious Jews. Indeed, this has been their portion, with but little intermission, for nearly 1,800 years." (Clarke)

ii. **They shall be upon you for a sign and a wonder**: "The Lord who had brought the Israelites out of Egypt by signs and wonders (4:34) would make the curses to be 'a sign and a wonder' to them and their descendants forever (v.46)." (Kalland)

iii. **Your sons and your daughters shall be given to another people**: "In several countries, particularly in *Spain* and *Portugal*, the children of the Jews have been taken from them by order of government, and educated in the Popish faith. There have been some instances of Jewish children being taken from their parents even in *Protestant* countries." (Clarke)

g. **The LORD will bring a nation against you from afar**: A covenant-disobedient Israel would be attacked and conquered by **a nation of fierce countenance**, and they would fight **until they** had **destroyed** Israel.

i. **You shall eat the fruit of your own body**: This became horribly true in the days of the later kingdom. 2 Kings 6:24-30 describes a famine so severe in a besieged Israelite city that there was a fight between two women over an agreement to eat their children. This was a terrible fulfillment of the promise, **he will not give any of the flesh of his children whom he will eat**. Lamentations 4:1-11 vividly describes the horrors of the siege of Jerusalem.

ii. "There are few more degrading pictures in the Bible than that of a mother who, even during a siege, ought to have put away the afterbirth of her child and to have cherished her new-born baby, but in her desperate need eats both, secretly denying to her own husband any share in the ghastly meal." (Thompson)

iii. "Women so refined and genteel as to avoid touching the ground with unshod feet would not hesitate to consume their own offspring." (Merrill)

iv. Adam Clarke said this was also fulfilled in the Roman siege of Jerusalem. "This was literally fulfilled when Jerusalem was besieged by the Romans; a woman named Mary, of a noble family, driven to distraction by famine, boiled and ate her own child!"

h. The LORD will scatter you among all the peoples, from one end of the earth to the other: As a result of their repeated, chronic covenant disobedience, Israel would be dispersed. Because of their disobedience to the covenant, the covenant they agreed to, these curses became the history of the nation of Israel.

i. Many of these horrible curses upon a disobedient Israel were fulfilled in the years of history recorded in the Old Testament. Yet, their fulfillment did not cease with the end of biblical history, recorded in the Old and New Testaments.

ii. For example, around A.D. 68 the Romans had finally had enough of the rebellious Jews in the Roman province of Judea, so they laid siege to Jerusalem. At the time, the Jews fervently expected the coming of the Messiah to save them and conquer the Romans, based on God's promise to destroy the armies laying siege to Jerusalem (Zechariah 12:1-9). Sadly, the Jews of that time refused to fulfill Zechariah 12:10 which described their humble, repentant embrace of a pierced Messiah.

iii. Nevertheless the Jews of that day were so confident the Messiah would rescue them that their factions fought each other and burned each other's food, trying to be the group in power when the Messiah came. According to Josephus, it was "as though they were purposely serving the Romans by destroying what the city had provided against a siege and severing the sinews of their own strength" (*Wars* 5.24). "Through famine certainly the city fell, a fate which would have been practically impossible, had they not prepared the way for it themselves." (*Wars* 5.26)

iv. When the Roman general Vespasian came to Jerusalem, the Jewish factions were busy fighting each other. His staff urged him to attack immediately, but he knew that an attack would instantly unite the Jews. So, he held back and let them destroy each other for as long as possible. Vespasian said that God was a better general than he was, and that He was delivering the Jews into the hands of the Romans. Before Jerusalem was attacked, Vespasian became emperor, and he put his son Titus in charge of the assault.

v. In contrast, Christians in Jerusalem heeded the words of Jesus in Luke 21:20-24, in which He told people to flee Jerusalem when it was *surrounded by armies*, because *the days of vengeance* were at hand.

vi. In this siege of Jerusalem hunger became so great that many tried to escape the walls and forage for food. Five hundred or more were captured and crucified daily. "The soldiers out of rage and hatred amused themselves by nailing their prisoners in different postures; and so great was their numbers, that space could not be found for the crosses nor crosses for the bodies." (*War* 5.451) According to Josephus, more than 600,000 Jews died from starvation, and their dead bodies were dumped over the walls of the city. In total more than a million died and 97,000 were captured, with most of the captives being shipped as slaves to Egypt. The promise of Deuteronomy 28:68 was tragically fulfilled: **you shall be offered for sale to your enemies as male and female slaves, but no one will buy you**. This happened as too many Jewish slaves flooded the Egyptian slave market, and no one could buy all the available slaves.

vii. "When Jerusalem was taken by Titus, many of the captives, which were above seventeen years of age, were sent into the works in Egypt. See Josephus, Antiq., b. xii., c. 1, 2, War, b. vi., c. 9, s. 2." (Clarke)

viii. After the conquest the Jews still living in Judea were continually subjugated and humiliated by the Romans. The Romans continued to collect the temple tax from the Jews, even though their temple had been destroyed. The Romans took the temple tax and used it to support their *pagan* temples.

ix. After some years of this, the Jews of Judea again rebelled against the Romans in A.D. 132, led by a man named bar-Kochoba. He was proclaimed to be the messiah by the rabbis who supported the revolt. But after the bar-Kochoba rebellion, Rome finally and utterly crushed the Jewish population of Judea. Josephus said that because of the many battles, the once beautiful land was destroyed, and that it could not even be recognized.

x. But the curse for Israel did not end with the Roman conquest of the Jews. Tragically, in the centuries following, the institutional church and most Christians turned on the Jews. It was as if the branches of the tree attacked their own root. As the church grew in political power and became the official religion of the Roman Empire, the church decided to attack the Jews.

xi. They did this in part as retribution for the distant early years of Jewish persecution of the Christians. It was also because the current Jewish rejection of Jesus as Messiah was considered offensive. A significant motivation was a bizarre evangelistic strategy. Many Christians thought, "The Jews are cursed because they have killed their Messiah. The curses are meant to turn the heart of the nation back to God. We will help God by being His instrument to curse the Jewish people."

xii. For centuries, the worst enemies of the Jews were Christians who thought they could help God by cursing the Jewish people. Over centuries, the Jews of Rome were forced to pay homage to the Pope with a procession to him and presenting an Old Testament scroll to the Pope. Often, the Popes insulted the Jews after they presented the scroll. This hatred of the Jewish people was seen in the story of the Crusades, the slaughters, and the ghettos.

xiii. This helps to explain the great corruption and lack of spiritual power in the church through the Dark Ages. God promised to Abraham and his covenant descendants, the Jewish people, *I will bless those who bless you, and curse him who curses you* (Genesis 12:3). Satan's clever, and powerful strategy to *curse* the church was effective: to bring a curse against the church by inspiring them to curse the Jewish people. God judged Assyria, Babylon, and Rome for their mistreatment of the Jewish people. Later, for its crimes against the Jewish people, Germany suffered hunger, death, and destruction (among other ills) in the years directly following the Second World War. After these patterns, so the church was (in some sense) cursed as it persecuted the Jews. The church ignorantly disregarded the words of Jesus in Matthew 18:7: *For offenses must come, but woe to that man by whom the offense comes!* If the Jewish people were to be cursed, it was for God to do, not the church's mission.

xiv. "They have, it is true, grievously sinned; but, O ye Christians, have they not grievously suffered for it? Is not the stroke of God heavy enough upon them? Do not then, by any unkind treatment or cruel oppression, increase their miseries. They are, above all others, the men who have seen affliction by the stroke of his rod." (Adam Clarke, 1811)

xv. Gloriously, the curses described here were not and are not the end of God's plan for the Jewish people. As Ezekiel 37 describes, God will – and has begun to – revive the Jewish people as back from the dead and prepare them to be used in these last days. God is not done with Israel, and the curses *will not* be their final legacy.

i. **You shall become an astonishment, a proverb, and a byword among all nations where the Lord will drive you**: Even as with the blessings, God's purpose in cursing Israel would be for a greater goal than immediately punishing them for their sin. The curses would also become a witness to the nations.

i. God would do this for His glory, and because it would glorify Him, it can even be said that He would *rejoice* in the work: **just as the Lord rejoiced over you to do you good and multiply you, so the Lord will rejoice over you to destroy you and bring you to nothing**.

ii. "See here the venomous nature of sin, so far forth offensive to Almighty God, as to cause him, who otherwise afflicts not willingly (Lamentations 3:33), but delights in mercy (Micah 7:18), to rejoice in the ruin of his creatures, as here." (Trapp)

iii. "It is a vivid climax to a sustained picture of unspeakable suffering." (Thompson)

iv. "Certainly this graphic portrayal of disobedient Israel under the curse should have been a most effective warning—as it was intended to be." (Kalland)

v. "The story is a warning for us, revealing as it does the capacity of man for evil, and how, in spite of the clearest warnings, he is capable of disastrous disobedience. More is needed than the law which indicates the way and more than the prophet who urges obedience." (Morgan)

Deuteronomy 29 – Renewal of the Covenant

A. God's mighty works for Israel.

1. (1) The covenant **in the land of Moab**.

These *are* the words of the covenant which the LORD commanded Moses to make with the children of Israel in the land of Moab, besides the covenant which He made with them in Horeb.

> a. **These are the words of the covenant**: Some 40 years before this, at **Horeb** (Mount Sinai), Israel made a covenant with God (Exodus 24:7-8). This is a re-stating and re-affirmation of that covenant.
>
>> i. In using the vocabulary of covenant, the idea **to make** a covenant here is literally "to cut" a covenant. Genesis 15:9-11 is an example of an ancient covenant that was made by cutting sacrificial animals in half (normally, at the spine) and the two parties reciting the terms of the covenant as they stood or walked between the animal parts. That idea remained to the time of Moses in the concept of "cutting" a covenant.
>>
>> ii. "The victim is *separated* exactly into *two equal parts*, the separation being in the direction of the *spine;* and these parts are laid opposite to each other, sufficient room being allowed for the contracting parties to pass between them." (Clarke)
>
> b. **Besides the covenant which He made with them in Horeb**: For the most part, the people who had the blood of the covenant sprinkled upon them had died in the wilderness. The generation of unbelief had died, and the covenant must be renewed with the generation that would enter and conquer Canaan.

2. (2-4) Israel saw wonders, but they did not see them.

Now Moses called all Israel and said to them: "You have seen all that the LORD did before your eyes in the land of Egypt, to Pharaoh and to all

his servants and to all his land—the great trials which your eyes have seen, the signs, and those great wonders. Yet the LORD has not given you a heart to perceive and eyes to see and ears to hear, to this *very* day.

a. **You have seen all that the LORD did before your eyes**: Israel saw **great wonders** from the hand of God since departing Egypt. They saw the plagues, the death of the firstborn, the Red Sea parted, the Egyptian armies destroyed, and victories won by prayer. Israel ate the manna, drank the miraculously provided water, and Israel saw and received miracle after miracle.

b. **Yet the LORD has not given you a heart to perceive**: The miracles in and of themselves did not accomplish anything in the heart of Israel. If God did not send His Spirit to change their hearts, then the greatest wonder imaginable would not make a difference.

i. Some people today think the greatest help to evangelism would be to see more miraculous events. After all, who could *not* believe in the face of such displays of spiritual power? But seeing **great wonders** accomplishes nothing without a supernatural work of God in someone's heart.

ii. "They needed the enlightenment that Yahweh could give but which, by reason of their disobedience, He had not given to them. Such blindness on the part of those who reject God's revelation is not uncommon. Men may hear but not understand, because of a hardness of heart." (Thompson)

iii. "There was not a lamb slaughtered, nor a lamp kindled, nor a handful of incense burned on the altar, nor a curtain folded up, nor a silver socket set in its place without some moral and spiritual significance. Had they desired to learn it, they might have discovered in the tabernacle in the wilderness great store of teachings as to those things which make for the peace and salvation of men: but they had no heart to perceive, nor eyes to see, nor ears to hear; and so the whole apparatus of teaching was lost upon them." (Spurgeon)

iv. Spurgeon suggested three reasons why Israel – and those since them – were blind to God's truth.

- They never recognized their own blindness, thinking they could see.
- They never asked God for a heart to perceive.
- They resisted the little light that they had.

v. "Paul quoted this very text to speak of the hardness and blindness of his fellow Jews (Rom 11:8)." (Kalland)

3. (5-9) God's great works for Israel in the wilderness.

And I have led you forty years in the wilderness. Your clothes have not worn out on you, and your sandals have not worn out on your feet. You have not eaten bread, nor have you drunk wine or *similar* **drink, that you may know that I** *am* **the LORD your God. And when you came to this place, Sihon king of Heshbon and Og king of Bashan came out against us to battle, and we conquered them. We took their land and gave it as an inheritance to the Reubenites, to the Gadites, and to half the tribe of Manasseh. Therefore keep the words of this covenant, and do them, that you may prosper in all that you do.**

> a. **And I have led you forty years in the wilderness**: During their forty years through the **wilderness**, their **clothes** did not wear out, their **sandals** did not wear out, and though they had no **bread** to eat or **wine** to drink, their needs were provided for. Israel **conquered** over their enemies, and they **took their land**.
>
>> i. "The best situation possible for the people was their commitment to the Lord as God. No higher and more satisfactory state was conceivable than that of obedient Israel under the covenant-treaty with the Lord." (Merrill)
>>
>> ii. Plainly, these were remarkable miracles. Clothing and sandals simply do not last 40 years of hard marching in the wilderness apart from a miracle (Deuteronomy 8:4). The wilderness does not provide enough food and water to meet the needs of some two million people apart from a miracle. A nation of slaves for 400 years does not conquer standing kingdoms and take their land apart from a miracle.
>>
>> iii. These *great wonders* were proof in themselves of God's power and love for Israel. Each of them has a spiritual counterpart in the life of the believer.
>>
>>> - God provides *clothing* for His people in a spiritual sense (Revelation 3:18).
>>> - God gives His people *shoes* (Ephesians 6:15).
>>> - God gives believers bread to eat and wine to drink (1 Corinthians 11:23-26).
>>> - God enables His people to *conquer* their enemies by the power of Jesus (Romans 8:37).

- God makes it possible for His people to take the *land* of their spiritual enemies (2 Corinthians 10:4-5).

b. That you may know that I am the Lord your God: By all the miraculous works God did for Israel, Yahweh gave them every reason to know that He alone was God, and none other.

i. "This could not have been done by Israel alone but only as Yahweh the Warrior led his people to conquest and occupation. From beginning to end, Israel's covenant history had been a record of miracle." (Merrill)

c. Therefore keep the words of this covenant: Seeing these great works of God, there is one logical response. Knowing the greatness of God's love and power should have made Israel more committed than ever to God's covenant.

B. Renewing the covenant.

1. (10-15) The parties to the covenant.

"All of you stand today before the Lord your God: your leaders and your tribes and your elders and your officers, all the men of Israel, your little ones and your wives—also the stranger who *is* in your camp, from the one who cuts your wood to the one who draws your water—that you may enter into covenant with the Lord your God, and into His oath, which the Lord your God makes with you today, that He may establish you today as a people for Himself, and *that* He may be God to you, just as He has spoken to you, and just as He has sworn to your fathers, to Abraham, Isaac, and Jacob.

"I make this covenant and this oath, not with you alone, but with *him* who stands here with us today before the Lord our God, as well as with *him* who *is* not here with us today

a. All of you stand today before the Lord your God: This means that the covenant was made with all of Israel. This included the leaders, the men, the women, the children, servants, and the **stranger** (foreigner) who had joined themselves to Israel.

i. This was a *national* covenant Israel made with God. The nation of Israel was largely defined by ethnicity, being the genetic descendants of Abraham, Isaac, and Jacob. It was not exclusively defined by ethnicity – foreigners were allowed to forsake all their pagan gods and surrender to the covenant and law of Israel – but it was mainly defined by ethnicity.

ii. "His appeal was to all classes of the community—to the rulers, the people, men, women, children, and also to the servants. There was to be no escape and no excuse." (Morgan)

iii. This was not a covenant that made individuals righteous before God. That righteousness was and is received by faith (Genesis 15:6). Individuals among Israel who learned of their need and saw God's provision foreshadowed in the sacrifices, ceremonies, and priesthood of Israel, trusting in God's provision, these were accounted righteous. The Mosaic Covenant (or, old covenant) was not a covenant that brought salvation, but through which God worked in and through Israel, furthering His great plan of the ages.

iv. The phrase, **that you may enter into covenant** is another example of the idea that covenant was made, in times before this, by walking through or standing between divided sacrificial animals. Clarke says that **enter into** here is "*to pass through*, that is, between the *separated* parts of the covenant sacrifice."

v. **And into His oath**: "The text reads literally 'for your crossing over into the covenant of Yahweh your God and into his curse'. The noun 'curse' refers to the curses of the covenant. When one enters a covenant he places himself in the position where the curses will fall upon him if he violates the covenant obligations." (Thompson)

b. **That He may establish you today as a people for Himself**: All of Israel was included in God's desire to **enter into covenant**, to be the **people for Himself**. He wasn't just looking for a few prominent and talented people, or for just one spiritual tribe like the Levites. God wanted the whole nation to be this **people for Himself**.

c. **As well as with him who is not here with us today**: The covenant extended beyond those who stood before the LORD and Moses on that day. It also included the one who was **not with** Moses and Israel that day (**today**). The *descendants* of those assembled before the LORD and Moses were also included in the covenant.

i. "The covenant demand is here extended to those who were yet to be born. Future generations were one with that early Israel who took the oath at Sinai." (Thompson)

2. (16-20) The promise of judgment against the covenant-breaker.

(for you know that we dwelt in the land of Egypt and that we came through the nations which you passed by, and you saw their abominations and their idols which *were* among them—wood and stone and silver and gold); so that there may not be among you man or woman or family or tribe, whose heart turns away today from the LORD our God, to go *and* serve the gods of these nations, and that there may not be among you a root bearing bitterness or wormwood; and so it may not happen,

when he hears the words of this curse, that he blesses himself in his heart, saying, 'I shall have peace, even though I follow the dictates of my heart'—as though the drunkard could be included with the sober.

"The LORD would not spare him; for then the anger of the LORD and His jealousy would burn against that man, and every curse that is written in this book would settle on him, and the LORD would blot out his name from under heaven.

a. **You saw their abominations and their idols which were among them**: Israel had seen the **abominations** and **idols** of their pagan neighbors. God promised that anyone who **turns away from the LORD our God, to go and serve the gods of these nations**, should never presume on a sense of peace in his heart.

i. The **root** of **bitterness or wormwood** here is connected with compromise, idolatry, and resentment against God's nature as a jealous God who demands to be exclusively worshipped. This bitterness leads people to reject God yet remain confident that they will have **peace**.

ii. "Idolatry is here described as a plant which takes root and issues in a harvest of poison weed and wormwood." (Thompson)

b. **He blesses himself in his heart, saying "I shall have peace"**: Perhaps one who has turned from the LORD to idols hears the curses against the covenant-breaker, yet thinks he has escaped any penalty. He considers himself blessed and as having **peace**, God's *shalom*. Such a one may have an immediate sense of peace at the moment, but it is the peace of the blind, the peace of the ignorant, who cannot see the peril of coming judgment.

i. A compromiser or idolater may feel confident in his own heart, having a marvelous sense of "peace." But this peace is an illusion. It is the peace of the blind, of the unknowing. If a bomb is on a plane, almost everyone on the plane is at peace the moment before the bomb explodes – but their peace is based on their ignorance. In the same way, a sinner may be completely untroubled in his heart, but this is only because he is blind.

ii. "So man's foolish heart reasons. He hears the curse pronounced against sin; he knows that the man who turns from God is threatened with gall and wormwood, and yet he persists in his evil ways, secretly blessing himself, and laying the flattering unction to his heart that he at least will come off scot-free." (Meyer)

iii. **As though the drunkard could be included with the sober**: The **drunkard** may be happy when he is drunk, but his happiness is based on an illusion. God warns against equating the peace of the righteous with the peace the wicked might seem to have.

c. **The LORD would not spare him**: God says simply that there is no peace for the wicked (Isaiah 48:22) Justice may come on either side of eternity, but it will come. No one can forsake the LORD and escape the consequences.

i. "If sin were in the long run pleasurable, and really produced advantage to man, it would be a very strange arrangement in the divine economy. The Judge of all the earth must do right, but would it be right that sinning should be rewarded with blessedness?" (Spurgeon)

ii. For those in Christ and under the new covenant, Jesus Christ is in their place as the one whom the **LORD would not spare**. He was a substitute, dying in the place of guilty sinners (2 Corinthians 5:21).

3. (21-28) The purpose for judgment against the covenant-breaker.

And the LORD would separate him from all the tribes of Israel for adversity, according to all the curses of the covenant that are written in this Book of the Law, so that the coming generation of your children who rise up after you, and the foreigner who comes from a far land, would say, when they see the plagues of that land and the sicknesses which the LORD has laid on it:

'The whole land *is* brimstone, salt, and burning; it is not sown, nor does it bear, nor does any grass grow there, like the overthrow of Sodom and Gomorrah, Admah, and Zeboim, which the LORD overthrew in His anger and His wrath.' All nations would say, 'Why has the LORD What does the heat of this great anger mean?' Then *people* would say: 'Because they have forsaken the covenant of the LORD God of their fathers, which He made with them when He brought them out of the land of Egypt; for they went and served other gods and worshiped them, gods that they did not know and that He had not given to them. Then the anger of the LORD was aroused against this land, to bring on it every curse that is written in this book. And the LORD uprooted them from their land in anger, in wrath, and in great indignation, and cast them into another land, as *it is* this day.'

a. **The LORD would separate him from all the tribes of Israel for adversity**: There is an evident reason to punish the covenant-breaker for his own sake. But God has a purpose beyond the individual; God wants His dealing with the covenant-breaker to be a lesson to all Israel.

b. **So that the coming generation of your children who rise up after you, and the foreigner who comes from a far land**: God's purpose in bringing judgment against a covenant-breaking Israel was also for the sake of **the coming generation of your children** and the **foreigner**. When they saw the devastation that came from breaking God's covenant, when they saw what happened to the land **which the Lord overthrew in His anger and His wrath**, they would be warned and directed to obedience.

> i. An example of God's judgment that should be learned from is what He did against **Sodom and Gomorrah**. As God devastated the land of those wicked cities in His judgment, so the land of a disobedient, covenant-breaking Israel would also be devastated.

> ii. People today may also learn from the calamity that comes on the lives of others when they break God's covenant. The price of disobedience is not worth it. The commands of God are good and protect us.

c. **All nations would say**: God's purpose in bringing judgment against a covenant-breaking Israel was also for the sake of **all nations**. When they saw what happens to a people who had received so much blessing from God, and yet who forsook the Lord, they would be warned and directed to obedience.

> i. "Nothing could be more ironic than for the land of Canaan, a land 'flowing with milk and honey'…to become one divested of any sign of fertility and productivity. In the face of such incredible reversal of blessing to curse, the nations in the day of wrath would ask in amazement why the Lord had done such things." (Merrill)

4. (29) God's revelation to Israel.

"The secret *things belong* to the Lord our God, but those *things which are* revealed *belong* to us and to our children forever, that *we* may do all the words of this law.

> a. **The secret things belong to the Lord our God**: Amid this encouragement to obedience, Moses paused to declare a principle of how God speaks. First, God never declares *everything* to man. There are things God keeps **secret** to Himself.

> i. God is greater and wiser than man and always will be, and this must be accepted. *"For My thoughts are not your thoughts, nor are your ways My ways," says the Lord. "For as the heavens are higher than the earth, so are My ways higher than your ways, and My thoughts than your thoughts."* (Isaiah 55:8-9)

> ii. "To the mind of man, in all life there are secret things, things veiled, things which cannot be explained. These things are not veiled to God. He knows them." (Morgan)

b. **Those things which are revealed**: Second, God does reveal *some* things to humanity. Because God exists and He has spoken, we must do all we can to pay close attention to Him.

c. **Those things which are revealed belong to us**: Third, God's revelation is meant to *say* something to us. God did not speak just to amaze or amuse mankind. There is a message which *belongs* to man. While we cannot perfectly understand God's revelation, in the main it can be comprehended and understood.

d. **To us and to our children**: Fourth, God's revelation is *trans-generational*. God had a specific message for Moses' generation, but the message went beyond its original audience to speak to all generations which follow.

    i. **To us and to our children**: According to Clarke, the Jews considered these words to be of such importance that they were specially marked in many Jewish scrolls or manuscripts.

e. **To us and our children forever**: Fifth, God's revelation is *eternal*. His word not only lasts **forever**, but it is also **forever** relevant. God's word is more relevant than any new fad or interest which might sweep through the world or the church.

f. **That we may do all the words of this law**: Finally, God's revelation should *matter* to humanity. He has not spoken merely to satisfy man's curiosity about spiritual things. God has spoken to impact the way men and women *live*. Those who are hearers only of God's word, without also being doers, have not really received God's word.

Deuteronomy 30 – The Choice

A. Restoration for a repentant Israel.

1. (1) When the blessing and the curse comes upon Israel.

"Now it shall come to pass, when all these things come upon you, the blessing and the curse which I have set before you, and you call *them* to mind among all the nations where the LORD your God drives you,

> a. **Now it shall come to pass, when all these things come upon you**: Under the inspiration of the LORD, Moses carefully explained the blessings and curses that would come upon an obedient or disobedient Israel. Under the same inspiration, Moses knew that **all these things** *would* **come upon** Israel.
>
>> i. From the height of blessing during the reigns of David and Solomon, to the depth of cursing at the fall of Jerusalem, Israel's history has been a legacy of either being blessed or cursed under the terms of the old covenant.
>
> b. **You call them to mind among all the nations where the LORD your God drives you**: God knew that Israel would be eventually scattered and exiled and that more than once. Here through Moses, God called the Jews dispersed among the nations (the *Diaspora*) to remember the promises of **the blessing and the curse**.

2. (2-5) God's promise to restore Israel in the Promised Land.

And you return to the LORD your God and obey His voice, according to all that I command you today, you and your children, with all your heart and with all your soul, that the LORD your God will bring you back from captivity, and have compassion on you, and gather you again from all the nations where the LORD your God has scattered you. If *any* of you are driven out to the farthest *parts* under heaven, from there the LORD your God will gather you, and from there He will bring you.

Then the LORD your God will bring you to the land which your fathers possessed, and you shall possess it. He will prosper you and multiply you more than your fathers.

   a. **Return to the LORD your God**: As Israel would return to the LORD, God would bless them and **bring** them **back from captivity** having **compassion on** them.

      i. This was fulfilled in part by the return of the Babylonian exiles during the times of Ezra and Nehemiah. But a greater fulfillment of this would await the twentieth century, when God gathered Israel in the Promised Land. This modern regathering is a larger, broader, more evidently sovereign, and a more miraculous restoration than what was recorded in Ezra and Nehemiah after the Babylonian captivity.

      ii. "The Hebrew phrase translated 'restore your fortunes' [**bring you back from captivity**] signifies a total change, a return to a former state, and indicates that Israel would return to the position of being under the blessing of the Lord in their own land." (Kalland)

      iii. **Return to the LORD your God**: "By sin we run away from God; by repentance we return to him." (Trapp)

   b. **From all the nations where the LORD your God has scattered you**: The modern restoration of Israel more accurately fulfills this promise than the return from the Babylonian exile. Today, Israel is populated by Jews from virtually every country in the world. The breadth of this promise is emphasized by repetition, highlighted by the gathering of the Jews from **the farthest parts under heaven**.

      i. Adam Clarke, writing in 1811, recognized that this gathering must be fulfilled in a future time: "As this promise refers to a return from captivity in which they had been scattered among all nations, consequently it is not the Babylonish captivity which is intended; and the repossession of their land must be different from that which was consequent on their return from Chaldea."

   c. **To the land which your fathers possessed**: The restoration had to happen in the land of Israel. The modern restoration of Israel more accurately fulfills this promise than the return from the Babylonian exile. On the return from the Babylonian exile, Israel was still a vassal state of the Persians. But in the modern restoration of Israel, **you shall possess it** was literally fulfilled by an independent Jewish state.

      i. In the early days of the Zionist movement, the British government offered the territory of Uganda as a place to establish a Jewish state. If that would have happened, and if Jews from all over the world had flocked there to establish a Jewish state, it would *not* fulfill the promise of restoration stated here and in other Old Testament passages. This could only be fulfilled in the **land which your fathers possessed**.

d. He will prosper you and multiply you more than your fathers: This promise was fulfilled in a greater sense in the modern restoration of Israel, more than in the return from the Babylonian exile. In the days of the return from the Babylonian exile, the Jewish community was small, weak, and poor. But today, under the modern restoration of Israel, the state of Israel does indeed **prosper** and the promise to **multiply you more than your fathers** is fulfilled. Israel, as a nation, is larger, stronger, and richer than at any time after the Babylonian exile.

3. (6) The spiritual restoration of Israel.

And the LORD your God will circumcise your heart and the heart of your descendants, to love the LORD your God with all your heart and with all your soul, that you may live.

a. And the LORD your God will circumcise your heart…to love the LORD your God with all your heart: As remarkable and as prophetically meaningful as the modern restoration of Israel is, it is yet incomplete. The spiritual dimension of the restoration – the circumcision of the heart – has not yet been accomplished.

i. "Paul equated circumcision of the heart with spiritual renewal, especially in the Epistle to the Romans." (Merrill)

ii. Today Israel is a largely secular nation. Among many Israeli Jews there is some measure of respect for the Bible as a book of history and national identity. Yet there is not, and has not been, a true turning to the LORD God, particularly as a nation.

iii. The religious or Orthodox Jews have not truly turned to the LORD. Though they have had an important and precious part in God's plan for Israel in helping a spiritual consciousness for the Jewish people to survive through the centuries of the *Diaspora*, they have yet to truly turn to the LORD. This is true because the character and nature of the LORD are perfectly expressed in His Messiah, Jesus. Jesus said, *He who believes in Me, believes not in Me but in Him who sent Me. And he who sees Me sees Him who sent Me* (John 12:44-45). Since the Jewish people (except for a precious remnant) reject Jesus, they are rejecting the LORD God.

iv. As Paul wrote in Romans 11:28-29: *Concerning the gospel they are enemies for your sake, but concerning the election they are beloved for the sake of the fathers. For the gifts and calling of God are irrevocable.*

v. But God's promise still stands. As the final aspect of the promise to restore Israel, God will restore them spiritually. He promised to **circumcise** the **heart** of Israel. This idea is repeated in the promises of the new covenant (Ezekiel 36:26-27). The ultimate salvation in Jesus Christ of most Jewish people is promised (Romans 11:26). Jesus promised He would return to a Jewish people who welcomed Him in the name of the Lord (Matthew 23:39).

vi. Some people claim that because the modern restoration of Israel has not yet demonstrated this spiritual aspect that it has nothing to do with these prophecies. But the spiritual aspect is properly listed last in this passage after Israel has been restored to the land. The same order is seen in Ezekiel 37, the vision of the dry bones, seeing Israel restored and strong, *before* the Lord breathes the breath of His Spirit in them. The modern restoration of Israel is a remarkable sign, and an extremely significant – but thus far only partial – fulfillment of these prophecies.

4. (7-10) Blessings upon repentant Israel.

"Also the Lord your God will put all these curses on your enemies and on those who hate you, who persecuted you. And you will again obey the voice of the Lord and do all His commandments which I command you today. The Lord your God will make you abound in all the work of your hand, in the fruit of your body, in the increase of your livestock, and in the produce of your land for good. For the Lord will again rejoice over you for good as He rejoiced over your fathers, if you obey the voice of the Lord your God, to keep His commandments and His statutes which are written in this Book of the Law, *and* **if you turn to the Lord your God with all your heart and with all your soul.**

a. **Also the Lord your God will put all these curses on your enemies**: As Israel was restored to the land and restored to a true relationship with God through Jesus their Messiah, God would defend them and curse their enemies, the men who **hate** the Jewish people and have **persecuted** them.

i. These promises – much like the promise God made to Abraham, to *bless those who bless you* and to *curse him who curses you* (Genesis 12:3) – show how foolish it was for Christians and the institutional church to persecute the Jewish people.

b. **You will again obey the voice of the Lord and do all His commandments**: This is the ultimate restoration of the Jewish people to the Lord, through Jesus Christ, the Lord's Messiah (Romans 11:26, Ezekiel 37, Zechariah 12:10). The Lord will **again rejoice over** the Jewish people, as He did over their **fathers**. All this will be seen when Israel turns to the LORD with their all their **heart** and **soul**, as He is revealed in Jesus the Messiah.

> i. **You will again obey the voice of the LORD**: "Come again to thyself, as the prodigal, who had been for some while beside himself." (Trapp)

c. **The LORD your God will make you abound**: In part, these prophecies are fulfilled now in the modern restoration of Israel. Yet their ultimate fulfillment will happen in the Millennium when restored Israel has truly turned to the LORD and His Messiah, Jesus.

B. Moses concludes his great sermon: *choose life!*

1. (11-14) Israel's capability to keep the covenant.

"For this commandment which I command you today *is* not *too* mysterious for you, nor *is* it far off. It *is* not in heaven, that you should say, 'Who will ascend into heaven for us and bring it to us, that we may hear it and do it?' Nor *is* it beyond the sea, that you should say, 'Who will go over the sea for us and bring it to us, that we may hear it and do it?' But the word *is* very near you, in your mouth and in your heart, that you may do it.

> a. **For this commandment which I command you today**: The covenant God made with Israel – the old covenant – was not **too mysterious** for them, nor was it **far off**. Israel could indeed keep this covenant. God did not expect the impossible from Israel when He expected them to keep this covenant.
>
> > i. "This passage is used by Paul in Romans 10:6–8…. God now approached men in Christ and as the living Lord He asked not for some superhuman effort but only for a glad acceptance of his grace in Christ." (Thompson)
>
> b. **But the word is very near you, in your mouth and in your heart, that you may do it**: However, this is not intended to mean that the Mosaic Law could be perfectly kept and that a person could be obedient enough to the Mosaic Law to earn a righteous standing before God.
>
> > i. The *law* was only one aspect of the old covenant. There were also the aspects of *sacrifice* and *choice*. God never expected Israel to perfectly obey the law and find righteousness through law-obedience. That is why He provided for the *sacrifice* – the punishment of a perfect, innocent victim in the place of the sinner. God did not expect an Israelite to trust in his obedience to the law to save him (though God wanted Israel to love His law). God expected an Israelite to trust in the atonement made by *sacrifice* to make him righteous, and to understand

that this sacrifice pointed towards a perfect sacrifice God would one day make through the Messiah. In this, a godly Israelite, in the old covenant, trusted in the work of Jesus the Messiah to save him even before the time of Jesus.

ii. The outline of salvation by grace through faith was clear and was **near** to the Israelite. There were things right before them that they could easily grasp.

- They knew that they were sinners both because of the law, and the existence of the sacrificial system.
- They knew that salvation came by sacrifice, a substitute judged in their place.
- They knew that animal sacrifices could never be enough, because they had to be continually repeated.
- They knew that it was faith that brought the benefit of the great sacrifices that all the priesthood and its ceremonies pointed to.

iii. What the Israelite could see, they could see as if it was by moonlight. Since the incarnation, life, ministry, suffering, death, resurrection, and ascension of Jesus, all this is seen by the brightest sunlight. It was true that the word had come near to Israel; even more so, it has come near to us.

c. **That you may do it**: The old covenant including the aspects of law, sacrifice, and choice could be kept. It wasn't beyond Israel's capability to keep. When they failed to keep the law, there was a partial remedy through the sacrificial system, all pointing towards the life and sacrifice of Jesus Christ.

2. (15-18) The choice.

"See, I have set before you today life and good, death and evil, in that I command you today to love the LORD your God, to walk in His ways, and to keep His commandments, His statutes, and His judgments, that you may live and multiply; and the LORD your God will bless you in the land which you go to possess. But if your heart turns away so that you do not hear, and are drawn away, and worship other gods and serve them, I announce to you today that you shall surely perish; you shall not prolong *your* days in the land which you cross over the Jordan to go in and possess.

a. **I have set before you today life and good, death and evil**: Under the terms of the old covenant, Israel had a choice. God set before them **life** or **death**, **good** or **evil**. It was up to them. God was determined to glorify

Himself through Israel one way or another. How it would happen was their *choice*, and their choice would be seen in their obedience and faithfulness to the covenant.

    i. This was an appeal to all Israel but spoken to them as individuals. "As elsewhere, now at the end of his addresses, Moses stressed the personal involvement of the people with the Lord." (Kalland)

b. **The Lord your God will bless you in the land which you go to possess**: Under the terms of the old covenant, Israel, if obedient, would see blessing. If disobedient, then Israel would **surely perish**. It was up to Israel and based on their conduct.

    i. It must be understood that believers in Jesus Christ *do not* relate to God on the terms of the old covenant, but on the terms of something better: the new covenant. Under the new covenant, a relationship with God is not based on what the believer *does* for God, but on what *Jesus has done* on behalf of His people. There is more to the new covenant than this, but this is at least one crucial distinction between the old and new covenants.

    ii. The curses of Deuteronomy show that there was a terrible price to pay for unfaithfulness to the old covenant. Yet because the new covenant is a greater covenant, the price for rejecting it is even greater (Hebrews 10:28-29).

3. (19-20) **Choose life**.

I call heaven and earth as witnesses today against you, *that* **I have set before you life and death, blessing and cursing; therefore choose life, that both you and your descendants may live; that you may love the Lord your God, that you may obey His voice, and that you may cling to Him, for He** *is* **your life and the length of your days; and that you may dwell in the land which the Lord swore to your fathers, to Abraham, Isaac, and Jacob, to give them."**

    a. **I call heaven and earth as witnesses today against you**: In these most solemn words, Moses set the choice before Israel. They had to choose between **life and death**, between **blessing and cursing**.

    i. Moses did not call upon angels, demons, or a supposed "council of the gods" to witness this covenant. He called upon creation itself (**heaven and earth**) as witnesses. "In similar ancient Near Eastern legal transactions the witnesses usually were the gods of the respective litigants, but the monotheism of Israel's faith dictated that such appeal be to creation, to heaven and earth, for only it would endure into future ages." (Merrill)

b. **Therefore choose life**: Though the choice belonged to Israel, God cared about *what* they chose. When Moses pled with Israel, crying out that they would **choose life**, he displayed God's heart toward Israel. In some sense, how God would glorify Himself through Israel was up to them, but it was clearly God's preference that He glorify Himself through an obedient, blessed Israel. Therefore, God (through Moses) pled with Israel to **choose life**.

> i. "Man is accountable for his actions, because they are *his;* were he necessitated by fate, or sovereign constraint, they could not be *his*." (Clarke)

> ii. "The final decision was Israel's to make. It was one for the free choice of the people. The covenant mediator speaking on Yahweh's behalf could only make the alternatives clear and then appeal to Israel to *choose life*." (Thompson)

> iii. Man today is confronted with the choice. But since the life, death, and resurrection of Jesus, the choice focuses first not on "Will I obey God or not?" but on "Will I trust in Jesus for my standing before God?" Jesus said, *He who is not with Me is against Me, and he who does not gather with Me scatters*. (Luke 11:23) Jesus still asked the question, *who do you say that I am* (Matthew 16:15), and man's choice in answering that question determines his eternal destiny.

> iv. "The gospel, which is the perfect revelation of God in Christ, brings every one of us face to face with the great alternative, and urgently demands from each his personal act of choice whether he will accept it or neglect or reject it. Not to choose to accept is to choose to reject. To do nothing is to choose death." (Maclaren)

> v. To **choose life** meant much more than saying, "I would prefer life than death." It required faith and the true intent of being faithful to the covenant. "Choosing life meant choosing to enter into the covenant with the Lord and to be true to its principles." (Merrill)

c. **That you may love the Lord your God**: To love God this way, to really trust Him, is explained well in Deuteronomy 30:20. To love and trust God means to **obey His voice**, for a child who really loves and trusts their father will obey him. It means to **cling to Him**, for if we really love and trust Him, we will be attached to Him. It means to regard Him as our **life** and **length of…days**, because if we love and trust Him, He is not *part* of our life, He *is* our life.

> i. Adam Clarke noted the connection between love and obedience: "Without *love* there can be no *obedience*.… Without *obedience* love is *fruitless* and dead."

Deuteronomy 31 – Some Final Instructions from Moses

A. Moses charges the people, Joshua, and the priests.

1. (1-2) Moses at one hundred and twenty.

Then Moses went and spoke these words to all Israel. And he said to them: "I *am* one hundred and twenty years old today. I can no longer go out and come in. Also the LORD has said to me, 'You shall not cross over this Jordan.'

> a. **I am one hundred and twenty years old today**: Moses, at 120 years, was not significantly limited by his physical condition. Shortly after this, he climbed to the top of a mountain. Yet, he could **no longer go out and come in** because he was limited by God's command – the decree that Moses would not enter the land of Canaan (Numbers 20:7-12).
>
> b. **You shall not cross over this Jordan**: These specific words of God to Moses are not recorded in the Numbers 20 account. This must be a further elaboration of the decree spoken by God to Moses, *you shall not bring this assembly into the land which I have given them* (Numbers 20:12).
>
>> i. There is a difference between *you shall not bring this assembly into the land* and **you shall not cross over this Jordan**. By the first statement, it is allowable that Moses could go into the Promised Land, but not as the leader of the nation, having yielded his leadership to Joshua. But God made it clearer to Moses: **you shall not cross over this Jordan**.
>>
>> ii. God's correction of Moses was severe. This was more than being denied the leadership of bringing Israel into Canaan; it was to not enter Canaan at all. Moses had long known his calling to deliver God's people out of Egypt and into Canaan, perhaps even as a child in the palaces of Egypt. Here Moses heard again that another man would finish the job that he had started, and his feet would never touch the

soil of the land God had promised to the covenant descendants of Abraham, Isaac, and Jacob.

iii. This severe correction was appropriate because at Meribah (Numbers 20:7-12), when Israel complained and cried out for water, Moses significantly misrepresented God. He misrepresented God by lecturing the nation harshly and unnecessarily. Moses misrepresented God by acting as if God *needed* him to provide water for the people. And Moses both misrepresented and disobeyed God by angrily striking the rock twice, instead of simply speaking to the rock as God had told him to.

iv. Moses was being judged by a stricter standard because of his leadership position in Israel, and because he had a uniquely close relationship with God. At Meribah, the people acted worse than Moses did, but Moses had greater responsibility. It is right for teachers and leaders to be judged by a stricter standard (James 3:1), though it is obviously wrong to expect perfection from leaders and teachers among God's people.

v. Moses also defaced a beautiful picture of the redemptive work of Jesus. The rock that provided water in the wilderness was a representation of Jesus the Messiah (1 Corinthians 10:4). Jesus, being struck once, provided life for all who would receive from Him (John 7:37). But it was unnecessary – and unrighteous – that Jesus would be struck again, much less again twice more, because the Son of God needed only to suffer once (Hebrews 10:10-12). Jesus can now be approached with words of faith (Romans 10:8-10), as Moses should have only used words of faith as the means of bringing life-giving water to Israel. Moses distorted God's intended picture of the work of Jesus. Therefore, Moses **shall not cross over this Jordan**.

vi. "What Moses could not do because of the people's unbelief – viz, to bring them to Canaan, Joshua did. So what Moses's law could not do – viz, to bring us to heaven because of the infirmity of our flesh, Christ by his gospel hath done for us." (Trapp)

2. (3-6) The encouragement to the children of Israel.

The Lord your God Himself crosses over before you; He will destroy these nations from before you, and you shall dispossess them. Joshua himself crosses over before you, just as the Lord has said. And the Lord will do to them as He did to Sihon and Og, the kings of the Amorites and their land, when He destroyed them. The Lord will give them over to you, that you may do to them according to every commandment which I have commanded you. Be strong and of good courage, do not fear nor

be afraid of them; for the LORD your God, He *is* the One who goes with you. He will not leave you nor forsake you."

a. **The LORD your God Himself crosses over before you**: Moses had led Israel for 40 years and there was no one left in Israel who had known a previous leader. Yet Israel could be confident, and Moses could go his way in peace because He knew God was with Israel. Israel, Moses, or Joshua did not have to be afraid. Instead, they could be **strong and of good courage**, knowing that God Himself went with them.

i. Moses was a great man; one of the greatest to ever walk this earth. But Moses was not irreplaceable. God being with them, Israel was in good hands, with or without Moses.

ii. **Joshua himself crosses over before you**: "Once more, then, Moses reminded the assembly that Joshua was God's choice to succeed him, a choice that appeared evident from many years past (Exodus 17:8-16; 24:13; Numbers 11:28) and one that was solidified by repeated verbal affirmation (Num 27:15-23; Deuteronomy 1:38; 3:23-29)." (Merrill)

b. **Be strong and of good courage**: It was now time for Israel to take courage in the LORD and **not fear nor be dismayed**. Moses would pass from the scene, but God would not abandon Israel.

i. **He will not leave you nor forsake you**: "Five times in holy Scriptures is this precious promise repeated; and in Hebrews 13:5, made common to all believers, with a very deep asseveration [solemn declaration]." (Trapp)

3. (7-8) The encouragement to Joshua.

Then Moses called Joshua and said to him in the sight of all Israel, "Be strong and of good courage, for you must go with this people to the land which the LORD has sworn to their fathers to give them, and you shall cause them to inherit it. And the LORD, He *is* the one who goes before you. He will be with you, He will not leave you nor forsake you; do not fear nor be dismayed."

a. **Then Moses called Joshua and said to him in the sight of all Israel**: Bringing the people into Canaan was God's work. He would certainly do it. But God almost always does His work through men and women who make themselves available to Him. The man God would use in bringing Israel into Canaan was **Joshua**, the former assistant to Moses.

i. God does *His* work, but He normally does it *through* people. It is still God's work even when He uses human instruments (1 Corinthians 15:10).

b. **Be strong and of good courage**: Since God was going to use Joshua, he must **be strong and of good courage**. But Moses knew Joshua and knew that he would fulfill this. So, Moses confidently said to Joshua, **you shall cause them to inherit it**.

> i. Moses blessed Joshua with this encouragement. Moses knew that Joshua might be wavering, so he encouraged him, and pushed him forward to fulfill the great calling God gave to him. God uses encouraging people to help His people fulfill their destiny.
>
> ii. "David also picked up these words to urge Solomon to follow the decrees the Lord gave Moses, as David encouraged Solomon to build the temple (1 Chronicles 22:13; 28:20)." (Thompson)

4. (9-13) The encouragement to the priests.

So Moses wrote this law and delivered it to the priests, the sons of Levi, who bore the ark of the covenant of the LORD, and to all the elders of Israel. And Moses commanded them, saying: "At the end of *every* seven years, at the appointed time in the year of release, at the Feast of Tabernacles, when all Israel comes to appear before the LORD your God in the place which He chooses, you shall read this law before all Israel in their hearing. Gather the people together, men and women and little ones, and the stranger who *is* within your gates, that they may hear and that they may learn to fear the LORD your God and carefully observe all the words of this law, and *that* their children, who have not known it, may hear and learn to fear the LORD your God as long as you live in the land which you cross the Jordan to possess."

> a. **Moses wrote this law**: Just as the kings of Israel were to write their own copy of God's law (Deuteronomy 17:18), so **Moses wrote this law**. He, as an uncrowned king over Israel, loved God's word and wanted to pass it on to the generation following him.
>
> i. Commentators debate whether **this law** refers to all five books of Moses (Genesis through Deuteronomy), only the book of Deuteronomy, or only chapter 31 (which can be taken as summary of Deuteronomy).
>
> ii. "Most of the material in chapter 31 is given elsewhere in Deuteronomy. This material appears to be in the nature of a summary with, here and there, some specific additions—just as one who knows that his ministry is coming toward its end repeats, for emphasis' sake, things said before." (Kalland)

iii. "Writing had been in common use in the ancient Near East for at least a thousand years before Moses. Even the use of the alphabet was known for perhaps three centuries before Moses' day." (Thompson)

b. **You shall read this law before all Israel in their hearing**: Part of the job of the Levites was to minister the word of God to Israel, as the Levites would settle in cities and villages appointed throughout all of Israel. In addition, every seven years the Levites were to have a public reading and explanation of the law of God, as was modeled in Nehemiah 8:1-8.

i. The law – either all the books of Moses, or just focusing on Deuteronomy – was to be read every seven years at the Feast of Tabernacles.

ii. The first we know of a public reading of the law is in Joshua 8:30-35. The next we hear of it is during the reign of Jehoshaphat (2 Chronicles 17:7-9), more than 500 years later. Then, in the reign of Josiah there was another public reading of the law (2 Chronicles 34:30), more than 250 years after Jehoshaphat. There may have been public readings of the law in fulfillment of this instruction that are not mentioned. Yet the fact that some are mentioned probably means they were unusual, not normal. If, in disobedience to God's command, the word of the LORD was so neglected by the Levites to Israel, no wonder Israel was so often in trouble.

iii. "An unusually full account of this being done in later times (and perhaps an almost unique instance) is that of Nehemiah 8:13–9:38." (Merrill)

c. **And that their children…may hear and learn to fear the LORD**: This seventh-year national focus on God's word was especially important for the children among the people of Israel. They had to be taught God's law, and through the proclaimed truth of God's word, they could come to a personal relationship with the LORD.

B. Moses insures his legacy.

1. (14-15) The preface to Joshua's inauguration as leader of Israel.

Then the LORD said to Moses, "Behold, the days approach when you must die; call Joshua, and present yourselves in the tabernacle of meeting, that I may inaugurate him."

So Moses and Joshua went and presented themselves in the tabernacle of meeting. Now the LORD appeared at the tabernacle in a pillar of cloud, and the pillar of cloud stood above the door of the tabernacle.

a. **Present yourselves in the tabernacle of meeting**: Through the wilderness journey, Moses and Joshua often presented themselves together before the LORD. Joshua was often at the tabernacle with Moses (Exodus 33:11). This was an important aspect of Joshua's qualification for leadership. Joshua had a real relationship with God, and he was at home in the presence of the LORD.

b. **Now the LORD appeared**: This begins a solemn and important chapter in the history of the journey from Egypt to Canaan. What follows will be the retirement ceremony for Moses and the inauguration ceremony for Joshua. The importance of the event was marked by the visible presence of God in the **pillar of cloud**.

2. (16-22) An introduction to the song of Moses, warning Israel of future apostasy.

And the LORD said to Moses: "Behold, you will rest with your fathers; and this people will rise and play the harlot with the gods of the foreigners of the land, where they go *to be* **among them, and they will forsake Me and break My covenant which I have made with them. Then My anger shall be aroused against them in that day, and I will forsake them, and I will hide My face from them, and they shall be devoured. And many evils and troubles shall befall them, so that they will say in that day, 'Have not these evils come upon us because our God** *is* **not among us?' And I will surely hide My face in that day because of all the evil which they have done, in that they have turned to other gods.**

"Now therefore, write down this song for yourselves, and teach it to the children of Israel; put it in their mouths, that this song may be a witness for Me against the children of Israel. When I have brought them to the land flowing with milk and honey, of which I swore to their fathers, and they have eaten and filled themselves and grown fat, then they will turn to other gods and serve them; and they will provoke Me and break My covenant. Then it shall be, when many evils and troubles have come upon them, that this song will testify against them as a witness; for it will not be forgotten in the mouths of their descendants, for I know the inclination of their behavior today, even before I have brought them to the land of which I swore *to give them.***"**

Therefore Moses wrote this song the same day, and taught it to the children of Israel.

a. **This people will rise and play the harlot with the gods of the foreigners of the land**: After Moses died (resting **with** his **fathers**), and even after Joshua died, Israel would decline into idolatry, going after the gods of the

Canaanites. Israel's unfaithfulness would be like harlotry, forsaking God and dishonoring their covenant with Him.

b. Then My anger shall be aroused against them: In response to Israel's idolatry, God would show His anger and, in some sense, withdraw from His people. Israel would receive the curses previously mentioned (Deuteronomy 27-28), receiving the great **evils** God had promised in response to their **evil**.

> i. **I will hide My face**: "Hiding his face (vv.17–18; 32:20) is the converse of making his face to shine on his people and turning his face toward them as in the Aaronic blessing (Num 6:25–26)." (Kalland)

c. Write down this song…teach it to the children of Israel: In anticipation of their future idolatry, God inspired Moses to compose this song. The poetic arrangement would help Israel remember the words and themes, reminding them that any present calamity was due to their disobedience to the covenant.

> i. **Put it in their mouths**: "Implies sufficient repetition to fix it in the minds of the people. Only then would they be able to sing it, and only then would it be a witness." (Kalland)

> ii. "Songs often remain after commandments are forgotten, and it was that this might be so that Moses was instructed to write." (Morgan)

> iii. "Things which were of great importance and of common concern were, among the ancients, put into verse, as this was found the best method of keeping them in remembrance, especially in those times when *writing* was little practised." (Clarke)

d. Therefore Moses wrote this song the same day, and taught it to the children of Israel: This was a strange national song, because the purpose of this anthem was to **testify against** Israel **as a witness**. The song Moses composed as inspired by the LORD is found in Deuteronomy 32.

> i. "As they sang it, its words would remind them of the covenant pledges they had made and the judgments they freely and voluntarily invoked upon themselves." (Merrill)

> ii. "The song should testify against them, by showing that they had been sufficiently warned, and might have lived to God, and so escaped those disasters…. Never was a people more fully and faithfully warned." (Clarke)

3. (23) The inauguration of Joshua.

Then He inaugurated Joshua the son of Nun, and said, "Be strong and of good courage; for you shall bring the children of Israel into the land of which I swore to them, and I will be with you."

a. **Joshua the son of Nun**: Joshua – who was not a young man at this time – had spent his entire career previously as the assistant of Moses. Joshua found that now it was his time to lead, but only after God had prepared him.

> i. Joshua was the leader of the group of 12 spies sent to Canaan before Israel's opportunity to enter the Promised Land (Numbers 13:4-16). The Numbers 13 passage explains that Joshua was originally named *Hoshea* (salvation) but Moses changed his name to *Joshua* (Yahweh is salvation).
>
> ii. Among those 12 spies, only Caleb and Joshua returned from Canaan with a faith-filled report, confident God would empower Israel to overcome the challenges in the conquest of Canaan. Because of their faithfulness, Joshua and Caleb were the only adult Israelites of the generation that left Egypt to survive the wilderness years and enter Canaan (Numbers 14:30).
>
> iii. Some 38 years before his inauguration, Joshua believed God would work through Israel to give them the land, and he still believed it. Moses was not allowed to lead Israel into the Promised Land because of his disobedience (Numbers 27:12-14).
>
> iv. The Hebrew name *Yehoshua* is translated into English as "Joshua." That Hebrew name is translated into biblical Greek as "Iesous." In English, we translate the Greek name *Iesous* as "Jesus." In other words, in English the names "Joshua" and "Jesus" are translations of the same Hebrew name, *Yehoshua*. "The Conqueror of Canaan and the Redeemer of the world bear the same name. The Jesus whom we trust was a Joshua." (Maclaren)

b. **He inaugurated Joshua the son of Nun**: At God's command, Moses had already formally recognized Joshua as his successor to lead Israel (Numbers 27:18-23). Though Joshua was not of noble birth or a literal son of Moses, there were many things that in God's eyes qualified him to be the successor of Moses.

Joshua had led the army of Israel against the Amalekites (Exodus 17:8-16).

- Joshua was an assistant to Moses (Exodus 24:13).
- Joshua helped Moses at the tabernacle after the golden calf disaster (Exodus 33:7-11).

- Joshua was zealous to preserve the authority and leadership of Moses (Numbers 11:28).

- Joshua was one of the two faith-filled spies among the total of twelve who spied out the land of Canaan (Numbers 13:30-14:38).

- Joshua was a "man in whom is the Spirit" (Numbers 27:18), the most important qualification of all. The Holy Spirit would empower and enable him to fulfill the challenging role of leading the nation into Canaan.

i. God used the consistent, demonstrated faithfulness of Joshua in many small things to prepare him for this essential role of leading Israel into Canaan, a land with strong enemies reluctant to leave their land.

c. **Be strong and of good courage**: This was a manly, straightforward exhortation to a man who would soon take on tremendous responsibility. It is remarkable how often this exhortation is directed towards Joshua. Seven different times, it is recorded that God spoke this to Joshua (Deuteronomy 31:6, 7, and 23; Joshua 1:6, 7, 9, and 18).

i. Wonderfully, the last time this phrase was used in connection with Joshua, *he* was encouraging *others* to be strong and of good courage (Joshua 10:25). Joshua could encourage others with the encouragement that the LORD, through others, had given to him.

d. **You shall bring the children of Israel into the land**: These words came from Moses, but by the inspiration of the LORD. God assured Joshua that he would bring Israel into the land of Canaan.

4. (24-27) Moses preserves the Law of God as a witness against Israel.

So it was, when Moses had completed writing the words of this law in a book, when they were finished, that Moses commanded the Levites, who bore the ark of the covenant of the LORD, saying: "Take this Book of the Law, and put it beside the ark of the covenant of the LORD your God, that it may be there as a witness against you; for I know your rebellion and your stiff neck. *If* today, while I am yet alive with you, you have been rebellious against the LORD, then how much more after my death?

a. **When Moses had completed writing the words of this law**: Moses finished the first five books of the Bible and gave them to Israel, and to all creation, as the inspired words of God.

i. Some raise objections at this point, wondering who wrote the last three chapters of Deuteronomy, because the text says that Moses finished here. No doubt, Joshua had the remainder of Moses' words and deeds recorded and added to the end of his great written work.

b. **Put it beside the ark of the covenant**: The Ten Commandments were placed inside the ark of the covenant (Hebrews 9:4). But the whole Book of the Law – Genesis through Deuteronomy – was placed **beside the ark of the covenant**.

i. "There is no hint anywhere that those tablets were ever removed from the ark in the interim, so one may infer that the scroll of the *tora* was placed alongside the ark in the holy of holies as a supplement to them…. The holy of holies thus became a kind of sacred archives housing the documents that attested to the Lord's relationship to his people throughout the years." (Merrill)

c. **That it may be there as a witness against you**: Moses knew Israel would eventually rebel. He knew this both from the promise of God (Deuteronomy 31:16-17), and from common sense (**If today, while I am yet alive with you, you have been rebellious against the Lord, then how much more after my death?**). Therefore, the law would stand as a **witness against** a rebellious Israel.

i. It is wonderful to find refuge in God's word in times of stress and trouble. Yet believers don't often consider that God's word can, in some sense, be our adversary. It will be a **witness against** any who depart from its truth, a witness that rises to testify.

5. (28-30) The elders and officers of Israel gather for the song of Moses.

Gather to me all the elders of your tribes, and your officers, that I may speak these words in their hearing and call heaven and earth to witness against them. For I know that after my death you will become utterly corrupt, and turn aside from the way which I have commanded you; and evil will befall you in the latter days, because you will do evil in the sight of the Lord, to provoke Him to anger through the work of your hands."

Then Moses spoke in the hearing of all the assembly of Israel the words of this song until they were ended:

a. **For I know that after my death you will become utterly corrupt**: Moses said this either by divinely given prophetic insight or through intuition based on experience. Either way, his words were true. Joshua succeeded Moses, and Israel stayed generally faithful to God through Joshua's leadership. Afterward, in the days of the book of Judges, Israel did **turn aside**, they did **do evil**, and they did **provoke** the Lord to anger.

i. "His pessimism was well founded both in experience and in the predictive warnings from the Lord. The conduct of Israel fluctuated between obedience and disobedience with gray areas of partial obedience all through their history as a nation." (Kalland)

ii. "In fact, the song of chapter 32 is strongly reminiscent in its structure and content of a well-known secular political form, namely, the formulation of a complaint against a rebel vassal by his overlord with the threat of punishment. It is not impossible that some, at least, in Israel would have understood such a pattern and Moses would certainly have met it in the pharaoh's court." (Thompson)

b. **Then Moses spoke in the hearing of all the assembly of Israel the words of this song until they were ended**: The sense is that Moses knew he could not *prevent* the turning away to come, but through his warning he could *delay* it. The warning would also set a foundation for Israel's repentance and return to the LORD.

Deuteronomy 32 – The Song of Moses

A. The song of Moses.

1. (1-4) Introduction: Praise to Yahweh.

"Give ear, O heavens, and I will speak;
And hear, O earth, the words of my mouth.
Let my teaching drop as the rain,
My speech distill as the dew,
As raindrops on the tender herb,
And as showers on the grass.
For I proclaim the name of the Lord:
Ascribe greatness to our God.
He is **the Rock, His work** *is* **perfect;**
For all His ways *are* **justice,**
A God of truth and without injustice;
Righteous and upright *is* **He.**

> a. **Give ear, O heavens…and hear, O earth**: Moses began by asking for attention, not only from Israel, but from all of creation. Moses previously appealed to creation as his witness to the covenant with Israel (Deuteronomy 30:19, 31:28), not to a supposed divine council.

> b. **Let my teaching drop as the rain**: Moses prayed that his words, his teaching, would be as helpful and nourishing to Israel as the **rain** and **dew** are to vegetation. This is a good prayer for any preacher and follows along God's promise later stated in Isaiah 55:10-11.

>> i. "Like rain, dew, showers, and abundant rain bringing fertility to the new grass and tender plants, Moses hoped that his teaching—his words—would prove pleasant and beneficial." (Kalland)

>> ii. "It is good preaching, and good hearing too, when the gospel comes like a gentle shower which saturates and soaks into the soil, and

refreshes and makes it fruitful; may God the Holy Spirit make it to be so whenever we gather together for worship!" (Spurgeon)

c. **Ascribe greatness to our God**: As Moses proclaimed the name of Yahweh, he gave Him praise. This praise was given for who God is (the **Rock**, **Righteous**, and **upright**) and for what God does (**His work is perfect**, and **all His ways are justice**).

i. **He is the Rock**: "In those lands, rocks were the ordinary places of *defence* and *security*, God may be metaphorically represented thus, to signify his *protection* of his followers." (Clarke)

2. (5-6) The accusation: The children have forsaken their father.

"**They have corrupted themselves;**
They are **not His children,**
Because of their blemish:
A perverse and crooked generation.
Do you thus deal with the LORD**,**
O foolish and unwise people?
Is **He not your Father,** *who* **bought you?**
Has He not made you and established you?

a. **They have corrupted themselves**: The Song of Moses speaks prophetically about Israel's future (Deuteronomy 31:19-22). The deep corruption Moses spoke of in this song was not among Israel in the days of Moses or his immediate successor Joshua, but afterward. Looking to the future, Moses spoke as a witness against a rebellious Israel.

i. These were strong words but deserved. "Preachers should take the same liberty to cry down sins that men take to commit them." (Trapp)

b. **Is He not your Father, who bought you?** Moses made a fascinating poetic contrast. Israel acted as if they were not God's **children** (32:5), yet Moses could still appeal to God as their **Father**. Because God had **made** and **established** Israel, it was **foolish** and **unwise** for them to rebel against the God who did so much for them.

i. "Yahweh's charges against Israel were that they had become so disobedient that they no longer acted like his children but, to the contrary, had repudiated him as their Father and Creator." (Merrill)

3. (7-14) Moses remembers God's past faithfulness to Israel.

"**Remember the days of old,**
Consider the years of many generations.
Ask your father, and he will show you;
Your elders, and they will tell you:

When the Most High divided their inheritance to the nations,
When He separated the sons of Adam,
He set the boundaries of the peoples
According to the number of the children of Israel.
For the LORD's portion *is* His people;
Jacob *is* the place of His inheritance.

"He found him in a desert land
And in the wasteland, a howling wilderness;
He encircled him, He instructed him,
He kept him as the apple of His eye.
As an eagle stirs up its nest,
Hovers over its young,
Spreading out its wings, taking them up,
Carrying them on its wings,
So the LORD alone led him,
And *there was* no foreign god with him.

"He made him ride in the heights of the earth,
That he might eat the produce of the fields;
He made him draw honey from the rock,
And oil from the flinty rock;
Curds from the cattle, and milk of the flock,
With fat of lambs;
And rams of the breed of Bashan, and goats,
With the choicest wheat;
And you drank wine, the blood of the grapes.

>   a. **Remember the days of old**: Considering that this song was meant to be a *witness against* a future rebellious Israel, it is surprising that Moses reminded Israel of all God's goodness to them. This was to both bring a greater conviction of sin, and to remind them of God's love and grace they could return to.
>
>   b. **He set the boundaries of the peoples according to the number of the children of Israel**: Going back to the separation of the nations at the Tower of Babel (Genesis 11:1-9), God had a plan for Israel, choosing them as His **portion** and valuing Israel as His **inheritance**. God's call of Abraham and His covenant with him (Genesis 11:27-12:4) appear in the Genesis record shortly after the Tower of Babel account.
>
>   > i. **According to the number of the children of Israel**: "The meaning of the passage seems to be, that when God divided the earth among mankind, he reserved *twelve lots*, according to the *number* of the *sons* of

Jacob, which he was now about to give to their descendants, according to his promise." (Clarke)

ii. **He set the boundaries of the peoples**: "Not only did the Lord give Canaan to Israel, he also gave certain lands to other nations. While this reference probably falls back on Genesis 10, that does not suggest that this division was made all at once in the distant past. It suggests, rather, that the Lord rules over the disposition of land to all nations in the sovereign exercise of his will in every generation." (Kalland)

iii. **The LORD's portion is His people**: "What an astonishing saying! As *holy souls* take GOD for *their portion*, so GOD takes *them* for *his portion*. He represents himself as happy in his followers; and they are infinitely happy in, and satisfied with, God as their *portion*." (Clarke)

c. **The LORD alone led him**: God cared for Israel in the **desert land**, in the **howling wilderness**. He valued and protected Israel in the wilderness as a man cares for the pupil of his eye (the **apple of His eye**), and as an **eagle** protects and cares for its young (Exodus 19:4). God provided for Israel, and brought them to **Bashan**, part of the land on the eastern side of the Jordan River that became the territory of Israel. All this was the generous gift of Yahweh alone, with no **foreign god with Him**.

i. "Three great facts are stated: the election of Israel (8, 9), their deliverance at the time of the exodus (10–12), and Yahweh's gift of Canaan to his people (13, 14)." (Thompson)

ii. "The 'apple of his eye' (v.10) is an English idiom for 'anything held extremely dear' or 'much cherished' and is a fitting translation for the Hebrew 'the little man of his eye,' that is, the pupil." (Kalland)

iii. **He made him ride in the heights of the earth**: "Israel was able to scale the heights (lit., 'ride the backs') of the desert land (v. 13a). This connotes Israel's dominion as well, for elsewhere they are described as walking 'on the heights' (*bamot*, as here), a figure of speech suggesting strength and triumph (Habakkuk 3:19; cf. Deuteronomy 33:29)." (Merrill)

4. (15-18) Israel responds to God's kindness with apostasy.

"But Jeshurun grew fat and kicked;
You grew fat, you grew thick,
You are obese!
Then he forsook God *who* made him,
And scornfully esteemed the Rock of his salvation.
They provoked Him to jealousy with foreign *gods*;
With abominations they provoked Him to anger.

They sacrificed to demons, not to God,
To gods **they did not know,**
To new *gods,* **new arrivals**
That your fathers did not fear.
Of the Rock *who* **begot you, you are unmindful,**
And have forgotten the God who fathered you.

> a. **Jeshurun**: This is a title for Israel, which literally means *the upright one* (Isaiah 44:2). Israel took the many blessings described in the previous section and **grew fat**, and then **forsook God**. Their devotion to **foreign gods** was to treat God **scornfully**.
>
>> i. There is a shocking contrast between the generous blessings of God in 32:7-14 and the ungrateful rebellion in 32:15-18. "In all her well-being Israel forsook God her Creator and the ground of her salvation. 'A full stomach does not promote piety, for it stands secure and neglects God' (Luther)." (Thompson)
>>
>> ii. "Many can endure the trials of adversity who cannot escape the perils of prosperity.... many a man has failed in that time of testing. When you come to be wealthy, to be admired, to receive honour among men, then is the time of your severest trial." (Spurgeon)
>>
>> iii. **Kicked**: "In the only other place where this verb is used, the Lord says to Eli, the high priest, 'Why do you kick at my sacrifice?' which the NIV meaningfully translates 'Why do you scorn my sacrifice?' (1 Sam 2:29)." (Kalland)
>
> b. **They sacrificed to demons**: As Israel forsook God and honored idols, their devotion was not directed to merely imaginary beings, beings that did not actually exist. There were **demons** behind the **foreign gods**. Their idolatry was worse than useless; it gave honor to demonic spirits. There was a dark spiritual reality behind the idols of the nations, and Israel embraced that dark spiritual reality.

5. (19-27) Yahweh's reaction would be to withdraw from Israel and to punish them.

"And when the LORD saw *it,* **He spurned** *them,*
Because of the provocation of His sons and His daughters.
And He said: 'I will hide My face from them,
I will see what their end *will be,*
For they *are* **a perverse generation,**
Children in whom *is* **no faith.**
They have provoked Me to jealousy by *what* **is not God;**
They have moved Me to anger by their foolish idols.

But I will provoke them to jealousy by *those who are* not a nation;
I will move them to anger by a foolish nation.
For a fire is kindled in my anger,
And shall burn to the lowest hell;
It shall consume the earth with her increase,
And set on fire the foundations of the mountains.

'I will heap disasters on them;
I will spend My arrows on them.
They shall be wasted with hunger,
Devoured by pestilence and bitter destruction;
I will also send against them the teeth of beasts,
With the poison of serpents of the dust.
The sword shall destroy outside;
There shall be terror within
For the young man and virgin,
The nursing child with the man of gray hairs.
I would have said, "I will dash them in pieces,
I will make the memory of them to cease from among men,"
Had I not feared the wrath of the enemy,
Lest their adversaries should misunderstand,
Lest they should say, "Our hand *is* high;
And it is not the LORD who has done all this."'

a. **I will hide My face from them**: When God's people forsake Him, He withdraws the closeness of His presence. This is the opposite of the favor of God expressed in His face shining upon His people (Numbers 6:25).

b. **Children in whom is no faith**: Israel's embrace of **foolish idols** was a denial of true **faith** in Yahweh. Idolatry proved they did not truly trust in and rely on Yahweh, which are marks of true faith.

i. It is a dangerous and dreadful thing to be counted among those **in whom is no faith**. "I beg you to lay to heart this fact, that unless you have faith in Jesus you will perish just as surely as if you were an open denier of the word of God and a reviler of his Son. There are, doubtless, degrees in the terribleness of the punishment, but there are no degrees in the certainty of the fact that every unbeliever will be shut out from the blessing of the gospel of Christ." (Spurgeon)

c. **I will heap disasters on them**: Using poetic images and repetition to express intensity, God described the judgments He would bring upon a disobedient, idol-worshipping Israel. The judgment would come as **fire** and God would shoot all His **arrows** against Israel. **Hunger** and disease would make God's people waste away.

i. "Their life of covenant rebellion would lead to bitter consequences that they appeared unable to foresee." (Merrill)

ii. **Shall burn to the lowest hell**: "The very deepest destruction; a total extermination, so that *the earth*—their land, and *its increase*, and all their property, should be seized; and the *foundations of their mountains*—their strongest fortresses, should be razed to the ground." (Clarke)

iii. **My arrows**: "The judgments of God in general are termed the *arrows of God*, Job 6:4; Psalm 38:2, 3; 91:5; see also Ezekiel 5:16; Jeremiah 50:14; 2 Samuel 22:14, 15." (Clarke)

d. **Lest their adversaries should misunderstand**: One thing that would soften the judgment of Yahweh against Israel would be the pride and arrogance of the other nations God would use to punish Israel. If not for their arrogant claim that their **hand** was **high** and that *they* had done this against Israel and **not the Lord**, then God might have made the **memory** of Israel to **cease**. One reason God would spare and restore Israel was because the pride of their **adversaries**.

6. (28-35) The Lord warns Israel of coming judgment.

"For they *are* a nation void of counsel,
Nor *is there any* understanding in them.
Oh, that they were wise, *that* they understood this,
***That* they would consider their latter end!**
How could one chase a thousand,
And two put ten thousand to flight,
Unless their Rock had sold them,
And the Lord had surrendered them?
For their rock *is* not like our Rock,
Even our enemies themselves *being* judges.
For their vine *is* of the vine of Sodom
And of the fields of Gomorrah;
Their grapes *are* grapes of gall,
Their clusters *are* bitter.
Their wine *is* the poison of serpents,
And the cruel venom of cobras.

'*Is* this not laid up in store with Me,
Sealed up among My treasures?
Vengeance is Mine, and recompense;
Their foot shall slip in *due* time;
For the day of their calamity *is* at hand,
And the things to come hasten upon them.'

a. **Oh…that they would consider their latter end**: God wanted Israel to think about where their backsliding would lead them, what the **end** of their path would be. For Israel, it would lead them to defeat, disaster, and disgrace before enemies God appointed for their judgment. This is something that the disobedient and backslidden should consider.

b. **One chase a thousand…two put ten thousand to flight**: This was the opposite of the blessing God promised to an obedient Israel (Leviticus 26:8). God would not fight for a disobedient Israel. When Israel was unfaithful to their covenant with Yahweh, He would give them to their enemies, who would bring bitter defeat to Israel.

i. "Under the figure of vines, grapes, and wine, the wickedness of Israel's enemies is described. Their vine (character) has its source in the vine of Sodom and Gomorrah—those cities so wicked that they were annihilated by the Lord with cataclysmic force (Gen 19:24–25). The grapes from their vine were filled with poison, bitterness, and snake venom—synonyms significant of their patently evil and dangerous nature." (Kalland)

c. **Their foot shall slip in due time**: In their seasons of disobedience, Israel often was arrogantly confident. Yet God's **vengeance** could come against them at any moment, even if the vengeance of God came through Israel's enemies.

i. One of the most famous sermons preached from an American pulpit was based on this line from Deuteronomy 32:35, **their foot shall slip in due time**. This sermon by Jonathan Edwards was titled *Sinners in the Hands of an Angry God* and was mightily used by God. Edwards began by developing the following ideas:

- Sinners are *always* in danger of judgment; they presently stand in a slippery place.

- Sinners are in danger of *sudden* judgment; slips come suddenly.

- Sinners are to be blamed for their fall; when one slips, no other person throws them down – they fall of themselves.

- Sinners who have not yet slipped and fallen into God's judgment have their fall delayed only by God's mercy. Their judgment will come in due time.

ii. "The enemies may think that it was their decision and their strength that brought terrible punishment on the Lord's people (v.27), but that was not really so. They were only the instruments of God's punishment." (Kalland)

iii. **Vengeance is Mine**: "Verse 35 is quoted in the New Testament in Romans 12:19 and Hebrews 10:30.... There may be occasions when God's wrath is carried into effect by human agency (Rom. 13:4), but even then it is by divine appointment (Rom. 13:1). No individual should assume that he can carry out the divine sentence by the exercise of his own vengeful feelings." (Thompson)

7. (36-43) Hope for Israel under Yahweh's judgment, and hope for the Gentiles.

"For the LORD will judge His people
And have compassion on His servants,
When He sees that *their* power is gone,
And *there is* no one *remaining,* bond or free.
He will say: 'Where *are* their gods,
The rock in which they sought refuge?
Who ate the fat of their sacrifices,
And drank the wine of their drink offering?
Let them rise and help you,
And be your refuge.

'Now see that I, *even* I, *am* He,
And *there is* no God besides Me;
I kill and I make alive; I wound and I heal;
Nor *is there any* who can deliver from My hand.
For I raise My hand to heaven,
And say, *"As* I live forever,
If I whet My glittering sword,
And My hand takes hold on judgment,
I will render vengeance to My enemies,
And repay those who hate Me.
I will make My arrows drunk with blood,
And My sword shall devour flesh,
With the blood of the slain and the captives,
From the heads of the leaders of the enemy."'

"Rejoice, O Gentiles, *with* His people;
For He will avenge the blood of His servants,
And render vengeance to His adversaries;
He will provide atonement for His land *and* His people."

a. **The LORD will judge His people and have compassion on His servants**: God's judgment of His people is an expression of His **compassion**. He judges them to discipline them, to train them, to purify them. God would put the severe judgments described in the previous verses to a good purpose:

to destroy Israel's confidence in the **gods** of the nations. They would be of no **help** to Israel.

> i. It is also possible to understand the phrase the **LORD will judge His people** in the sense of, "the LORD will vindicate His people." There is a true application in either sense. This second sense matches well with the next phrase and **have compassion on His servants**.
>
> ii. "In the Hebrew, the first two lines of v.36 are quoted verbatim in Psalm 135:14—a psalm that has other likenesses to Deuteronomy. The Lord's vindication comes when his people have no more strength and, hyperbolically, no longer exist." (Kalland)

b. **There is no God besides Me**: Backslidden Israel could be brought to understand this. God alone has power to **kill** and **make alive**, not the idols of the pagan nations. Only Yahweh has the power of **judgment**.

> i. For Yahweh to **raise** His **hand to heaven** and to say, "**As I live forever**," was for God Himself to take an oath. This puts the words of Jesus in the Sermon on the Mount regarding oaths (Matthew 5:33-37) in perspective. Jesus did not mean that there is never a good or appropriate time to make an oath; He meant that our daily speech should be so marked by integrity that such oaths are unnecessary.
>
> ii. **My glittering sword**: "The expression *my glittering sword* means literally 'the lightning of my sword' and may be translated 'my flashing blade' (cf. Nah. 3:3; Hab. 3:11; Ezek. 21:9f.). Yahweh is pictured as a warrior arming himself for battle (Exod. 15:3; Isa. 42:13; 59:17)." (Thompson)

c. **Rejoice, O Gentiles**: The Gentiles could come to understand what Israel came to know through the judgments of God against them. They could **rejoice** as they understood that God will defend **His servants** and came to know that God will **provide atonement**. This atonement would be ultimately provided in Jesus Christ, who is the Savior not only of Israel, but of the whole world (John 4:42).

8. (44-47) Moses encourages Israel.

So Moses came with Joshua the son of Nun and spoke all the words of this song in the hearing of the people. Moses finished speaking all these words to all Israel, and He said to them: "Set your hearts on all the words which I testify among you today, which you shall command your children to be careful to observe—all the words of this law. For it *is* not a futile thing for you, because it *is* your life, and by this word you shall prolong *your* days in the land which you cross over the Jordan to possess."

a. **Spoke all the words of this song in the hearing of the people**: The Song of Moses was presented to all Israel so they could learn from it and be warned by it.

b. **Set your hearts on all the words which I testify among you today**: As Israel received and responded to the word of God through Moses, their departure from Yahweh and His judgment following it would be delayed. If they and their **children** would **observe** God's law, they would be blessed and not cursed.

> i. **It is not a futile thing**: One of Satan's great lies is that it is **a futile thing** to serve God and obey His word. It sometimes seems that those who are against God prosper more than those who are for Him. It should be seen and understood – from an eternal perspective – that **it is not a futile thing** to love and obey God.
>
> ii. **Not a futile thing**: "God's favour is no empty favour; it is not like the winter sun, that casts a godly countenance when it shines, but gives little comfort and heat." (Trapp)

9. (48-52) God's final command to Moses.

Then the LORD spoke to Moses that very same day, saying: "Go up this mountain of the Abarim, Mount Nebo, which *is* in the land of Moab, across from Jericho; view the land of Canaan, which I give to the children of Israel as a possession; and die on the mountain which you ascend, and be gathered to your people, just as Aaron your brother died on Mount Hor and was gathered to his people; because you trespassed against Me among the children of Israel at the waters of Meribah Kadesh, in the Wilderness of Zin, because you did not hallow Me in the midst of the children of Israel. Yet you shall see the land before *you*, though you shall not go there, into the land which I am giving to the children of Israel."

a. **Go up this mountain…and die on the mountain**: Moses, as the last act of his 120 years, would climb Mount Nebo, and die at the summit of the mountain.

> i. "The modern Mount Nebo provides a fine view over the Jordan valley and is traditionally identified with the site." (Thompson)

b. **You shall see the land before you, though you shall not go there**: Though because he **trespassed against** the LORD (Numbers 20:2-13) Moses was not allowed to cross the Jordan and enter the Promised Land, yet he would **view the land of Canaan**.

i. The ministry of Moses was now over. Only two more things remained before his death: to bless the tribes, and to see Canaan from the summit of Mount Nebo.

Deuteronomy 33 – Moses Blesses the Tribes of Israel

A. Introduction to the blessing of the tribes.

1. (1) **Now this is the blessing.**

Now this *is* the blessing with which Moses the man of God blessed the children of Israel before his death.

> a. **Moses the man of God**: As he looked at Israel with a shepherd's heart, Moses could not leave without blessing them. This blessing of Israel was the appropriate gift of Moses to the people he loved and served for 40 years.
>
>> i. "The introductory statement very fittingly calls Moses 'the man of God.' Never before in the Pentateuch had this designation been used. The second occurrence also is a reference to Moses as the man of God (Joshua 14:6). Subsequently, messengers of God (prophets especially) are called men of God (Judges 13:6, 8, and more often in 1 and 2 Kings). Moses is again designated as the man of God in the superscription to Psalm 90." (Kalland)
>>
>> ii. Deuteronomy 33 appears to have been based on the words of Moses, but written by an editor, possibly Joshua or Eleazar the priest. "This chapter has every appearance of being reported by one other than the speaker." (Kalland)
>
> b. **This is the blessing**: This chapter is like the blessing Israel (Jacob) gave his twelve sons in Genesis 49. Since Moses was the one who recorded the blessing of Israel in Genesis 49, it is not unreasonable to think he consciously modeled his blessing on Jacob's prior words.
>
>> i. "He is pictured as giving a *blessing* (*beraka*) before his death, rather like the patriarchs (Genesis 27:7; 49:1; 50:16). Such blessings were more than empty wishes and, once uttered, they carried the promise of fulfilment." (Clarke)

ii. The order in which the tribes are blessed is different than Jacob's blessing in Genesis 49. These words of Moses are more in the form of blessings, while Jacob's words were more predictive, prophetic. Finally, the tribe of Simeon is not included among the tribes blessed by Moses (with a possible exception of verse 6). The fact that Simeon is not mentioned may also be because this tribe's fate was to be essentially absorbed into Judah (Joshua 19:9).

2. (2-5) The context of the blessing: The glory of God's revelation to Israel.

And he said:

"The LORD came from Sinai,
And dawned on them from Seir;
He shone forth from Mount Paran,
And He came with ten thousands of saints;
From His right hand
Came **a fiery law for them.**
Yes, He loves the people;
All His saints *are* **in Your hand;**
They sit down at Your feet;
Everyone **receives Your words.**
Moses commanded a law for us,
A heritage of the congregation of Jacob.
And He was King in Jeshurun,
When the leaders of the people were gathered,
All the tribes of Israel together.

a. **The LORD came from Sinai**: The blessing Moses gave to the tribes of Israel came in the context of images of God's glory in revealing Himself and His word to Israel (**He shone...with ten thousands of saints...a fiery law.... He was King**). This added a sense of drama and grandeur to Moses' prophetic words to each tribe.

i. **Came...dawned...shone forth**: "The verbs...indicate that the coming of the Lord on Mount Sinai was like the sun flooding the desert area bounded by Sinai on the south, Seir on the northeast, and Paran on the north." (Kalland)

b. **He loves the people; all His saints are in Your hand**: The glory of God was displayed not only in awesome and glorious events. It was also evident in His great love for His people, and His care for them. His **saints** are securely in His **hand**.

i. **He loves the people**: "The word is in a form in the Hebrew which implies that the act spoken about is neither past, present, nor future only, but continuous and perpetual." (Maclaren)

B. The blessing of the individual tribes of Israel.

1. (6) Reuben: Nor let his men be few.

**"Let Reuben live, and not die,
Nor let his men be few."**

a. **Let Reuben live**: This was a general blessing for the tribe of Reuben. Moses prayed, **nor let his men be few**, asking that the tribe of Reuben be blessed with growth.

b. **Live, and not die**: This tepid blessing was consistent with Jacob's prophecy concerning the tribe of Reuben (*you shall not excel*, Genesis 49:4). The tribe of Reuben never did excel. As far as is known, there never came a prophet, a judge, or a king from the tribe of Reuben.

i. The tribe of Simeon is not mentioned in this blessing. According to Adam Clarke, in one ancient copy of the Septuagint, the name Simeon is inserted in verse 6 and the line should be understood as, "Let Simeon be few." If so, it would fit with the radical decline of the tribe of Simeon through the 40 years of the wilderness, from a tribe of 59,300 (Numbers 1:23) to 22,200 (Numbers 26:14). This decline of 37,100 men (more than 62%) was the largest decline of any tribe of Israel in the wilderness years.

2. (7) Judah: May You be a help.

And this he said of Judah:

**"Hear, LORD, the voice of Judah,
And bring him to his people;
Let his hands be sufficient for him,
And may You be a help against his enemies."**

a. **Hear, LORD, the voice of Judah**: Since the name **Judah** means *praise*, Moses prayed that the LORD would hear the *voice of praise*.

b. **Let his hands be sufficient**: Moses prayed for the blessing and sustaining of the tribe of Judah, so that it would fulfill its prophetic destiny to bring the Messiah. He prayed that God would **help** Judah **against his enemies**.

i. "Let him have a sufficiency of warriors always to support the tribe, and vindicate its rights; and let his enemies never be able to prevail against him!" (Clarke)

ii. Moses knew this destiny for the tribe of Judah from Jacob's prophecy in Genesis 49:10: *The scepter shall not depart from Judah.*

3. (8-11) Levi: **They shall teach…Israel Your law**.

And of Levi he said:

"*Let* **Your Thummim and Your Urim** *be* **with Your holy one,**
Whom You tested at Massah,
And with whom You contended at the waters of Meribah,
Who says of his father and mother, 'I have not seen them';
Nor did he acknowledge his brothers,
Or know his own children;
For they have observed Your word
And kept Your covenant.
They shall teach Jacob Your judgments,
And Israel Your law.
They shall put incense before You,
And a whole burnt sacrifice on Your altar.
Bless his substance, LORD,
And accept the work of his hands;
Strike the loins of those who rise against him,
And of those who hate him, that they rise not again."

a. **They have observed Your word and kept Your covenant**: Because of their obedience and loyalty to God, Levi had a blessed place among the tribes of Israel. Moses prayed that the **substance** of Levi would be blessed and that their enemies would be defeated.

i. **They have observed**: In the golden calf incident, "Moses had asked 'whoever is for the Lord' (Exodus 32:26) to come forward and punish the Israelite idolaters even to the extent of 'brother and friend and neighbor' (v. 27). Levi volunteered and proceeded to slay their own 'sons and brothers' (v. 29)." (Merrill)

ii. **Bless his substance**: "The blessing of God to the tribe of Levi was peculiarly necessary, because they had no inheritance among the children of Israel, and lived more immediately than others upon the providence of God." (Clarke)

b. **They shall teach Jacob Your judgments, and Israel Your law**: The tribe of Levi had the blessed place of teaching Israel the word of God. The work of the teaching priest and Levite was important in ancient Israel (2 Chronicles 17:9, 15:3; Leviticus 10:11). The Levites would accomplish this as they were scattered in Israel, as Jacob had prophesied (Genesis 49:7).

i. The teaching role of the priests "is supported by the edict given to Aaron and his sons at the commencement of their priestly ministry that they 'teach the Israelites all the decrees (*huqqim*) the Lord [had] given them through Moses' (Leviticus 10:11; cf. Deuteronomy 31:9-13)." (Merrill)

ii. The prophecy *I will divide them in Jacob and scatter them in Israel* (Genesis 49:7) was given to both the tribes of Simeon and Levi. For the tribe of Levi, it was a blessing, as they were scattered throughout the nation to minister to the people and to bring God's word to the whole nation. For the tribe of Simeon, the scattering was a significant curse. Simeon had no land allotment of their own and were scattered in a region of the tribe of Judah (Joshua 19:1-9). Here, the tribe of Simeon is not even mentioned among the tribes that Moses blessed.

iii. The tribe of Levi also held the **Thummim** and **Urim**. Thompson had an interesting explanation of what they may have been: "One conjecture is that each was inscribed on each side with the words *Urim* (derived from *arar*, 'to curse') and *Thummim* (derived from *tamam*, 'to be perfect'). When the stones were taken from the high priest's breastplate (Exod. 28:30; Lev. 8:8) and thrown, if both sides showed *Urim* the answer was No, and if *Thummim* the answer was Yes."

4. (12) Benjamin: **The beloved of the Lord.**

Of Benjamin he said:

"The beloved of the Lord shall dwell in safety by Him,
***Who* shelters him all the day long;**
And he shall dwell between His shoulders."

a. **The beloved of the Lord**: The place of special love and blessing Benjamin had would be prophetically fulfilled in a Benjaminite city becoming the center of the nation – Jerusalem. When the tabernacle was at Nob (1 Samuel 21:1), that was also in the territory of Benjamin.

b. **Shall dwell in safety by Him**: Thus, though the tribe of Benjamin was indeed fierce and warlike (Jacob's prophecy described Benjamin as a *ravenous wolf*, Genesis 49:27), the tribe was greatly **beloved of the Lord**.

i. "The final phrase *and makes his dwelling between his shoulders* may mean that Benjamin rests between Yahweh's shoulders, i.e. in the place of affection and protection." (Thompson)

ii. "The anthropomorphism here is suggestive of the most tender compassion and solid security at the same time. The phrase speaks not of carrying on the back but of being held close to the breast or bosom." (Merrill)

5. (13-17) Joseph: **Let the blessing come.**

And of Joseph he said:

"**Blessed of the** LORD *is* **his land,**
With the precious things of heaven, with the dew,
And the deep lying beneath,
With the precious fruits of the sun,
With the precious produce of the months,
With the best things of the ancient mountains,
With the precious things of the everlasting hills,
With the precious things of the earth and its fullness,
And the favor of Him who dwelt in the bush.
Let *the blessing* **come 'on the head of Joseph,**
And on the crown of the head of him *who was* **separate from his brothers.'**
His glory *is like* **a firstborn bull,**
And his horns *like* **the horns of the wild ox;**
Together with them He shall push the peoples
To the ends of the earth;
They *are* **the ten thousands of Ephraim,**
And they *are* **the thousands of Manasseh."**

> a. **Blessed of the** LORD **is his land**: The two tribes that came from Joseph – **Ephraim** and **Manasseh** – were indeed blessed numerically and with land in Israel. The descendants of this one son among twelve sons of Jacob were far more numerous than all the other tribes.
>
>> i. "Joseph is thus described as the dominant figure in the tribal confederacy. The tribes of Ephraim and Manasseh occupied such a position more or less continuously, since they were the largest of the northern tribes." (Thompson)
>>
>> ii. **The favor of Him who dwelt in the bush**: It was at the burning bush that Moses found the **favor** of God (Exodus 3:1-6), and he blessed the tribes of Joseph with that same favor. "That was a strange shrine for God, that poor, ragged, dry desert bush, with apparently no sap in its gray stem, prickly with thorns, with 'no beauty that we should desire it,' fragile and insignificant, yet it was 'God's house.' Not in the cedars of Lebanon, not in the great monarchs of the forest, but in the forlorn child of the desert did He abide." (Maclaren)
>
> b. **Ten thousands of Ephraim…thousands of Manasseh**: This fulfilled Jacob's prophecy regarding the prosperity and growth of the descendants of the sons of Joseph in Genesis 49:22 (*Joseph is a fruitful bough, a fruitful bough by a well; his branches run over the wall*).

i. "Like a firstborn bull…or a wild ox, he would rise to ascendancy and exercise dominion (thus thrusting with a horn)." (Merrill)

6. (18-19) Zebulun and Issachar: **They shall partake of the abundance of the seas.**

And of Zebulun he said:

"Rejoice, Zebulun, in your going out,
And Issachar in your tents!
They shall call the peoples *to* **the mountain;**
There they shall offer sacrifices of righteousness;
For they shall partake *of* **the abundance of the seas**
And *of* **treasures hidden in the sand."**

a. **They shall partake of the abundance of the seas**: Both the tribes of Zebulun and Issachar were in the Galilee region and were blessed to take advantage of the Sea of Galilee.

i. "That is, as Zebulun should be prosperous in his *shipping* and *traffic*, so should Issachar be in his *tents*—his *agriculture* and *pasturage*." (Clarke)

ii. "While this cannot be documented as having taken place in biblical times, the promise has found startling fulfillment in the modern state of Israel, whose major port is Haifa, located in the area of ancient Zebulun." (Merrill)

b. **Treasures hidden in the sand**: This is consistent with what Jacob said of Zebulun in Genesis 49:13 (*Zebulun shall dwell by the haven of the sea*).

7. (20-21) Gad: **He dwells as a lion.**

And of Gad he said:

"Blessed *is* **he who enlarges Gad;**
He dwells as a lion,
And tears the arm and the crown of his head.
He provided the first *part* **for himself,**
Because a lawgiver's portion was reserved there.
He came *with* **the heads of the people;**
He administered the justice of the LORD,
And His judgments with Israel."

a. **He dwells as a lion**: The lion-like character of the tribe of Gad was shown by the fact that Gad furnished many fine troops for David (1 Chronicles 12:14). This is in fulfillment of Jacob's words in Genesis 49:19: *he shall triumph at last*.

b. **A lawgiver's portion**: Gad held the central area of land among the Israelite tribes on the eastern side of the Jordan, with Manasseh to the north and Reuben to the south. This was the best, choice part of the region.

i. "Gad's area was by far the largest and best, conforming well to its description as 'the leader's portion.'" (Merrill)

8. (22) Dan: **A lion's whelp**.

And of Dan he said:

"Dan *is* a lion's whelp;
He shall leap from Bashan."

a. **He shall leap from Bashan**: This may not be a complimentary phrase. History records that Dan was a troublesome tribe. They were the tribe to introduce idolatry into Israel (Judges 18:30); Jeroboam set up one of his idolatrous golden calves in Dan (1 Kings 12:26-30), and later Dan became a center of idol worship in Israel (Amos 8:14). Indeed, Jacob said of Dan in Genesis 49:17, *Dan shall be a serpent by the way*.

b. **From Bashan**: The tribe of Dan originally was allotted land in the southern part of Israel but migrated to the north hundreds of years after this (Judges 18). Moses' reference to **Bashan** (a region in northern Israel) prophetically anticipated this migration.

9. (23) Naphtali: **Full of the blessing of the LORD**.

And of Naphtali he said:

"O Naphtali, satisfied with favor,
And full of the blessing of the LORD,
Possess the west and the south."

a. **O Naphtali, satisfied with favor**: The tribe of Naphtali was indeed **satisfied with favor**. Naphtali's land was in a key portion near the Sea of Galilee, the region where Jesus did much of His teaching and ministry.

b. **Full of the blessing of the LORD**: Since the ministry of Jesus was based in the tribal lands of Naphtali, his blessing was indeed **full**. Jacob said of Naphtali in Genesis 49:21, *he uses beautiful words*.

i. "Scarcely any of the tribes was more particularly favoured by the wondrous mercy and kindness of God, than this and the tribe of Zebulun. The light of the glorious Gospel of Christ shone brightly here, Matthew 4:13, 15, 16. Christ's chief residence was at *Capernaum* in this tribe, Matthew 9:1; Mark 2:1; and this city, through Christ's constant residence, and the mighty miracles he wrought in it, is represented as being *exalted unto heaven*." (Clarke)

10. (24-25) Asher: **Most blessed of sons**.

And of Asher he said:

"Asher *is* most blessed of sons;
Let him be favored by his brothers,
And let him dip his foot in oil.
Your sandals *shall be* iron and bronze;
As your days, *so shall* your strength *be*."

a. **Asher is most blessed of sons**: The abundance of the tribe of Asher was also expressed by Jacob in Genesis 49:20 (*he shall yield royal dainties*). Here, Moses blessed Asher with an abundance of olive **oil**, plenty to **dip** one's **foot** in.

i. "The Galilean highlands were famous for olives and both Josephus and one of the Jewish Midrashim refer to this fact." (Thompson)

b. **Your sandals shall be iron and bronze**: The tribe of Asher would be blessed with wealth so that even their **sandals** would be made of the best, strongest, most durable materials.

i. **Sandals** of **iron and bronze** have a spiritual sense for the believer. Spurgeon suggested several applications.

- Such sandals would protect tender feet, and God protects.
- Such sandals would be sturdy for travel, and God enables us to walk difficult paths.
- Such sandals would be good for soldiers, and we wage war in the Spirit and crush spiritual adversaries under our feet.
- Such sandals would be good for climbing mountains, and God has heights for His people to climb.
- Such sandals would last a long time, needed for our long journey with the Lord.

c. **As your days, so shall your strength be**: This wonderful promise meant that their **strength** would match their **days**. This can be understood in many blessed aspects.

i. "The saying, I have no doubt, has comforted the souls of multitudes. The meaning is obvious: 'Whatever thy trials or difficulties may be, I shall always give thee grace to support thee under and bring thee through them.'" (Clarke)

ii. Spurgeon suggested many applications of the truth, **as your days, so shall your strength be**.

- We receive strength from God as we do our days – day by day, piece by piece. We receive one day at a time and receive strength for that day.
- We receive strength from God proportionally. A day of little service or little suffering may receive little strength; but days of greater service or greater suffering will receive greater strength.
- We receive strength from God in many ways. As our days differ, so does the strength God gives us, always suited to the day.
- We receive strength from God as long as our days continue; it is a constant provision.

11. (26-29) Conclusion: **Happy are you, O Israel!**

"*There is* **no one like the God of Jeshurun,**
Who **rides the heavens to help you,**
And in His excellency on the clouds.
The eternal God *is your* **refuge,**
And underneath *are* **the everlasting arms;**
He will thrust out the enemy from before you,
And will say, 'Destroy!'
Then Israel shall dwell in safety,
The fountain of Jacob alone,
In a land of grain and new wine;
His heavens shall also drop dew.
Happy *are* **you, O Israel!**
Who *is* **like you, a people saved by the LORD,**
The shield of your help
And the sword of your majesty!
Your enemies shall submit to you,
And you shall tread down their high places."

a. **The eternal God is your refuge**: What blessing God gave to Israel! As Paul wrote in Romans 3:2: *To them were committed the oracles of God.* The true greatness of Israel is the same as the greatness of the Christian: not in and of themselves, but in their God, that there **is no one like the God of Jeshurun**.

b. **Who rides the heavens to help you**: God is great and uses His greatness on behalf of His people, upholding them with **the everlasting arms**. When believers are **a people saved by the LORD**, it means that God is for them, and heaven is on their side. *If God is for us, who can be against us?* (Romans 8:31) He is **the shield of** the believer's **help**.

i. "The figure of deity riding on a chariot through the heavens is an ancient Near Eastern motif known to the Canaanites, but occurring also in the Old Testament (Psalms 18:10; 68:33; Isaiah 19:1; Ezekiel 1)." (Thompson)

ii. **The fountain of Jacob**: "It is a figurative way of describing Jacob's offspring, the descendants of his sons who came to comprise the nation Israel." (Merrill)

iii. **Then Israel shall dwell…alone**: "This people shall not be *incorporated* with any other people under heaven. A prophecy which continues to be fulfilled to the very letter. Every attempt to unite them with any other people has proved absolutely ineffectual." (Clarke)

c. **Underneath are the everlasting arms**: The hymn *Leaning on the Everlasting Arms* gets its title and theme from this phrase. The sense of this simple and powerful image gives great comfort and courage to those who believe and receive its truth.

i. The everlasting arms of God are **underneath**, as a foundation for everything. Everything in the universe, all creation, the church, the individual believer – all built on a firm foundation, with God's everlasting, strong, arms **underneath**. They are also underneath the believer as a place of rest. Our Father's arms are a perfect pillow, giving perfect rest. We can put all our weight on these strong **arms**, leaning heavily on them.

ii. If we sink deep from humiliation, from trials, inner conflict, weary working, illness, or impending death – no matter what brings us low – we have God's everlasting arms underneath us. "You cannot go so low but that God's arms of love are lower still. You get poorer and poorer; but 'underneath are the everlasting arms.' You get older and feebler; your ears are failing, your eyes are growing dim; but 'underneath are the everlasting arms.'" (Spurgeon)

iii. "I recollect being at the funeral of one of our brethren, and a dear friend in Christ offered prayer in which there was a sentence which struck me, 'O Lord,' he said, 'thou hast laid our friend low, but we thank thee that he cannot go any lower, for underneath him are the everlasting arms.' Yes, underneath the bodies of the saints are the everlasting arms of God." (Spurgeon)

iv. **Everlasting arms**: "They are arms which always were, and always will be: arms which always were strong, and never will grow faint or weary; arms which once outstretched will never be drawn back again; arms which once engaged for the defense of the chosen people shall never cease to work for their good world without end. Not failing arms, nor dying arms, but everlasting arms, are underneath the saints of God." (Spurgeon)

d. **Happy are you, O Israel**: With this salvation, with God as their shield and sword, with victory assured, all this gave God's people great reason to be **happy**. These blessings, in their spiritual sense, were not limited to Israel. Believers, God's people under the new covenant, also have such blessings and reasons to be **happy**.

i. **A people saved by the LORD**: "If you are indeed believers in Christ, you are 'a people saved by the Lord.' If you only read as far as the word 'saved' and there pause, what music there is in the words—'a people saved'! Not a people who may be saved, who are in process of being saved, but a people saved; for he that believes in Jesus is saved. The work is done." (Spurgeon)

ii. "Remember that, O believer. Not half saved, but completely saved; saved in the Lord with an everlasting salvation; you shall not be ashamed nor confounded, world without end. Why, that one word 'saved' is enough to make the heart dance as long as life remains." (Spurgeon)

e. **Your enemies shall submit to you**: The last recorded words of Moses were full of confidence that Israel would defeat the Canaanites and occupy the land Yahweh had promised them.

i. "On the eve of conquest it was assuring to know that Yahweh, the Divine Warrior (cf. v. 27), would lead his elect nation to victory. Their enemies would submit to them, and they would tread upon the high places of their foes." (Merrill)

Deuteronomy 34 – The Death of Moses

A. Moses on Mount Nebo.

1. (1-3) God gives Moses a vision of the Promised Land.

Then Moses went up from the plains of Moab to Mount Nebo, to the top of Pisgah, which is across from Jericho. And the Lord showed him all the land of Gilead as far as Dan, all Naphtali and the land of Ephraim and Manasseh, all the land of Judah as far as the Western Sea, the South, and the plain of the Valley of Jericho, the city of palm trees, as far as Zoar.

> a. **Then Moses went up from the plains of Moab to Mount Nebo**: As Israel camped on the **plains of Moab**, Moses climbed the heights of **Mount Nebo** – from which he could see Canaan, **as far as the Western Sea**.
>
>> i. Deuteronomy 34 describes the death of Moses, and unless he wrote it prophetically, the most logical and uncomplicated explanation is that this chapter was written by someone such as Joshua or Eleazar the priest, who accompanied Moses to the place of his death and as God's agent buried Moses. There is nothing in this chapter that says Moses was alone at his death.
>>
>> ii. Moses was commanded in Deuteronomy 32:48-52 to climb Mount Nebo for his death. Here that command was fulfilled. Moses began his work as Israel's deliverer at one mountain (Mount Sinai, Exodus 3:1-10) and ended it here at another mountain.
>
> b. **And the Lord showed him all the land**: This was God's kind grace to Moses. Though he could not set foot in the Promised Land, God allowed him to see it. Standing on the peak of **Nebo** on the collection of mountains called **Pisgah**, Moses stood on what is the modern Kingdom of Jordan, looking westward to Canaan.

i. Moses lived 120 years (Deuteronomy 31:2), and his life was divided into three 40-year periods.

- The first 40 years of Moses ended with a murder and a flight from justice (Exodus 2:11-15).
- The second 40 years of Moses ended with a revelation of God at the burning bush (Exodus 3:1-10).
- The last 40 years of Moses ended with the vision of the Promised Land.

2. (4) God's last words to Moses: **This is the land**.

Then the LORD said to him, "This *is* the land of which I swore to give Abraham, Isaac, and Jacob, saying, 'I will give it to your descendants.' I have caused you to see *it* with your eyes, but you shall not cross over there."

a. **This is the land of which I swore to give**: These words, being in the present tense, were spoken to Moses at the summit of Mount Nebo as he looked westward and saw the Promised Land.

i. The list of places here follows a large counterclockwise circle from the north to the south. In this sweeping panorama, Moses saw the scope of Canaan.

ii. "The invitation to Moses to view the land was not merely a kindly provision of God to allow His servant to view Israel's inheritance. It may have had some legal significance. There is some evidence that this was part of a legal process. A man 'viewed' what he was to possess." (Thompson)

iii. "The only time in Old Testament history that this ideal ever reached realization was in the heyday of the United Monarchy under David and Solomon (cf. 2 Samuel 10:19; 1 Kings 4:24)." (Merrill)

b. **I will give it to your descendants**: God **swore** to give it to the descendants of **Abraham, Isaac, and Jacob**, and now the promise was going to be fulfilled. Moses was allowed to take the descendants of Abraham, Isaac, and Jacob up to the threshold of the Promised Land, but no further.

i. "His death leaves nothing to regret; neither is any desirable thing lacking. Failing to pass over Jordan seems a mere pin's prick, in presence of the honours which surrounded his departing hours. His death was the climax of his life. He now saw that he had fulfilled his destiny, and was not as a pillar broken short. He was ordered to lead the people through the wilderness, and he had done so." (Spurgeon)

c. **I have caused you to see it with your eyes, but you shall not cross over there**: This was a bittersweet moment. Moses saw this, and his heart was thrilled at the sight of Canaan as he had never seen it. Yet, there was probably a sadness in his heart, knowing that it was his own sin – his own misrepresentation of God (Numbers 20:7-12) – which led to his not being able to set foot in the Promised Land himself. Here he stood so close, yet so far away.

> i. "What drama! What pathos! What inward pain! What sense of accomplishment mixed with disappointment must have been in Moses' mind as he looked over the land the Lord had promised to Israel!" (Kalland)
>
> ii. Looking out over the vast panorama, on what must have been a crystal-clear day, Moses saw the result of his life's work – leading Israel to Canaan – and heard God say, **this is the land**.
>
> iii. Moses appealed to God, asking Him to lessen his penalty – but God emphatically told Moses to speak no more to Him on that matter (Deuteronomy 3:26).
>
> iv. Moses died under the penalty of sin, but his own sin. He died and remained buried. Jesus also died under the penalty of sin, but not His own – He died as a payment, a satisfaction, for the sins of His people. As God's Holy One, even in death, Jesus did not remain buried and rose gloriously from the dead. As great as Moses was, Jesus is the One greater than Moses (Hebrews 3:1-6).

3. (5-8) The death and burial of Moses, **the servant of the LORD**.

So Moses the servant of the LORD died there in the land of Moab, according to the word of the LORD. And He buried him in a valley in the land of Moab, opposite Beth Peor; but no one knows his grave to this day. Moses *was* **one hundred and twenty years old when he died. His eyes were not dim nor his natural vigor diminished. And the children of Israel wept for Moses in the plains of Moab thirty days. So the days of weeping** *and* **mourning for Moses ended.**

> a. **So Moses the servant of the LORD died there in the land of Moab**: Moses' epitaph – what we might call the writing on his tombstone, though he had no tombstone – was simple.
>
> - It was not "Moses, prince of Egypt."
> - It was not "Moses, murderer of an Egyptian."
> - It was not "Moses, shepherd in the wilderness."
> - It was not "Moses, spokesman for a nation."

- It was not "Moses, miracle worker."
- It was not "Moses, prophet."
- It was not "Moses, the man who saw a piece of God's glory."
- It was not "Moses, who never entered the Promised Land."
- At the end, the title was simple: **Moses the servant of the Lord**.

i. "He might be barred from Canaan and even sentenced to death on Nebo, but he was Yahweh's servant nonetheless." (Merrill)

ii. To be satisfied with simply being **the servant of the Lord** is worthy and important. This should be enough for the believer. It is often *said*, and it sounds humble to *say* it, but it is more difficult to really live it. It is the happiest of all stations in life, for when the Master is glorified, the servant is satisfied.

iii. If someone is truly a **servant of the Lord**, one way it may be demonstrated is by how they react when someone else *treats* them like a servant. Many are pleased to be servants for people of their choosing or in circumstances of their choosing. But that isn't really being **the servant of the Lord**.

b. **Moses the servant of the Lord died**: Moses died just as God promised. The promises of God are sure, including His more severe promises. It all happened **according to the word of the Lord**.

i. Literally, the phrase **according to the word of the Lord** means *upon the mouth of the Lord*. From this, some ancient Jewish traditions say that Moses died as God took away his soul with a kiss. The medieval Jewish rabbi Maimonides wrote that of the 903 different ways to die, this was the best.

ii. According to ancient Jewish legends – which should be regarded *only as legends* – the death of Moses was tender and full of God's compassion.

"In the meanwhile, Moses' time was at an end. A voice from heaven resounded, saying: 'Why, Moses, dost thou strive in vain? Thy last second is at hand.' Moses instantly stood up for prayer, and said: 'Lord of the world! Be mindful of the day on which Thou didst reveal Thyself to me in the bush of thorns, and be mindful also of the day when I ascended into heaven and during forty days partook of neither food nor drink. Thou, Gracious and Merciful, deliver me not into the hand of [Satan].' God replied: 'I have heard thy prayer. I Myself shall attend to thee and bury thee.' Moses now sanctified himself as do the Seraphim that surround the Divine Majesty, whereupon God from the highest heavens revealed Himself to receive Moses' soul. When Moses beheld the Holy One, blessed be His Name, he fell upon his face and said: 'Lord of the world! In love didst Thou create the world, and in love Thou guidest it. Treat me also with love, and deliver me not into the hands of the Angel of Death.' A heavenly voice sounded and said: 'Moses, be not afraid. "Thy righteousness shall go before thee; the glory of the Lord shall be thy rearward."'"

"With God descended from heaven three angels, Michael, Gabriel, and Zagzagel. Gabriel arranged Moses' couch, Michael spread upon it a purple garment, and Zagzagel laid down a woolen pillow. God stationed Himself over Moses' head, Michael to his right, Gabriel to his left, and Zagzagel at his feet, whereupon God addressed Moses: 'Cross thy feet,' and Moses did so. He then said, 'Fold thy hands and lay them upon thy breast,' and Moses did so. Then God said, 'Close thine eyes,' and Moses did so. Then God spake to Moses' soul: 'My daughter, one hundred and twenty years had I decreed that thou shouldst dwell in this righteous man's body, but hesitate not now to leave it, for thy time has run....I Myself shall take thee to the highest heavens and let thee dwell under the Throne of My Glory'....When Moses heard these words, he permitted his soul to leave him, saying to her: 'Return to thy rest, O my soul, for the Lord hath dealt bountifully with thee.' God thereupon took Moses' soul by kissing him on the mouth." (Ginzberg, *The Legends of the Jews*)

iii. "As a mother takes her child and kisses it, and then lays it down to sleep in its own bed; so did the Lord kiss the soul of Moses away to be with him for ever, and then he hid his body we know not where." (Spurgeon)

iv. God said that when Moses died, he would be gathered to his people (Deuteronomy 32:50). "How, then, was he 'gathered to his people'? Surely only thus, that, dying in the desert alone, he opened his eyes in 'the City,' surrounded by 'solemn troops and sweet societies' of those to whom he was kindred. So the solitude of a moment leads on to blessed and eternal companionship." (Maclaren)

c. **And He buried him in a valley**: God may have done this through a human agent, such as Joshua or Eleazar the priest. There were several reasons why the burial of Moses was unique and unmarked (**no one knows his grave**).

- So that Israel would not worship Moses or his tomb.

- So that Israel would not take the body of Moses into Canaan, in disobedience to God's command that he would not enter the Promised Land.
- So that a later purpose of God for Moses may be fulfilled, suggested by Jude 9, and perhaps fulfilled at the transfiguration of Jesus (Luke 9:28-31).

i. The burial of Moses was more complicated than it first appears because the devil contended with God over the body of Moses. Jude 9 speaks of an occasion when *Michael the archangel, in contending with the devil, when he disputed about the body of Moses*. Apparently, there was a contention over the body of Moses, and according to Jude Michael the archangel won this contest as he appealed to the Lord's authority: *"The Lord rebuke you!"* Yet *why* Michael contended with Satan over the body of Moses is less clear.

ii. Some say that the devil wanted to use Moses' body as an object of worship to lead Israel astray into idolatry. Others think that Satan wanted to desecrate the body of Moses and claimed a right to it because Moses had murdered an Egyptian.

iii. But consider that God had another purpose for Moses' body, which Satan wanted to defeat: Moses appears in bodily form with Elijah (whose body was caught up to heaven [2 Kings 2]) at the transfiguration (Matthew 17:1-3), and perhaps Moses and Elijah are the two witnesses of Revelation 11.

iv. Apparently, God had a purpose to fulfill with the body of Moses before the time of general resurrection, so God made special provision to bury the body of Moses. And, perhaps, God preserved the body of Moses in some way. God wanted to protect the body of Moses, so **no one knows his grave to this day**. Seemingly, they searched for it (as would be expected) out of a desire to memorialize this great leader of the nation.

v. "Whoever had such a burial as that of Moses? Angels contended over it, but Satan has failed to use it for his purposes. That body was not lost, for in due time it appeared on the Mount of Transfiguration, talking with Jesus concerning the greatest event that ever transpired." (Spurgeon)

d. **Moses was one hundred and twenty years old when he died**: Moses' life was neatly divided into thirds. He spent 40 years as the crown prince of Egypt, 40 years as a humble shepherd in the wilderness, and 40 years leading the children of Israel to their destiny in the Promised Land. The first two-thirds were in preparation for the last one-third. Moses was willing to let God prepare him for 80 years.

> i. "The passing of Moses was full of beauty. As we have seen, his exclusion from the land towards which his face had so long been set was in fact a punishment. Yet how wonderfully it was tempered with mercy." (Morgan)
>
> ii. "This testimony, and indeed this whole chapter, is thought to have been added by Joshua or Eleazar, being divinely inspired, for the completing of the history." (Trapp)

e. **His eyes were not dim nor his natural vigor diminished**: Moses was not hindered by physical infirmity, but by the command of God. Moses was old when he died, but he did not die from old age. He died because Israel was going into the Promised Land, and Moses could not go with them. Like the rest of his generation (with the exceptions of Joshua and Caleb), Moses died in the wilderness.

> i. "He did not fail to enter Canaan because he died, but he died because he failed to enter Canaan." (Merrill)
>
> ii. "Perhaps it meant that for a man of his age he had retained his powers in a remarkable way, even if he was no longer able 'to go out and come in' (even this latter expression is a figure of speech)." (Thompson)
>
> iii. Given the great challenges and responsibilities Moses faced, his relative health at the time of his death was remarkable. "He had seen plenty of sorrow and toil; but such was the simple power of his faith, in casting his burden on the Lord, that they had not worn him out in premature decay. There had been no undue strain on his energy. All that he wrought on earth was the outcome of the secret abiding of his soul in God. God was his home, his help, his stay. He was nothing: God was all. Therefore his youth was renewed." (Meyer)

f. **The children of Israel wept.... the days of weeping and mourning for Moses ended**: As great as Moses was, the days of mourning for him ended. It was time to move on. God's program did not end with Moses, nor does it end with any man. The torch was passed, and God's work continued.

> i. It was an august and glorious ending to a great and dignified life." (Morgan)

B. The legacy of Moses.

1. (9) Joshua's leadership in Israel.

Now Joshua the son of Nun was full of the spirit of wisdom, for Moses had laid his hands on him; so the children of Israel heeded him, and did as the LORD had commanded Moses.

   a. **For Moses had laid his hands on him**: Moses' prayer for Joshua was answered. Joshua was indeed **full of the spirit of wisdom**. Moses **laid his hands** on Joshua in Numbers 27:18-23.

      i. The **spirit of wisdom**: "Is the equipment that makes it possible for one to do what the Lord delegates him to do. The skilled workmen who made the priestly garments for Aaron and his sons were given wisdom to make those garments (Exodus 28:3). The spirit of wisdom for Joshua was the military and administrative ability necessary for the task the Lord had laid on him as well as the spiritual wisdom to rely on and be committed to the Lord." (Kalland)

   b. **The children of Israel heeded him**: The leadership of Joshua was seen in that Israel followed him. In general, the generation that followed Joshua into Canaan was more faithful to the LORD and to Joshua than the generation that perished in the wilderness.

2. (10-12) The unique legacy of Moses.

But since then there has not arisen in Israel a prophet like Moses, whom the LORD knew face to face, in all the signs and wonders which the LORD sent him to do in the land of Egypt, before Pharaoh, before all his servants, and in all his land, and by all that mighty power and all the great terror which Moses performed in the sight of all Israel.

   a. **Since then there has not arisen in Israel a prophet like Moses**: Joshua was a capable leader for Israel, and God's work went on, but that did not diminish Moses' unique legacy.

      i. "Not until the Lord Jesus Christ came (the one whom Moses spoke about, John 5:46) was there anyone greater than Moses, the emancipator, prophet, lawgiver, and father of his country." (Kalland)

   b. **Since then there has not arisen in Israel a prophet like Moses**: Several things made Moses unique.

      i. **Whom the LORD knew face to face**: Moses was unique because of his personal intimacy with God. The term **face to face** does not literally mean "physical face to physical face," but it has the idea of free and unhindered communication. Moses had a remarkably intimate relationship with God.

      ii. **All the signs and wonders which the LORD sent him to do**: Moses was unique in the number and kind of miraculous works he was associated with.

iii. **All that mighty power and all the great terror which Moses performed**: Moses was unique in the power and authority with which he led the nation of Israel.

c. **Since then there has not arisen in Israel a prophet like Moses**: There were greater rulers over Israel than Moses, greater leaders, greater prophets, and greater priests. But before the coming of Jesus Christ the Messiah, there was never one man who held all offices so gloriously as Moses did.

i. "In him were concentrated all the great offices of Israel – prophet, ruler, judge and priest. If some who held these offices were great, Moses was the greatest of them all." (Thompson)

Deuteronomy Bibliography

Albright, William F. *From the Stone Age to Christianity* (Garden City, New York: Doubleday & Company, 1957)

Calvin, John *Commentaries on the Four Last Books of Moses, Arranged in the Form of a Harmony, Volume 2* (Grand Rapids, Michigan: Baker Book House, 1979)

Clarke, Adam *The Holy Bible, Containing the Old and New Testaments, with A Commentary and Critical Notes* (New York: Eaton and Mains, 1826)

Cole, R. Alan *Exodus, An Introduction and Commentary* (London: Inter-Varsity Press, 1973)

Ginzberg, Louis *The Legends of the Jews, Volumes 1-7* (Philadelphia: The Jewish Publication Society of America, 1968)

Harrison, R.K. *Leviticus – An Introduction and Commentary* (Leicester, England: Inter-Varsity Press, 1980)

Robert Jamieson, A. R. Fausset, and David Brown, *Commentary Critical and Explanatory on the Whole Bible*, vol. 1 (Oak Harbor, WA: Logos Research Systems, Inc., 1997)

Kaiser, Walter C. Jr. "Exodus" *The Expositor's Bible Commentary Volume 2* (Grand Rapids, Michigan: Zondervan, 1990)

Kalland, Earl S. "Deuteronomy" *The Expositor's Bible Commentary Volume 3* (Grand Rapids, Michigan: Zondervan, 1990)

Leupold, H.C. *Exposition of Genesis, Volumes 1 and 2* (Grand Rapids, Michigan: Baker Book House, 1976)

Lewis, C.S. *Christian Behaviour* (London: Geoffrey Bles, The Centenary Press, 1945)

Maclaren, Alexander *Expositions of Holy Scripture, Volume 1* (Grand Rapids, Michigan: Baker Book House, 1984)

McMillen, S.I. *None of These Diseases* (Old Tappan, New Jersey: Fleming H. Revell Company, 1968)

Merrill, Eugene H. *Deuteronomy*, vol. 4, The New American Commentary (Nashville: Broadman & Holman Publishers, 1994)

Meyer, F.B. *Our Daily Homily* (Westwood, New Jersey: Revell, 1966)

Morgan, G. Campbell *An Exposition of the Whole Bible* (Old Tappan, New Jersey: Revell, 1959)

Morgan, G. Campbell *Searchlights from the Word* (New York: Revell, 1936)

Poole, Matthew *A Commentary on the Holy Bible*, Volume 1 (London: Banner of Truth Trust, 1968)

Redpath, Alan *Law and Liberty: The Ten Commandments for Today* (Grand Rapids, Michigan: Revell 1993)

Spurgeon, Charles Haddon *The New Park Street Pulpit, Volumes 1-6* and *The Metropolitan Tabernacle Pulpit, Volumes 7-63* (Pasadena, Texas: Pilgrim Publications, 1990)

Thompson, John Arthur *Deuteronomy – An Introduction and Commentary* (Leicester, England: Inter-Varsity Press, 1981)

Trapp, John *A Commentary on the Old and New Testaments, Volume 1 – Genesis to Second Chronicles* (Eureka, California: Tanski Publications, 1997)

Whiston, William A.M. (translator) *The Works of Flavius Josephus Volume I* and *Volume III* (Grand Rapids, Michigan: Baker Book House, 1988)

Author's Remarks

As the years pass I love the work of studying, learning, and teaching the Bible more than ever. I'm so grateful that God is faithful to meet me in His Word.

I am also tremendously grateful to Alison Turner for her proofreading and editorial suggestions, especially with a challenging manuscript. Alison, thank you so much!

Thanks to Brian Procedo for the cover design and the graphics work.

Most especially, thanks to my wife Inga-Lill. She is my loved and valued partner in life and in service to God and His people.

David Guzik

David Guzik's Bible commentary is regularly used and trusted by many thousands who want to know the Bible better. Pastors, teachers, class leaders, and everyday Christians find his commentary helpful for their own understanding and explanation of the Bible. David and his wife Inga-Lill live in Santa Barbara, California.

You can email David at
david@enduringword.com

For more resources by David Guzik,
go to www.enduringword.com